British History in Perspective

General Editor: Jeremy Black

PUBLISHED TITLES

(List continued overleaf)

Please note that a sister series, *Social History in Perspective*, is now available. It covers the key topics in social, cultural and religious history.

British History in Perspective
Series Standing Order
ISBN 0–333–71356–7 hardcover
ISBN 0–333–69331–0 paperback
(outside North America only)

You can receive future titles in this series as they are published by placing a standing order. Please contact your bookseller or, in case of difficulty, write to us at the address below with your name and address, the title of the series and the ISBN quoted above.

Customer Services Department, Macmillan Distribution Ltd
Houndmills, Basingstoke, Hampshire RG21 6XS, England

THE LIBERAL PARTY
TRIUMPH AND DISINTEGRATION, 1886–1929

SECOND EDITION

G. R. SEARLE

palgrave

First published 2001
PALGRAVE
Houndmills, Basingstoke, Hampshire RG21 6XS and
175 Fifth Avenue, New York, N. Y. 10010
Companies and representatives throughout the world

PALGRAVE is the new global academic imprint of
St. Martin's Press LLC Scholarly and Reference Division and
Palgrave Publishers Ltd (formerly Macmillan Press Ltd).

ISBN 0–333–78661–0

This book is printed on paper suitable for recycling and made from fully managed and sustained forest sources.

A catalogue record for this book is available from the British Library.

Library of Congress Cataloging-in-Publication Data has been applied for.

10 9 8 7 6 5 4 3 2 1
10 09 08 07 06 05 04 03 02 01

Printed in Malaysia

CONTENTS

ACKNOWLEDGEMENTS

I would like to thank Professor John Charmley, Dr Steve Cherry, Dr Brian Hill, Dr Terry Jenkins and the late Dr Roger Virgoe for their advice and encouragement.

1
INTRODUCTION

Major political parties seldom disintegrate; at least that has been the experience of Britain over the last 200 years or more. They may go through a period of prolonged electoral unpopularity, as the Conservative Party did after the schism over the Repeal of the Corn Laws in 1846, or as Labour did during the 1950s and 1980s. But parties of government, though sometimes written off, have usually bounced back. The case of the Liberal Party is different. On the eve of the First World War it was enjoying its ninth successive year in office. But in the course of the war it underwent a fatal split and, despite spluttering attempts at revival in the 1920s, soon found itself on the fringes of national political life. By the mid-1930s the Liberals had dwindled to a rump of a mere twenty-one MPs. Only in the collapse of the Irish National Party and its replacement by Sinn Fein between 1917 and 1919 do we have anything remotely like this swift descent from glory to impotence.

But the collapse of the Liberal Party was not only unusual, it also had momentous consequences, since it heralded the arrival of the party duopoly which has survived, after a fashion, until the present day. The replacement of the Liberals by Labour as the only serious alternative party to the Conservatives is the most important single development in early twentieth-century political life. No wonder that posterity has been preoccupied with the issue.

Unfortunately, so obsessive has been the search for the 'origins' of the Liberal disintegration that it has distorted our understanding of the late Victorian and Edwardian Liberal Party. As Trevor Wilson observed in his pioneering study first published in 1966, some have traced the start of the process back to the 'Great Labour Unrest' of the pre-First World

War period; some to the foundation of the Labour Party at the start of the century; and some to the split in the Party over Irish Home Rule in 1886; 'to satisfy every view about when and why the Liberal party met its doom', he comments, 'one might as well go back to the time when there was a party bearing the name Liberal at all'.[1] Wisdom of hindsight can so dominate our thoughts that we are tempted to assume the imminent 'death' of the Liberal Party almost before it had been born!

This distortion of vision has particularly affected the reading of the electoral data. Obviously no party can expect an uninterrupted tenure of power. Even the most successful of parties loses a general election from time to time. A single electoral reverse, or even a sequence of reverses, does not usually signal the start of an irreversible decline. But because we know the decline of the Liberal Party to be just around the corner, the difference between losing an election and sliding into insignificance can easily be overlooked.

For example, in the years immediately preceding the Great War, the Liberal Ministry headed by Asquith ran into a patch of deep electoral unpopularity. Irish Home Rule was on balance a vote-loser, and many voters were displeased that money was being deducted from their wages to finance the recent National Insurance Act. Between 1911 and 1914 the Liberals lost no fewer than fourteen seats to the Opposition in by-elections, in some of them on swings to the Opposition that were very high by the standards of the day (10.8 in South Manchester in March 1912, for example). Historians disagree over whether the government would have been able to repair its fortunes in time for the general election which, had war not broken out, would have been held by December 1915 at the latest. The omens were not entirely favourable. On the other hand, the Liberals had earlier recovered from a somewhat similar trough of mid-term unpopularity to win a qualified victory in the general election of January 1910.[2] In any case, even if the probability is that the Liberals' long run in office was indeed about to end in August 1914, that by itself does not necessarily tell us much about the reasons for the party's subsequent decline.

Moreover, there is something very unsatisfactory about judging the Liberal Party by 'performance indicators' that no sane person would apply to the Conservatives or the Labour Party, simply because we know that the latter 'survived', whereas the Liberals did not. Yet the Conservatives were themselves in deep crisis during the Edwardian decade, with weak leaders, serious policy divisions, and a sad record of electoral failure (in 1914 they had lost three general elections in a row). The

Labour Party on the eve of the war faced an even more problematic future. Its MPs owed their seats to the operation of an electoral pact with the Liberals, to whom they stood very much in the role of junior partners. True, in the immediate pre-war by-elections many Labour candidates took their courage in their hands and ran independently of the two major parties, but those that did, without exception, came bottom of the poll. On the basis of evidence such as this, one might be tempted to trace the origins of the Labour Party's inevitable decline back to the Edwardian years – did we not know what the future had in store.[3]

For most of the twentieth century the Conservatives tended to sub-scribe to values of hierarchy, tradition and deference, while Labour historically drew upon the loyalty generated by class solidarity. The old Liberal Party, by contrast, was a party of ideas and ideals, much given to discussion and argument. This often made it appear fractious and quarrelsome. As we shall see, some of the Liberals' policy divisions were indeed damaging, especially when they led to personal rancour among the leadership: think of the feud between Rosebery and Harcourt in the mid-1890s, or the later estrangement between Asquith and Lloyd George. But in many ways the debate about policy priorities was a sign of health, not of sickness. Walter Bagehot thought that the glory of the British political system resided in the fact that it involved 'government by discussion', and the Liberals were perhaps simply honouring the spirit of that system when they engaged in open public debate – amongst themselves, as well as with their political opponents. Nor should deep significance be read into all the leadership clashes. As A. B. Cooke and John Vincent pertinently observe:

> It is naive to think that the Liberals were bound to split because they were always quarrelling. Commentators who themselves lead the lives of church mice, note and are shocked by cabinet dissensions and tend to magnify the normal hurly-burly of politics as the end of the world. In fact, quarrelling was one of the party's greatest strengths, and the Tories' refusal to argue with each other led to an unenviable torpor.[4]

So the question of when the Liberal Party went into irreversible decline should not be prejudged. Nor should we forget that in the late Victorian and Edwardian years Liberalism was in many ways a vibrant and successful political movement, with major achievements and tri-umphs to its credit.

The Marxist Account

There may, however, be additional reasons for believing in the 'inevitability' of Liberal decline – as well as the lazy assumption that what happened was inevitable. For the collapse of the Liberal Party in Britain did not occur in isolation. Liberal parties in other European countries suffered a similar fate at approximately the same time. So it can plausibly be contended that the fate of British Liberalism formed part of a wider social and political upheaval affecting all industrialised societies. And a commonly accepted explanation of what underlay this worldwide 'crisis of Liberalism' is the one put forward by Marxists, though in its broad outlines it has also been followed by many historians who are not socialists of any kind.

This interpretation can be summarised as follows.[5] Liberalism was the ideology of the new entrepreneurial middle class thrown up by industrialisation, the Liberal Party serving as its principal political agency. Liberalism expressed the hostility of businessmen towards the world of aristocratic and landed privilege. The main objective of this creed was 'free trade' in its widest sense, that is to say, a liberation of commercial and industrial life from all trammels and interference, whether customary or legislative, so as to maximise production and to secure optimum conditions for economic growth. True, resentment against old monopolies and privileges was usually expressed in a 'universalistic' language. Liberals, with perfect sincerity, claimed to be furthering the interests of 'the People': they spoke, not of the needs of capital, but of individual rights and of citizenship. Indeed, many members of the lower orders (manual workers included) joined energetically in the assault on the old 'feudal' order. But the 'freedoms' and liberties which Liberals espoused were all, in essence, class-specific, rooted in the economic needs of the bourgeoisie.

Yet Liberalism, Marxists claim, could only flourish in the early, pioneering, optimistic phase of capitalist development. By the last quarter of the nineteenth century social and economic circumstances no longer favoured the Liberal cause. Joint-stock company legalisation and amalgamations had led to the replacement of the individual entrepreneur (the owner-manager characteristic of the early industrial revolution) by the large impersonal corporation. As the size of the average business unit increased, so the gap between employers and their workforce grew too large for employer paternalism to be successful. Paralleling these developments was growing social segregation in the big cities, as the middle classes withdrew to the outer suburbs, leaving behind them working-class areas over which they could exercise little direct influence. Moreover, sharpening the social tensions generated by these changes in late Victorian Britain was the onset of a worldwide industrial depression (more prolonged, if less acute, than the cyclical slumps which had marked the early and mid-Victorian years), resulting in reduced profit margins, intensified competition (as more and more countries underwent their own industrial revolutions), and high unemployment.

According to the Marxist account, the former buoyant confidence in the future of manufacturing industry collapsed under these pressures, as the commercial and industrial classes found themselves driven into adopting increasingly defensive strategies in the face of the twin threats of working-class unrest at home and foreign competition abroad.

Middle-class Liberals had long agonised over whether manual workers should be given the parliamentary vote, which served as a passport into the community of free citizens. Was it wise, they asked, to confer political rights on 'uneducated' men who patently did not understand the teachings of political economy – in other words, was capitalism compatible with democracy?

By the last quarter of the nineteenth century this issue had effectively been resolved. In nearly every industrial country manual workers had the vote, though not all enjoyed the universal male suffrage that prevailed in the unified German Reich. But for how long would these newly enfranchised masses be content to vote for representatives of the older political parties – parties which, like the British Liberal Party, claimed to have the working man's interests at heart? Sooner or later, Marxists argue, an appreciation of the divergent interests of employee and employer was bound to weaken the popular base of Liberalism, as working men sought to create new forms of political organisation which would better reflect their own class needs. The forming of 'independent' Labour parties would then be followed by a widespread acceptance within working-class communities of the socialist creed, which laid bare the realities of capitalist exploitation and offered its victims a practical means of redress.

Central to the Marxist interpretation is the claim that these changed economic and political circumstances faced Liberal parties everywhere with an intolerable dilemma. They could seek to hold on to their traditional working-class support by a concessionary policy of social reform. But though this might delay, it could not decisively halt, the efforts of class-conscious manual workers to break free from the political control of their superiors. Furthermore, the very attempt to 'woo' them in this way carried with it the risk of alienating the more timid members of the middle class, who began to drift in increasing numbers out of the Liberal Party into the security offered by Conservatism. In consequence, the Conservatives, no longer so heavily dependent upon the agricultural interest and other 'pre-industrial' social groupings, were able to broaden their electoral appeal until they eventually came to be looked upon as the 'natural' defenders of all forms of property – landed, commercial and industrial.

But, paradoxically, the Conservatives and their allies in the length and breadth of Europe were simultaneously attracting significant support from the working classes (over and above the 'deference voters' to whom they had always made an appeal). For at a time of mounting international tension and economic stress, nationalism and imperialism held a great attraction to people from all walks of life, and both these creeds became appropriated by the parties of the 'right'. In particular, Conservatives began to associate themselves with protectionism, which enjoyed a revival as manufacturers sought to counter foreign penetration of their markets. To the Conservatives, this brought obvious advantages. The employer's loss of profits and the working man's loss of wages and employment could both be blamed upon 'the foreigner'. Fears of foreign invasion also contributed to the new mood of nationalist hysteria, in which, once again, Conservatives presented themselves as custodians of the 'national interest', though, needless to say, this conception of the 'national interest' very largely rested upon middle-class premises.

In short, so runs the Marxist interpretation, in the last quarter of the nineteenth century economic and social developments were splitting the populations of the advanced industrial countries into two antagonistic camps: a working-class camp, represented by the Labour/Socialist parties, and the camp of those who, fearing a working-class political ascendancy, rallied behind the modernised parties of the right. This polarisation left the Liberal Party stranded high and dry. Its individualistic ideology now seemed archaic, while its programme of 'peace, retrenchment and reform' was ill-suited to an 'Age of Imperialism'. And so Liberalism, a bankrupt creed, went into decline as its social base atrophied. The pace of Liberal disintegration may have differed from country to country, but the social and economic forces producing this disintegration were everywhere the same, being ultimately located within the dynamic of capitalism itself.

The 'Revisionist' Case

The Marxist interpretation is bold and in many ways appealing, but it has always been open to a variety of objections. First, even if its broad truth be accepted, we still need to know how and when the Liberal collapse occurred. Historians (unlike social scientists, perhaps) are concerned with the specific form which events take. They are less interested, for example, in the general circumstances which produced the economic and political emancipation of women in mature industrial societies than in precisely how and why this happened in particular countries.

Similarly with the downfall of the British Liberal Party, where the exact chronology of events is highly important. For the later course of British political life would almost certainly have been different, but for the fact that the Liberals were strong enough in the early twentieth century to form a stable and long-lived ministry, and did not disappear as a potential party of government until the mid-1920s. Had the collapse occurred earlier, both the Labour and the Conservative Parties would have developed in different ways. In untangling these difficulties, the general explanations furnished by the Marxists offer only limited help.

Second, no steady decline in Liberal fortunes in fact took place in the later nineteenth century. On the contrary, not only did the Liberals enjoy a period of almost unparalleled electoral success between 1906 and 1914, but the legislative achievements of the Campbell-Bannerman and Asquith ministries during these years (most obviously in the field of social policy) probably eclipsed those of Gladstone's last three governments. Indeed, during the 1970s a 'revisionist' school of historians emerged which argued that the Liberal Party had successfully adapted itself to the requirements of class politics during the Edwardian years, before unexpectedly falling victim to the First World War.[6]

Third, there are many historians who have been struck by the way in which the Liberal Party was damaged, not so much by the operation of deep impersonal forces, but rather by 'bad luck', misunderstandings, and suchlike 'contingencies'. True, those who place most emphasis upon these 'accidents' tend to be historians deeply sympathetic to the Liberal Party.[7] But that does not mean that their work can simply be dismissed as 'special pleading'.

Let us take but two instances where 'accidents' seem to have played a large role (both will be dealt with more carefully later in the book). It does seem as though Asquith and Lloyd George were tantalisingly close to agreement over the composition and functions of a remodelled War Committee in December 1916, before a chapter of misunderstandings brought about the breach between them that eventually split Liberalism into two distinct parties, each with its own leader – a disaster from which the Liberals never fully recovered.[8]

An even more telling example of an unanticipated happening wrenching history away from what had seemed to be its natural course of development was Parliament's very narrow failure to end the 'first-past-the-post' system of voting in 1918; it would be hard to show that this was in any way 'predetermined'.[9] But the outcome was momentous since, arguably, it brought about the stark class-based duopoly which reduced the Liberals to their later peripheral role in British politics.

Finally, can the fate of 'Liberalism' as an ideology be linked so closely to the fate of the Liberal Party as an electoral machine? Employing, for once, a bit of 'wisdom of hindsight' ourselves, we can clearly see that the disappearance of the Liberal Party as a major force at Westminster did not mean the 'death of Liberalism' in any simple sense. On the contrary, many of the values and beliefs of the old Liberal Party were carried over into a succeeding period by the Labour Party, while others found a central place in the political thinking of Stanley Baldwin, the highly successful leader of the Conservative Party between 1923 and 1937.

Moreover, many of the tenets of the 'Manchester School' Liberals of the early nineteenth century were later revived (albeit in new forms and in a quite different context) by the Conservatives close to Mrs Thatcher. Symbolically, even the arguments for Free Trade (once dismissed as an early and mid-Victorian period piece) now enjoy widespread credibility. Liberalism has proved to be surprisingly resilient as a political and economic creed, and, despite the failure of the 'Alliance' to achieve the breakthrough which once seemed possible in the early and mid-1980s, it seems at present to have outlived the 'hard' Marxist theories predicting its inevitable supersession. Can we, then, be quite so sure that there was no place in mid-twentieth-century British political life for some kind of modernised Liberal Party? After all, Tony Blair's class-free 'New Labour' surely has more in common with the Radical-Liberal tradition than it does with the programmes promulgated by earlier Labour Leaders from Keir Hardie to James Callaghan.

What befell the Liberal Party between 1886 and 1929 has long been considered important, difficult and contentious.[10] But in the course of the 1990s new historical approaches further enriched this debate.

Political events, it is now argued, cannot simply be 'read off' from underlying social and economic developments: parties shape social reality as well as reflecting, and responding to, external social movements and trends. Looking back on the earlier exchanges between Marxists and many of their revisionist critics, it seems that both these groups relied too exclusively on notions of class, neither showing sufficient alertness to the role of culture and language in transmitting political values and beliefs.[11] The preoccupation with class, it is argued, also tended to result in a serious underplaying of the importance of 'gender' in fashioning social identities.

Both these criticisms have important implications for an understanding of Liberal decline since competing visions of the 'people' were at the very heart of the contest between popular Radicalism and socialism, while, as we will see in Chapter 7, disagreements about the constitutional rights of women played a significant part in Liberal disintegration and demoralisation at the start of the twentieth century.

2

THE RISE OF THE LIBERAL PARTY

The Liberal Party came into existence in the nineteenth century because the country's political system so obviously lagged behind its industrial development. True, following the Municipal Reform Act of 1835, rival middle-class groups vied for control in the major urban centres, but, in the counties, local government remained largely in the hands of the landed interest. The same was broadly true of national politics. Admittedly, offices such as the Presidency of the Board of Trade usually went to men of commercial backgrounds and experience, but the prestigious Secretaryships of State were, almost invariably, entrusted to members of one of the great aristocratic families. The landed interest also predominated in Parliament, especially in the House of Lords, which virtually functioned as its institutional embodiment – only after 1885 did middle-class men become ennobled in any significant numbers, and it would take decades before this significantly affected the composition of the Chamber as a whole. As for the Commons, here landowners and their dependants never comprised less than one-half of the membership of the House. It seemed as though political life was being controlled by a traditional 'ruling class', an elite all the stronger in that its tentacles encompassed other bastions of state power, such as the diplomatic service, the court, the armed services, and the Church of England.

As the century proceeded, many of these 'anomalies' were removed or mitigated. The 1832 Reform Act, in addition to extending the franchise, took away 143 seats from the 'rotten' boroughs, allowing extra representation to be given to the populous counties and to new manufacturing towns such as Birmingham and Manchester. The landed property qualification was abolished in 1858. Further Reform Acts in

1867 and 1884–5 gave recognition to the importance of the manufacturing districts and to London. Yet political reform in all these matters was slow in coming, often encountered considerable resistance, and, even by 1885, was far from complete.

Moreover, two aspects of British public life continued to reflect the survival of the old pre-industrial order. First, there was what some contemporaries called 'the land monopoly'. Land provided the basis of the political system, but it also enjoyed special legal privileges and immunities. For example, land did not pay its fair share of probate duty. Moreover, the system of primogeniture and entail meant that large concentrations of land remained in the hands of the great aristocrats – protected from the laws of supply and demand which regulated the accumulation and distribution of other forms of wealth.

Second, there was the privileged position occupied by the Church of England. This seemed unfair in the light of the 1851 religious census, which, taken literally, seemed to show that, over the whole of England and Wales, those worshipping in chapel slightly outnumbered those attending Anglican services. Indeed, in Wales, Anglicanism, practised by only 20 per cent of so of the churchgoing population, had the appearance of an 'alien' creed. But the same was only slightly less true of some of the new manufacturing districts; for example, in Rochdale and Bradford, Nonconformity supplied over 68 per cent of those attending a place of Christian worship.[1] Yet the Church of England still functioned as the 'national' Church, and, as such, played a central role in rituals of state. It also enjoyed a clear advantage over the other religious sects in the provision of 'elementary' education, while in the earlier decades of the century it virtually controlled the ancient universities of Oxford and Cambridge.

To protest at these 'anomalies' was the mission of the 'Radicals', the 'advanced guard' of the Victorian Liberal Party. It is important to remember that in the years before 1885 the Radicals formed a minority group (often a small minority) within the 'Whig–Liberal' alliance. Yet it was these men, of whom Richard Cobden and John Bright were the most prominent, who gave Liberalism its cutting edge and distinctiveness and who frequently set the agenda for political change. For what groups in the community did the Radicals speak?

Many Nonconformists looked to the Radicals for help in removing their legal disabilities, which were indeed gradually removed, though not in all cases through Radical agency. Compulsory payment of church rates ended in 1868, the following decade saw the repeal of the Test Acts which had previously closed Oxford and Cambridge to non-Anglicans, and an Act of 1880 at last permitted Dissenters to be buried in consecrated ground near to their chapels. But to the more intransigent Dissenters this was not enough. Through the Liberation Society, founded in 1853, many of them pressed for genuine religious equality, which they thought necessitated the abolition of the established Church. In 1869 the Church of Ireland was disestablished and disendowed, but the claims of the English, Welsh, and Scots[2] to a similar settlement remained unsatisfied. Moreover, as we shall see, in the sphere of elementary education the grievances of the Nonconformists intensified, rather than disappeared, in the later decades of the century.[3]

But perhaps the very heart of Victorian Radicalism lay in its attacks on the 'land monopoly'. Land, claimed the Radicals, differed from other kinds of wealth in that it constituted a 'natural monopoly'. Whereas industrial enterprise could be expanded indefinitely by hard work and entrepreneurial acumen, land was, by and large, fixed in extent. Yet since land was as necessary to life as oxygen, those fortunate enough to have inherited it were able to exploit the rest of the community. In T. H. Green's words, the real enemy of the working classes was therefore not the capitalist but the landlord, because 'the capital gained by one is not taken from another, but one man cannot acquire more land without others having less'.[4] Such a message appealed to middle-class groups otherwise solicitous of the rights of property, including many of the great capitalists – Cobden and Bright were themselves 'cotton lords'.

The landed system did, of course, change in the course of the century. The repeal of the Corn Laws in 1846 removed the special protection afforded to agriculture – a symbolic, as well as a practical, triumph for the manufacturing centres. Moreover, the Gladstone ministry's Settled Land Act of 1882 and the Conveyancing Act (prepared by the previous Tory administration) removed some of the more anomalous and indefensible aspects of the land market, thereby taking the steam out of the land reformers' campaign. The Game Laws, seen by the Radicals as a symbol of the way in which landowners used their parliamentary position to safeguard their own interests, also underwent successive reform. But the fundamental grievances remained barely touched. The outworks of privilege, it seemed, had been ceded, but not the citadel.

Because of the close links between landed society and the army officer corps, Radicals naturally moved on from attacking the 'land monopoly' to attacking the armed services. In their eyes, the landed aristocracy was an 'atavism', an anachronistic survival from an earlier era when societies were organised for warfare, but out of place in the modern industrial world. At times of emotional excitement, as in the early 1840s, they angrily portrayed the large landed families as the descendants of the conquering Normans, a military caste quartered upon the peace-loving industrial population. It was poor history, but made for potent propaganda.

Distrust of the army made Radicals keen to curb what they called 'bloated armaments'. But Radicals also disliked the Foreign Office and the diplomatic service, those other aristocratic strongholds, and this gave rise to a tradition of opposition to the 'official' conduct of foreign affairs. The 'Trouble Makers', as A. J. P. Taylor has called them, tended to view diplomacy as a mischievous pastime carried out by a landed elite for its own gratification. However, there tended to be two broad schools of thought over what should take its place. Some Radicals espoused a policy of 'non-intervention', believing that contacts between peoples should be confined to the civilising influences of trade and that the less foreign policy there was the better. But others (although, confusingly, the same people often switched from one line of argument to the other) insisted that the British government abandon its preoccupation with 'immoral' concepts such as the balance of power, and commit itself to an active policy designed to help oppressed nationalities rightly struggling to be free: Italians, Poles, Bulgars, Armenians, and so on, depending on the circumstances of time and place.[5]

Underlying all these specific campaigns was the Radical mission to put an end to what Cobden, the greatest of the Radical leaders, called 'feudalism'. In Cobden's view the country was in the grip of a sinister aristocratic system, its constitution being 'a thing of monopolies, and Church-craft, and sinecures, armorial hocus-pocus, primogeniture, and pageantry!'[6] Like other Radicals, he wanted the country's political institutions and practices to be brought into harmony with its economic base, so that the importance of manufacturing and trading would be fully recognised. In modern parlance, he was self-consciously concerned with institutional 'modernisation'.

Of course, this Radicalism did not find expression in modern class language. As Green's remark reveals, Radicals believed that 'the industrious classes', both employers and employees, were the common victims of an aristocratic conspiracy. But more common still was the Radical claim that they were advancing the interests of 'the people' against the forces of 'monopoly' and 'privilege'. Theirs was a secular creed of 'progress' which celebrated the great achievements of industrial capitalism, but which spoke less of the growth of trade and prosperity (important though both these things were) than of an enlargement of 'liberty'. Trade was to be freed from all trammels; so was land, which, it was hoped, could be made a commodity as easily tradeable as a bale of merchandise. Finally, there was to be 'religious equality', on the American model, with no one sect enjoying a preferential advantage, as well as freedom of speech and assembly.

This, then, was the gist of Radicalism, the creed of the 'advanced' wing of the Liberal Party. Its salient outlines did not fundamentally change from the 1830s through to the outbreak of the Great War. Indeed, Joseph Chamberlain in the early 1880s and, a quarter of a century later, David Lloyd George, often echoed the phraseology of Cobden and John Bright, from whom they were proud to trace their descent.[7]

These Radical beliefs also helped to determine the country's electoral geography well into the twentieth century. Although, as we shall later see, the Irish crisis in 1886 somewhat complicated matters, the Liberal Party continued to dominate the manufacturing districts, leaving the Conservatives in control of most rural constituencies, as well as the suburbs, seaside resorts and cathedral cities of southern England. In addition, Liberalism was strongly correlated with Nonconformity, Conservatism with Anglicanism. Finally, on the 'Celtic Fringe' in Scotland and Wales, the Liberals were able to harness the forces of nationalism against a Conservative Party which seemed, through its close association with the Church of England, to be the instrument of an alien nation as well as the custodian of an alien creed.

Yet during the mid-Victorian years the 'advanced Radicals', for all their achievements, never proved capable of forming their 'own' party. One reason for this was that, from the very start, the Radicals had difficulty in establishing priorities. For example, those who felt strongly about their religious disabilities often lacked militancy on the land question.[8] Conversely, there were entrepreneurial Radicals, such as the Anglican Cobden, who sympathised with Nonconformist grievances but were hostile to manifestations of Dissenting bigotry – which anyhow threatened the political unity of the industrial middle class. Moreover, the Radicals divided into two main groups. There were the 'Philosophic Radicals', who drew their inspiration from the writings of the Utilitarians, Bentham and the two Mills, a group which judged all institutions and practices by the criterion of whether or not they promoted the 'greatest happiness of the greatest number'; this group tended to come from the professional middle class (joined by some landowners) and was London-oriented. Second, there were the 'entrepreneurial Radicals', mostly capitalists from the big manufacturing cities, whose prime concern was to emancipate commerce and industry, a group which, at least initially, tended to look to Cobden for leadership.

There were also two important 'external' reasons for Radical ineffectuality. First, landed society possessed enormous social prestige, in the face of which many industrialists and Dissenters experienced a certain loss of self-confidence. Those anxious for social advancement were tempted to exchange the chapel for the Church of England, a transition which was often a prelude to a rapprochement with the Conservative Party. As Michael Hurst argues, right-wing Liberal defections to the Conservative Party 'began almost as soon as a full-blown Liberal party' emerged.[9] Moreover, many wealthy businessmen purchased a country house and succumbed to the lure of its accompanying lifestyle; even though this might not cause an actual change of party allegiance, it often blunted the militancy of those whose needs Radicalism claimed to represent.

In addition, the great public schools, with their Classics-dominated syllabus and emphasis on the 'gentlemanly' qualities of honour and service, tended to deaden the entrepreneurial appetites of those who received their education at these establishments – nearly all of them Anglican. The quest for places, titles and honorific offices, such as seats on the county bench or deputy lord-lieutenancies, may have had similar consequences. True, historians disagree over whether such activities should be seen as an aping of aristocratic values or as a healthy assertion by the urban middle class of the social position to which its wealth entitled it.[10] But, in either case, such emulation did little to foster the kind of 'class pride' which had meant so much to Cobden and Bright.

But, second, the very discriminations against which Radicals protested made it difficult for them to organise themselves politically in such a way as to 'capture' the institutions of the state. For example, the underrepresentation of the northern industrial centres (if measured by population or by wealth) meant that there were insufficient safe seats upon which to construct a parliamentary majority. The Radicals could form highly efficient pressure groups and run influential campaigns on specific issues; the most famous of these was obviously the Anti-Corn Law League. They were particularly good at mobilising opinion through the press; the provincial newspapers which carried so much authority in the mid- and late Victorian period had often been founded by Radical businessmen: the *Leeds Mercury*, the *Bradford Observer*, the *Manchester Guardian* and the *Eastern Daily Press* all exemplify this trend. But, at the level of national politics, the Radicals constituted only a small coterie. And brief experiments at 'independence' in the late 1840s and 1850s soon convinced them that, being unable to 'go it alone', their only hope of influencing events lay through association with one of the two major parties of government.

When the Conservative Party became a protectionist party in 1846, after its leader, Sir Robert Peel, had been expelled for repealing the Corn Laws, the Radicals had little option but to link up with the Whigs – a situation which was not without irony, since the Whig leadership comprised great aristocratic landowners, like the Russells, the Spencers and the Wodehouses.

Yet an alliance between Radicals and Whigs had much to recommend it. First, the 'principles of 1688' had bequeathed to the Whigs a strong commitment to 'constitutional liberty', a mistrust of the power of the executive, and a view of Parliament as custodian of the rights of the wider community. These 'principles' were capable of extension to meet new social and political needs. Then, too, the patrician Whig land-owners had always prided themselves on playing a skilful mediatory role between Crown and 'people', and the social unrest produced by population growth and industrialisation gave them plentiful scope for exercising these particular talents.

Second, the Whigs were open to modernising influences. The very fact that they tended to be members of great aristocratic families, with a metropolitan outlook and a wide spread of interests, meant that, unlike the Tories, who (especially after 1846) functioned as the 'country party', they saw the political problems of their day with a certain detachment, often rising above their immediate local and class interests. In fact, some Whig magnates, as owners of urban and industrial land, were directly implicated in the expanding capitalist economy, while others had houses or represented constituencies which brought them into close contact with the manufacturing districts. Few Whigs, in any case, were so obtuse that they failed to recognise how much their own survival as a kind of hereditary governing class required them to show some sensitivity to the wishes and needs of these centres.

In addition, many Whig leaders had diligently studied the social and economic problems of their day, reading the political economists, attending discussion groups such as the Political Economy Club, and generally keeping abreast of the times. Earl Grey, Lord John Russell and Lord Palmerston, for example, had all acquired a fluent mastery of the idiom of 'progress' which cannot simply be explained in terms of expediency. In short, even when dealing with the 1870s or 1880s, it would be a mistake to dismiss as an anachronism doomed to disappear a social grouping which not only dominated Cabinet discussions but which also showed an aptitude for new methods of political organisation and propaganda.[11]

Third, the Radicals were not in a position where open defiance of Whiggery was necessarily possible. For, while the the Radical leaders were nearly all manufacturers (for example, Cobden, Bright, Forster, Mundella and Chamberlain), their most loyal supporters during the mid-Victorian years were artisans and shopkeepers, not the more well-to-do members of the middle classes, who, given the option, tended to vote for 'moderate' Liberal and even Whig candidates.[12] Even businessmen, fierce Radicals though they might have been on first entering politics, sometimes came to find this 'moderate' approach acceptable, and made their peace with the Whig-dominated party. In other words, the old division between landowners and businessmen was losing its former asperity – though important status distinctions remained.[13]

Another sign of the growing convergence between Radicalism and Whiggery was the fact that, from the 1830s onwards, and especially after 1846, a significant number of politicians from both camps started to refer to themselves publicly by the common name of 'Liberals'.[14] And, insofar as the term 'Whig' was retained at all, it came to acquire new meanings: by the 1860s it no longer denoted a small powerful circle of interrelated landowning families, but was often applied to cautious and moderate Liberals, regardless of their social backgrounds.

Radicalism, too, ceased to depend so heavily on social position. Even in the 1840s some of the Anti-Corn Law League leaders, like Milner Gibson, had been drawn from the ranks of landowners. By the 1890s the Radicals were being led by William Vernon Harcourt, who had Plantagenet blood in his veins! Another cause of division disappeared when authentic urban Radicals – Forster in 1865, Bright in 1868, Mundella and Chamberlain in 1880 – receieved high office, a change in their circumstances which to some degree modified their political perspectives.

Yet Whiggery, even in its most progressive manifestations, was unlikely to meet with the full approval of the 'advanced' Radicals. The

Whigs were essentially men who had been brought up from birth with the notion that 'duty' might require them to govern their country just as they would have to administer their estates and supervise local affairs. But though they brought to political life an 'administrative ethic' and a pragmatic temper, they lacked 'warmth' as reformers and were temperamentally suspicious of 'enthusiasm' in others.[15]

Moreover, there were limits beyond which these great landowners were unlikely to advance in their measured pursuit of progress. True, a generous conception of the national interest had reconciled them to the abolition of the Corn Laws in the 1840s, and with it the notion that agriculture should play a central role in national life. Some also recognised the imperfections of the land system in Ireland, where many possessed estates, and were ready to sponsor bold remedies for these ills. But the Whigs were essentially 'repenters', not 'rebels', and it was inconceivable that they would deliberately subvert the landed system which underpinned their wealth and their power. (There existed, of course, a few genuinely Radical landowners, like Sir Wilfrid Lawson, but these can no more be taken as representative types than the millionaire socialists of more recent times.) Similarly with religious grievances: although the Whig leaders often acted as 'friends' of the Catholics and Dissenters, nearly all were Anglicans, and very few, except in the special circumstances of Ireland and Wales, showed any disposition to embrace the disestablishment and disendowment of the established Church, even as a long-term objective.[16]

Hence, as late as the 1880s, to the more doctrinaire of the Radicals, Whiggery, however defined, would never provide satisfaction. Apart from anything else, urban Radicals thought it a matter of shame and humiliation that people of their 'order' could not manage their own affairs but had to 'delegate' the conduct of public business to others or to occupy a subordinate position to the landowners who continued to dominate government. Walter Bagehot, writing about Bright and his capitalist friends in 1867, well understood this particular mentality: 'They cannot endure – they ought not to endure – that a rich, able manufacturer should be a less man than a small stupid squire.'[17]

The frail bond between Radicals and Whiggery might not have survived as long as it did, but for the role of William Ewart Gladstone, the effective creator of the British Liberal Party, into which both Whiggery and Radicalism became subsumed. Gladstone had entered politics as a Conservative, before his support for Corn Law repeal drove him into a more than ten years' sojourn in a political 'no man's land', prior to his eventual emergence as the Liberal leader. Gladstone's peculiar fitness to perform this role owed much to his family circumstances and personality. As the son of a Liverpudlian merchant prince, Gladstone enjoyed family ties with the great business centres, and, from the time of his 1853 Budget onwards, the public saw him as the prominent statesman who best understood the needs of the manufacturing and commercial world. As one historian has put it, 'his policies were those which the middle class would have pursued for themselves if they could have found in their midst a leader as appealing and representative'.[18]

But this was not all, since this remarkable man acquired an unparalleled ascendancy over the so-called 'plebeian Radicals' – who constituted another, as yet undiscussed, element in the wider constituency of Liberalism. These people – a mixture of working men, independent craftsmen, tradesmen and small employers – had inherited a 'democratic' tradition, going back through Thomas Paine to the seventeenth century, which asserted the right of ordinary men and women to live lives that were free from external supervision and control. These demands often found expression in the language of religion, but it was a religion which centred less on doctrine than on human emancipation. The God they worshipped was a democratic God who liked poor people and talked with them. Bunyan and Cromwell were heroes to the plebeian Radicals, but so too were contemporaries like Mazzini, Garibaldi (who was mobbed on his visit to Britain in 1864) and Abraham Lincoln.[19]

Not all manual workers in Victorian Britain subscribed to these beliefs. But in areas where the underprivileged could engage in political struggle without coming into contact with established middle-class elites (some farm labourers, the coal miners of the North-East and London artisans, for example), plebeian Radicalism exercised a strong appeal.

Of all the parliamentary leaders of Liberalism, apart from John Bright and Joseph Cowen of Newcastle, it was Gladstone who most struck a chord with such 'democrats'. They warmed even to his praise of 'retrenchment', finding little that the mid-Victorian state was doing that was of any benefit to them, just as they read their own meanings (of fair play, for example) into the doctrine of Free Trade.[20] But most of all, they responded to Gladstone's 'moral exaltation' in politics and the way in which he seemed to share their own belief in the dignity of labour, with its associations of 'independence' and 'respectability'. But it was a two-way relationship, since Liberal leaders such as Bright and Gladstone and their workingmen followers 'needed each other, and in a sense invented each other'.[21]

But it is rather puzzling that Gladstone should have been so popular with the plebeian Radicals – some of them ex-Chartists, some secularists and Republicans – since though, on certain issues, he could sound like a Radical, he was not really one at all. His experiences at Eton and later at Christ Church, Oxford, his strong High Church beliefs (with which he had replaced his family's Evangelicalism) and his marriage into a minor landed family had all brought Gladstone into an aristocratic world which, as an outsider, he tended to idealise. Far from sharing the Radicals' contempt for the values of landed society, Gladstone, throughout his life, held a high regard for the disinterested public service which he thought to be the hallmark of this class.[22] And far from seeking the overthrow of 'feudalism', Gladstone saw his role as that of a mediator between landed and industrial wealth, as well as a bridgehead between the 'classes' and the 'masses'. This, along with remarkable abilities and charismatic qualities, brought him popular adulation, which extended even to the ranks of the disfranchised. At Westminster Gladstonian enthusiasm was viewed with greater scepticism, but here, too, he succeeded in holding together his disparate followers, who, however exasperated they might often be with him, realised his indispensability.

In the aftermath of the Liberals' 1880 electoral victory, Gladstone, since February 1875 a backbencher, managed to impose himself on the Queen, becoming Prime Minister for the second time. But even Gladstone had his work cut out in maintaining a semblance of party unity. Some of the friction within Liberal ranks was generated by events in Ireland, where Charles Stuart Parnell, Michael Davitt and the Land League had succeeded in unleashing a 'Land War'. This development polarised opinion on mainland Britain, since many Radicals viewed with some satisfaction the collapse of landlord power in Ireland (the weak link in the chain of landlordism) and wanted to help it on its way with timely legislative interventions – whereas most Whig politicians took the very opposite view. Liberal disagreements over Ireland came to the surface in 1880, when the government's Compensation for Disturbances Bill provoked a rebellion of sixty Whig peers, a group which included twenty Irish landlords, eleven of whom held estates of over 20,000 acres each.[23] Lansdowne, one of the wealthiest of all Irish landlords, promptly resigned from the government, and in the following year the Duke of Argyll signalled his disaffection by joining the peers on the cross-benches.[24]

Such men worried that the curtailment of the rights of landed property in Ireland constituted a precedent and might serve as the prelude to an assault on landlordism on the other side of the Irish Channel. This was no empty fear – given the recent return to Parliament as Liberal MPs of a number of aggressive English land reformers, which included representatives of the tenant farmers. In Scotland the struggle of the crofters to secure greater legal rights was also disrupting Liberal unity.[25] Already suffering the consequences of an acute agricultural depression, many landowners trembled for the security of their estates.

But these problems were superimposed upon others. During the Liberals' previous administration, an Education Act had been passed (the Forster Education Act of 1870) which wounded the consciences of the Party's Nonconformist supporters by integrating Anglican schools into the new 'national' system.[26] In protest, a pressure group had been formed by a number of Birmingham businessmen (among them the up-and-coming star of Radicalism, Joseph Chamberlain), calling itself the National Education League. This body, which campaigned for a secular system of public education, evolved in 1877 into the National Liberal Federation (NLF). Through control of a new mass organisation in the country, Chamberlain and his friends sought to mobilise the opinion of rank-and-file activists against the 'notables' who dominated the party at Westminster. How much of a threat this represented to the old political order became apparent with the publication between August 1883 and July 1885 of the *Radical Programme* – a clear attempt to dictate to the reluctant party leadership. When in June 1885 Gladstone's second administration disintegrated and Lord Salisbury became Conservative Prime Minister, the world was entertained to the spectacle of a political duel between Chamberlain and Lord Hartington, the Whig leader.

What gave this contest its importance was the fact that Gladstone had been indicating his impending retirement ever since his return to front-bench politics in 1880. Moreover, with Parliament having agreed to franchise extension and a major Redistribution Bill in 1884–5, the two parties were about to face a new kind of electorate. This added to the mood of uncertainty. At stake, therefore, was not just the leadership of the Liberal Party, but also its future political trajectory.

The likelihood was that Hartington would take Gladstone's place, if only as a stop-gap leader. But how long would it be before the Radicals seized control of the party, which they had never in the past been powerful enough to do? Or, to put it another way, how much time would elapse before the more timorous Whigs parted company with the Liberal Party altogether and sought some sort of a rapprochement with the

Conservatives? Chamberlain may not have been that keen on driving the Whigs out of the party into the arms of the Conservatives, as some of his followers wanted him to do. But the logic of the situation pointed to some major party realignment in the not so distant future.[27]

Yet the division within the Liberal Party cannot just be reduced to one between landowning Whigs and urban Radicals. Indeed, Chamberlain was in some respects not really a conventional Cobdenite Radical at all. For the *Radical Programme* aimed at more than simply curtailing the privileges of the Church of England and of ending the 'land monopoly', since Chamberlain and his friends were also offering inducements (opponents called them bribes) to the poor. The most successful of these inducements, judging by the election returns in 1885, was the proposal (emanating from Chamberlain's friend, Jesse Collings) that local author-ities be empowered to acquire land for leasing as allotments or small-holdings, colloquially known as 'Three Acres and a Cow'. The *Radical Programme* also contained policies for free education, improved work-ing-class housing, and a graduated income tax. Chamberlain wanted these reforms because he believed that only a 'constructive' social pro-gramme would bind the propertyless masses to the established political system and prevent a disastrous drift into class politics – with the threat of a clash between Capital and Labour.[28]

Now, to understand why Chamberlain was advocating these reforms one must first examine the social issues which were forcing themselves upon public attention in the early 1880s. The problems of the big cities, particularly London, had become a major talking point following the publication of a series of exposures of what life meant for the 'people of the abyss'. Sensationalist pamphlets like Andrew Mearns's *The Bitter Cry of Outcast London* (1883) aroused feelings both of pity and of fear. The element of fear perhaps predominated in 1885–6, when a business recession pushed up unemployment, provoking riots and popular dem-onstrations in towns all over the country. This seemed all the more alarming since Britain's first Marxist party, the recently formed Social Democratic Federation (SDF), was helping to organise these protests. Although the threat of revolutionary socialism was as yet very small, these events did raise the spectre of class conflict and made many com-mentators worry about whether popular pressure might not, before too long, produce major changes in the structure and content of political life.[29] After all, such developments had already occurred in the German Empire and other continental countries, where Marxists had made heavy inroads at the expense of the older parties – and particularly at the expense of the Liberals.

Chamberlain's interest in new kinds of social legislation becomes intelligible against this background. But, to some extent, his new policies represented a sharp break with the mainstream Radical tradition. John Bright, for example, had earlier opposed the Factory Acts with great vehemence, denouncing state intervention in industrial and commercial life as both futile and damaging. True, during the late 1850s and 1860s such dogmatic laissez-faire convictions had already begun to subside. Some younger business Radicals, like W. E. Forster and A. J. Mundella, actually wanted to *extend* the Factory Acts.[30] Even so, the prospect of such developments created considerable nervousness among all Liberals (not least the businessmen). Indeed, one reason why so many Liberals (notably Robert Lowe) had opposed suffrage extension in 1866–7 was a fear that this would mean the enfranchisement of uneducated labourers who, not understanding the precepts of political economy, would try and use their new-found political power to force through ill-conceived schemes of social reconstruction.

By the 1880s, and with much greater reason, similar anxieties were being expressed by the likes of the City banker, George Joachim Goschen. Goschen had first been returned in a by-election in 1863 on a conventional Radical platform, although he very soon dissociated himself from Bright's extremism. As a minister in Gladstone's first administration (1868–74) Goschen had demonstrated his loyalty to the principles of political economy. But he had subsequently refused to take office in Gladstone's second ministry because he disapproved of the party's commitment to the equalisation of the franchise – that is to say, extending the household suffrage from the boroughs to the counties. Chamberlain's decision to contest the 1885 election on the basis of the so-called 'Unauthorised Programme' (a much abbreviated version of the *Radical Programme*) filled Goschen with horror.[31] Nor was he alone, since many members of the Liberal intelligentsia were also becoming worried over the direction of Liberal politics, grumbling that 'sentiment' was replacing 'science' as a guide to public action.[32]

Long before the Home Rule schism of 1885–6, Chamberlain's activities were therefore having a disturbing impact on party unity and alienating, not only many of the big landed families, but also segments of the more socially conservative middle class. Some businessmen even began to have their doubts about land reform, fearing that the Radicals' reckless presentation of its merits might weaken respect for all property.[33] Even more did they dislike Chamberlain's doctrine of 'ransom' (which held that owners of *all* kinds of property should pay high taxes as a form of 'protection money'), his wooing of manual workers and farm labourers, and his identification of social progress with an expansion of the role of the public authorities, necessitating increased taxation, the burden of which would fall on the wealthy. As Professor Southgate says, 'The governing class was now subjected to a renewal of the sort of attack in which Cobden and Bright had specialised, but with the object of reversing Cobdenite principles of public expenditure'.[34]

Yet, provided that no panic exodus took place, there was no reason why Chamberlain should regret the loss to Liberalism of some timid supporters from the urban middle class. On the contrary, in the summer of 1885, with Gladstone's long career of public service seemingly drawing to its close, the Radicals could view the future with optimism. A reconstruction of the Liberal Party on their own terms seemed only a matter of time.

Yet things did not work out like this at all. Why? Because in the winter of 1885–6 Gladstone changed the political agenda by announcing his conversion to a policy of Irish Home Rule, that is to say, giving Ireland a subordinate Parliament for the determination of its own affairs, subject to ultimate Westminster control. The full significance of this decision will be discussed at some length in the next two chapters. But before analysing the Home Rule crisis, it may be helpful to outline, in bald detail, what actually happened.

Gladstone's dramatic initiative quickly won the backing of the majority of his followers, but it alienated many of the Whigs, including Hartington, as well as Goschen and prominent Liberal intellectuals who feared that Home Rule would usher in a period of democratic chaos and imperial disintegration.[35] Yet, surprisingly, after a period of hesitation, Chamberlain and some of the Radicals also joined in the denunciation of Home Rule. The outcome was a serious party schism. When Gladstone, back in office, introduced his Home Rule Bill in the summer of 1886, nearly one-third of Liberal MPs voted against it, so securing its defeat and the fall of the government.[36]

At the ensuing general election, the dissident Liberal MPs and peers, who had created a new party of their own, the Liberal Unionist Party (so called because they were Liberals who wanted to maintain the Union with Ireland), formed an electoral pact with the Conservatives. The result was a new Conservative administration, headed by Lord Salisbury, generally supported by the Liberal Unionists, who held the balance of seats in the Commons. (Following Lord Randolph Churchill's resignation as Chancellor of the Exchequer, Goschen was brought in as his successor in January 1887, the first Liberal Unionist to serve with the Conservatives.) After hopes of Liberal reunion had been dashed following the breakdown of the Round Table Conference in 1887, the working alliance between Liberal Unionists and Conservatives (collectively known as the 'Unionists') grew tighter. When the short-lived Liberal administration of 1892–5 collapsed, Salisbury, back in Number 10 Downing Street for a third time, decided to give Cabinet office to four leading Liberal Unionists: Chamberlain opted for the Colonial Office, and Hartington (now the 8th Duke of Devonshire) became Lord President of the Council. The two Unionist parties finally fused in 1912.

On the surface, then, it would seem that, by making the Irish Question the central issue in British politics, Gladstone had thoroughly muddied the waters. People who could agree upon little else found themselves working together in the Gladstonian Liberal Party (as 'Home Rulers'), while an even more heterogeneous collection of politicians was running the Unionist Alliance.

Had the Home Rule crisis, then, really obliterated the social and economic issues which had been agitating the political world over the preceding five years? And, if so, what sort of Liberal Party came into existence as a result of Gladstone's extraordinary démarche?

3

THE ASSAULT ON FEUDALISM, 1886–1905

On the surface, the Home Rule schism of 1885–6 would seem to have brought the Radical assault on landed privilege to a decisive end, as perhaps Gladstone himself had intended. The extraordinary union between Hartington and Chamberlain, joint leaders of the new Liberal Unionist Party, was proof of how the violent passions raised by the Irish issue had succeeded in making friends out of old adversaries and adversaries out of old friends. For about twenty years the main dividing line between parties was that between 'Home Rulers' (the Liberals and their Irish Nationalist allies) and 'Unionists' (the Conservatives and Liberal Unionists).

The defection of Chamberlain and his drift into Unionism meant that the forces of Radicalism were divided. In Scotland, in particular, leading land reformers, temperance advocates and proponents of disestablishment now sat on the Unionist side of the House.[1] But, equally important, the schism robbed the Radicals of their only credible national leader. This had been seen with piercing clarity by several of Chamberlain's Radical friends on the eve of the great schism. Henry Labouchere ('Labby', as he was familiarly known) wrote an impassioned plea to Chamberlain in mid-April 1886, urging him to swallow his reservations about Home Rule and stay with the Liberal Party, the leadership of which must shortly drop into his lap:

> Your coming over [to the Home Rule party] would ensure the passing of the Irish Government Bill; it would go to the Lords. Then Queen, Lords and Whigs would be on one side, and the Radicals on the other.

Mr Gladstone must soon come to an end. You would be our leader. The Whigs would be hopelessly bogged. Radicalism would be triumphant. Does not this tempt you?[2]

In ignoring this advice, Chamberlain seems to have been influenced, not just by his own genuine antipathy to Home Rule, but also by the belief that his separation from the mainstream of the Liberal Party would only be temporary: Gladstone, it seemed, would shortly retire, perhaps in triumph, perhaps in disgrace, but in either case Chamberlain would be welcomed back into the party as its saviour.[3]

It was a fateful miscalculation. The weakness of the Radicals had always been that they formed a loose federation of cliques and factions, each peddling its own favourite panacea (land reform, temperance reform, disestablishment, and so on). It needed a politician of rare forcefulness and intelligence to draw these factions together and impose upon them a coherent programme. Lloyd George was to play this role twenty years later. Meanwhile the Radicals had to put up with the likes of the petulant John Morley and 'Labby', a lightweight figure who inspired considerable mistrust even within the Radical ranks. It was easy for opponents to ridicule Radicalism as an utterly negative creed, a patchwork of fads and crotchets.[4]

Radicalism was also weakened for a somewhat different reason. The Liberal Party's commitment to Irish Home Rule necessitated an alliance with the Irish Nationalist Party, without the support of which they could seldom expect to acquire a parliamentary majority. Only between 1906 and 1910 did the Liberals have an overall majority of seats in the Commons. Between 1892 and 1895 and again between 1910 and 1915 their continuance in office depended on the support of Irish MPs. In addition, although some contemporaries undoubtedly exaggerated its importance, the Irish vote (organised by the United Irish League) was an important asset in many English, Welsh and Scottish urban constituencies.[5]

Yet the social base of Irish Nationalism was formed by tenant farmers, shopkeepers and publicans, overwhelmingly Roman Catholic in religion, which made them in many ways uncongenial allies for the Liberals.[6] True, Dissenters and Roman Catholics could join hands without embarassment when it came to attacking the Anglican monopoly; for example, both groups had approved, though for slightly different reasons, of the 1869 Act disestablishing and disendowing the Church of Ireland. But many prominent English Dissenters abandoned the

Liberal Party entirely in 1886 rather than hand over Irish Protestants to 'priestly rule'; included in their number was the ex-Quaker, John Bright, author of the slogan 'Home Rule Means Rome Rule'. Chamberlain himself was also a Dissenter (a Unitarian). 'I feel the wrong proposed to be done to our Ulster brethren', said the great Baptist preacher, C. H. Spurgeon: 'What have they done to be thus cast off?'[7] Such sentiments were particularly prevalent in Scotland, where the dominance of Presbyterianism made for a natural alliance with the majority of Ulster Protestants.[8]

In time most Dissenters overcame their doubts and, mesmerised by Gladstone, rallied behind the Liberal Party, particularly in 1887–8, when the Unionist Government's Crime Bill provided them with just the kind of 'moral' issue with which they felt most at home. The Wesleyan leader, Hugh Price Hughes, opined that Home Rule was 'simply applied Christianity'.[9] But events like those which followed the scandalous divorce case involving the Irish leader, Parnell, in 1890–1, when the Roman Catholic Church had thrown its weight into the electoral scales on the side of Parnell's Nationalist opponents, reawakened all the old ancestral suspicions of 'priestly interference' and 'Popery'.

This tension was most acute in the field of education, where the Liberal preference for undenominational or secular schooling ran counter to the Irish Catholics' determination to maintain institutions which would disseminate the distinctive tenets of their creed. True, Ireland had an entirely separate educational system from that of mainland Britain, so theoretically the two countries could have peacefully coexisted. However, there were large Irish settlements in the big cities of England and Scotland, on whose behalf the Irish Nationalist Leaders felt obliged to intervene. As a result, whenever the prospect of Irish Home Rule seemed remote, there was always the danger that the Irish on mainland Britain would desert the Liberals and join forces with the Conservative Party in defence of the church schools. This certainly affected the pattern of voting in western Scotland in the 1900 general election. More seriously, Liberal MPs were aghast at the support given by Irish Nationalists to the Unionist Government's 1896 Bill, which offered financial aid to the voluntary schools of England and Wales. In what looks retrospectively like a dress-rehearsal for the later quarrel over the 1902 Education Act, Hughes declared that 'Gladstonian Home Rule was dead'.[10]

Such problems plagued the Liberal Party for as long as Home Rule figured prominently on the political agenda, just as they constituted a dilemma for Irish Nationalists, many of whom were torn between their political and their religious loyalties. Indeed, the irony is that, if Ireland's national claims could have been amicably settled, the Irish Nationalists might have found their natural allies in the Conservative Party, with which they broadly agreed on social policy as well as on education.

Some of these events lay in the future. But, in the short term, Gladstone's placing of Home Rule at the very centre of the Liberal programme in 1886 damaged the cause of Radicalism in yet another way. For, as Gladstone and his friend, John Morley (who twice served as Irish Secretary), openly admitted, it meant that all other reforms would have to wait until the Irish 'obstruction' had been removed.[11] True, after the Parnell scandal and when the disappointing 1892 election results came in, even Gladstone wavered in his faith. But Morley defiantly proclaimed: 'I cruise under the green flag – come what will',[12] and Home Rule soon resumed its centrality.

Many Radicals were pleased to follow such a strategy. Apart from a widespread inclination to trust Gladstone's judgement, Radicals could see advantages in revolutionising Ireland's entire political system, since Ireland was viewed as the part of the United Kingdom where the most pernicious manifestations of 'feudalism' were to be found. The cry of 'justice for Ireland' also appealed to many Radicals who instinctively sympathised with the national struggles of small oppressed peoples. 'The men who defeated Home Rule were [our] hereditary enemies', the advanced Radical, Channing, told his constituents in 1886.[13] The plebeian Radicals, in particular, needed little convincing that a close relationship existed between the liberties of Britons and Home Rule for the Irish.[14]

On the other hand, some Radicals resented the way in which Ireland was crowding all other issues off the Liberal agenda. For example, the ministries of Gladstone and Rosebery (1892–5) gave over the lion's share of their legislative time to the Second Home Rule Bill, in the teeth of fierce resistance from the Unionist opposition. No wonder their legislative record proved to be so barren. What made the situation even more frustrating was a sense that the sacrifice was all in vain, since the House of Lords was bound to reject the Home Rule Bill.

In theory, of course, the Liberals could have responded to the rejection by appealing to the electorate for a mandate to curb the powers of an unaccountable assembly. Yet this did not happen either. Liberals, at all levels, fulminated against the peers (in the process confirming their reputation as dangerous demagogues), but the Cabinet refrained from dissolving Parliament since it feared that this was not an issue which commanded sufficient electoral support. (Oddly enough, it was the Whig Rosebery who later tried to lead the party into a crusade on this issue, while Morley and Harcourt held back.) The deadlock left the Liberals with no other strategy than that of 'filling the cup', in other words, pressing forward with legislation which the Upper House was likely to reject until such time as a genuine constitutional crisis arose.

Meanwhile the Liberals found themselves hamstrung. Indeed, one reason for Chamberlain's refusal to back Home Rule had been his sense that public opinion in the big English cities did not approve. And in this respect Chamberlain's judgement was almost certainly sound. In the absence of opinion polls, one can only hazard a guess, but clearly defence of the Union brought the Conservatives and Liberal Unionists support from sections of the electorate which might otherwise never have been tapped. This particularly happened in areas of heavy Irish settlement – the Irish immigrants being widely, albeit unfairly, blamed for unemployment and low wages. Birmingham, a city which had returned Liberals for all seven constituencies in the 1885 General Election, never returned a Liberal again until the Ladywood by-election in 1969! The Liberals also suffered in localities where Wesleyans were thick on the ground, such as Lincolnshire and the West Country, which after 1885 both registered a swing against the 'official' Liberal Party that was well above average.[15] Admittedly, Herbert Gladstone (the Party's Chief Whip and Gladstone's son) believed that eighty-one of the seats won by the Liberals in 1892 were dominated by the Irish vote,[16] which, if true, might have cancelled out the anti-Irish prejudices which prevailed in other constituencies. But Gladstone's estimate was wildly inflated and, on balance, the Irish issue was undoubtedly a vote loser.

No wonder, then, that, following Gladstone's retirement in 1894 and the Liberal Party's crushing defeat at the general election of the following year, many Liberals started looking for ways to extricate themselves from the Irish entanglement. Surprisingly perhaps, the Radicals did not take the lead in this campaign. Instead, it was the so-called 'Liberal Imperialists' (Asquith, Grey, Haldane – and, loosely attached to them, Lord Rosebery) who called for a rethink on Irish policy. The Liberal Imperialists might have exercised more influence but for a division within their own ranks between those who advocated delay and those who wanted Home Rule completely abandoned.[17] Meanwhile, perversely or bravely, depending upon one's point of view, most Radicals, inside Parliament as well as the rank-and-file activists, fought to retain Home Rule, believing that to do otherwise would denote a craven abandonment of principle in the search for electoral popularity.

In late 1905, after years of wrangling, an adroit compromise was found, acceptable to all shades of opinion, even to the reluctant Irish Nationalist Leaders: there would be a 'step-by-step' approach to Home Rule. In the forthcoming general election the Liberals would promise that, if they won a majority, they would not introduce another Home Rule Bill in the lifetime of the new Parliament, though they would feel free to introduce more modest measures which were compatible with Home Rule and might eventually lead up to it. The Radicals, it seemed, had got themselves off the hook. At last the Gladstonian 'obstruction' had been removed, and a further assault on 'feudalism' could, at least in theory, be resumed with some prospect of success. It made for a welcome contrast to the sterile 1890s when so little that they valued had been achieved.

Yet, from the Radical viewpoint, the events of 1885–6 brought gains as well as losses. This was because so many of the Whigs had defected from the Liberal Party. The full extent of this development was partly camouflaged by the behaviour of many of the most famous Whig politicians who stayed loyal to official Liberalism in 1886, some out of loyalty to Gladstone, others out of respect for the wishes of Lord Spencer, the former Lord-Lieutenant of Ireland, whose experience in that office had convinced him that, without Home Rule, Ireland would be ungovernable. In Gladstone's last ministry there were no fewer than five major landowning peers (and several squires), which gave the impression that 'High Politics' had not changed one jot. Indeed, when Gladstone finally gave up the premiership in 1894, his personal choice of a successor (if the Queen had deigned to solicit his opinion) would have been Lord Spencer. In the event the succession went to another Whig, Lord Rosebery – to the indignation of many Radicals.[18]

Appearances, however, were deceptive. Most Whigs, convinced that Home Rule meant the destruction of the ascendancy in Ireland, left the Liberal Party in disgust in 1886, never to return. True, Gladstone himself continued to believe that, under Home Rule, the Protestant landlords of Ireland would rise to their new responsibilities and emerge as 'natural' leaders of the people, as had happened in the late eighteenth century when the Irish possessed a parliament of their own.[19] But such a prospect seemed remote even to most of the friends of Home Rule: Irish Unionists rejected it with derision.

This had an immediate impact on the balance of social forces within the British Liberal Party. Historians are divided over whether the division lists on the First Home Rule Bill can be explained by reference to social background. Possibly former Liberal MPs from landed backgrounds were proportionately more inclined to rebel than were Liberal MPs as a whole.[20] Something similar occurred outside Parliament. Northamptonshire was typical; despite having Spencer as its premier landlord, 'Home Rule turned the drift to the right . . . into a landslide.'[21] Gladstone was therefore exaggerating only slightly when he declared, 'We have say one-twelfth of the House of Lords, one twenty-fourth of the Squires, . . . perhaps one acre in fifty of the Soil.'[22]

In the House of Lords the 'flight of the Whigs' was even more apparent. For much of the century the Conservatives had controlled the Upper House, but after 1886 their dominance became still more pronounced, with the Liberals reduced to a tiny rump. After the Second Home Rule Bill had squeezed through the Commons in 1893, the Lords destroyed it by 419 votes to 41. It has been estimated that between 1886 and 1893 there were 356 Conservative peers and 115 Liberal Unionists, but only 84 Liberals. On non-Irish issues, it is true, the Liberal Unionist peers often sided, initially at least, with their former Liberal colleagues – just as the two groups continued to do for some time at the level of municipal politics.[23] But all parliamentary co-operation largely ended in 1891 with the appearance of the 'Newcastle Programme' (see below).[24]

Liberalism's weakness in the Upper House had further consequences in that it gave the party as a whole an incentive to curb the powers of that Chamber or change its composition. This in turn made the Liberal Party seem a more dangerously 'radical' organisation than it really was. The loss of so many great magnates also meant that after 1886 the overwhelming majority of Lord-Lieutenants were Unionists – which led to a grave party imbalance on the county benches, since Lord-Lieutenants were responsible for forwarding to the Lord Chancellor's Office the names of suitable JPs. Another festering Liberal grievance took root.[25]

But the converse to these landowning defections was an upsurge in the importance of 'advanced Radicalism', to which Gladstone found himself under a deep obligation. These groups were even more in the ascendant in the mass organisation of the party, the National Liberal Federation, which had broken with Chamberlain and stayed loyal to Gladstone and to official Liberalism in 1886. Their importance can be measured from Gladstone's guarded acceptance of a far-ranging Radical programme passed by the NLF at Newcastle in 1891. Included in the 'Newcastle Programme' were Welsh and Scottish disestablishment, local government reform, temperance, land reform, the amendment of the Employers' Liability Act, and Home Rule – though not, significantly, the Eight-Hour Day. Gladstone himself may by this time have grown into far more of a Radical than he had ever been in the past, having come to entertain warmer feelings towards trade unionism, now that he could see a connection between the cause of Irish freedom and the rights of labour – though the evidence for this is inconclusive.[26]

As a result of all these development there was a renewed burst of activity in the sphere of land reform. High in the priorities of the Liberal Party was the attempt to win back voters in the agricultural constituencies who had supported Liberalism so well in the 1885 election, only to desert them a year later. In 1890–1 the red vans of the 'Single Taxers' and the yellow vans of the 'Land Nationalisers' took missionaries into the country villages, eager to preach the gospel.[27] Raising the social and economic condition of 'Hodge', as the farm labourer was patronisingly called, particularly appealed to the Radical mind. Here, it seemed, was a class of downtrodden men, tyrannised over by their social superiors, who, lacking authentic spokesmen of their own (Joseph Arch, the union leader, had turned out a parliamentary failure), would respond to the lead given them by their middle-class friends. Despite all the difficulties they encountered, nothing could dampen the zeal of the reformers, and a commitment to some kind of land reform played a large part in the addresses of Liberal candidates right up until the Great War. In the 1906 election 68 per cent of Liberal election addresses in England mentioned the issue.[28]

But this emphasis on land reform still further alienated the landlords from the Liberal Party.[29] By 1906 the social composition of the party had decisively changed. When in 1905 Campbell-Bannerman formed his government, a few landed gentlemen (Sir Edward Grey) and traditional Whig aristocrats (Lords Carrington, Tweedmouth, Crewe, Ripon, and so on) still received high office, but most Cabinet Ministers were now unequivocally middle-class – arguably for the first time!

In the parliamentary party as a whole, the shift in Liberalism's social base was even more pronounced. The upper-class groups had fallen by 1914 to a mere 15 per cent of Liberal MPs (6 per cent landowners, 9 per cent official services), as compared with 45 per cent of their Unionist counterparts.[30] In the House of Lords the Liberal peers in 1908 numbered only 102 (out of a total of 615), and many were recently promoted businessmen or professional men or former MPs who had been given office and sent to the 'other place' to ensure that there was *someone* there who could speak authoritatively on the government's behalf. The Radicals who thirsted for a showdown with the forces of 'feudalism' were therefore in an infinitely stronger position than at any previous time, now that they no longer had to contend with a significant landed element within the party's own ranks urging caution and offering obstructions.

Nonconformity, too, emerged strengthened from the Home Rule crisis, despite the alienation of many Dissenters over the Irish issue. True, there is some evidence that, in certain parts of the country, prosperity was weakening the links between Dissent and Liberalism. A voluntary poll taken in 1887 revealed that perhaps 30 per cent of Wesleyan Conference delegates (that is to say, leading laymen) were Unionists. Similarly, as many as 35 per cent of Congregationalist deacons in London were Unionists, according to a survey taken seven years later. However, since most deacons would have been of higher social status than ordinary chapelgoers and since London was an area where a pronounced drift away from Liberalism had already occurred, the proportion amongst lay Congregationalists was almost certainly lower.[31] The close links between the Dissenting communities and the Liberal Party, though weakened, remained largely intact.

The sectarian balance within the Parliamentary Liberal Party also remained largely unaltered. The departure of Radical Unionists in the Birmingham area was a blow, but it was accompanied by the exodus of the Whigs, nearly all of whom were Anglicans. After the 1892 election 177 Nonconformists were sitting in the House, mostly as Liberals, and during the Edwardian period they constituted well over one-third of all Liberal MPs,[32] whereas amongst Unionists (if one leaves aside the Ulster Unionists) they numbered a mere handful – after the December 1910 election no more than seven.[33]

Similarly within the constituencies. In general the local Liberal activists tended to be Nonconformists – the Baptists being the most militant, the Congregationalists the most numerous. Such zealots worked hard to keep the old sectarian issues at the forefront of the Liberal programme. The electoral geography reveals a broadly identical pattern. Where Dissenters outnumbered Anglicans, more Liberals were usually returned to the Commons than Unionists. Wales, the West Riding of Yorkshire, the North-East, the South-West Peninsula, and certain districts of East Anglia, for example, long remained Liberal strongholds.

Except in the immediate aftermath of the Irish disruption, an over-whelming majority of Scottish MPs, too, sat on the Liberal benches.[34]

Moreover, in the mid-1890s a new attempt was made to unify the main Dissenting communities and to mobilise them for political action – in practice, in the Liberal interest – with the foundation in 1896 of the National Council of Evangelical Free Churches, to which nearly all the Nonconformist sects (except the Salvation Army, the Unitarians, and the Plymouth Brethren) affiliated.[35] Thomas Law, a minister from the United Methodist Free Churches, served as its vigorous organising secretary. Consequently, even before the end of the century, there were signs of revived Nonconformist militancy. The 1902 Education Act (which infuriated Dissenters by providing rate aid to church schools) then resulted in thousands of Dissenters who had abandoned Gladstonian Liberalism over Home Rule returning to the fold, especially in the West Midlands – as Chamberlain had warned would happen.[36]

In addition, the bitter disputes in the Commons over the Education Act provided an important milestone in the career of David Lloyd George, who emerged as the principal spokesman at Westminster of the angry Welsh Dissenters – from whose ranks he himself came. Why did he take so strong a stand on the issue, given that he had, it seems, lost his belief in the tenets of Christianity some time in his adolescence? The answer is that, as in present-day Northern Ireland, sectarian allegiance still involved much more than a set of theological beliefs; it also denoted membership of a distinct community. And Lloyd George, growing up as a boy in the rural area around Criccieth, identified passionately with the social and national feelings of the Welsh Dissenters, whose dislike of 'alien' Anglicanism he sincerely shared.[37] Significantly, the debate over the Education Act coincided in Wales with a great evangelical crusade which swept the Principality, led by an ex-miner, Evan Roberts: thousands of hardened sinners publicly repented and the chapels increased their membership by some 82,000. In such ways did religious feeling and political behaviour mutually reinforce one another.[38]

It was, in fact, in Wales that opposition to the Education Act was most fiercely expressed. Some Welsh County Councils exploited a legal loophole which enabled them to refuse rate-aid to voluntary schools, and the government had to pass a special measure giving the Board of Education powers to override the local authorities.[39] The Education Act did not apply to Scotland or Ireland, but in England, as in Wales, thousands of Dissenters refused on principle to pay their rates. This passive resistance movement was organised by the Norwich shoe manufacturer, George White, Liberal MP for North-West Norfolk. The Wesleyans refused to participate in it, but by 1906 there had been over 70,000 summonses, 2,568 auctions had taken place, and 176 Nonconformists had been sent to prison.[40] Isolated pockets of resistance survived until the eve of the Great War.

Anger over the Education Act spilled over into opposition to the 1904 Licensing Act, which provided generous financial compensation for publicans whose licences had been removed. Unionists, ever tender of property rights, thought that this was no more than the publicans' due, but Dissenters, most of whom were strong temperance advocates, were outraged by the state's 'favouritism' towards the hated drink trade. Temperance continued, in fact, to provide an important link between the world of the chapel and the secular activities of the Liberal Party.

The celebrated 'Nonconformist Conscience', which decreed that moral and religious convictions offered the sole guides to worthy political action, also drove the Liberal Party into taking a strong stand on the 'Chinese Slavery' issue.[41] Indeed, many Dissenters saw Liberalism as the only guarantor of public righteousness in a wicked world and would have agreed with the blunt verdict of one Congregationalist pastor: 'Toryism is wickedness.'[42]

Such feelings explain why so many Dissenting ministers enthusiastically threw themselves into the electoral campaigns of the Liberal Party just prior to and during the 1906 general election. When the Congregationalists were holding their annual convention at Leeds in October 1905, many delegates took time off to help the Liberal candidate in the important by-election in neighbouring Barkston Ash. And when polling opened in the 1906 general election, it was found that many Liberal candidates had had their nomination papers signed by Nonconformist pastors, many of whom also appeared by their side at public meetings. Leading divines went on motorised canvasses of the country, while Whitefield's Tabernacle in London, the celebrated Congregationalist Chapel, became virtually a Liberal committee room for the South St Pancras constituency.[43] In the run-up to the 1906 election the Council of Free Churches also supplied twenty-five parliamentary candidates, although the Chief Whip, Herbert Gladstone, drove a very hard bargain at their expense.[44] Well might Conservatives complain that many Nonconformist preachers had abused the privileges of the pulpit in the recklessness of their partisan zeal.

What, in conclusion, can be said about the way in which traditional Radicalism affected the survival chances of the Liberal Party after 1886?
Even at the time there were those who derided traditional Radicals
for living in the past. Around the turn of the century a reaction set
against what was called 'Gladstonianism'. Revisionist groups in the
party, notably the Liberal Imperialists, called not only for the demotion
of Irish Home Rule but also for the discarding of the Newcastle Programme and its replacement with a 'twentieth-century' approach which
put greater stress on ameliorating the social conditions of the urban
poor and improving the efficiency of the economy.[45] In retrospect, this
seems like plain common sense.

There were certainly ways in which the Nonconformists acted as a
drag on Liberal fortunes. Many of the issues which they forced the party
to prioritise, such as Welsh Disestablishment and Local Option (that is,
empowering the local authorities to restrict the issue of liquor licences),
lacked wider electoral appeal. As for Scottish Disestablishment, this was
thought by Liberal organisers to be unpopular even in Scotland.[46] Yet
such was the strength of the Nonconformist Committee within the
House of Commons, and so insistent the pressure from constituency
activists, that the party leaders often found themselves saddled with
commitments that later proved difficult to discard.

The various Nonconformist 'crusades' were perhaps better suited to
Liberal spells in opposition than to their periods in power. The 'politics
of indignation', in which Nonconformists specialised, led to the moral-
isation of politics and to a black-and-white approach to complex issues
(such as the relationship between schooling and the churches), together
with a disposition to reject compromise as a temporising with evil. This
reinforced the tendency of the Liberal Party to act as though it were
primarily a party of protest.

Such an approach to politics was often productive of strain between
the Nonconformists and the secular intelligentsia (some of them free-
thinkers like Morley) who had traditionally been drawn to the Liberal
Party. Both groups, admittedly, could unite behind the slogan of 'religious
equality'. But whereas most intellectuals followed Mill in believing
toleration to be the supreme virtue, to most Dissenters 'religious equality'
denoted a wish to destroy Anglican privilege. Indeed, as self-appointed
custodians of 'national righteousness', the Dissenters saw it as their
mission to wage war against 'sin', in all its guises; the result was a series
of unyielding attacks on Roman Catholicism, ritualism, gambling and
fornication.

The Liberal Party itself became associated with this sort of narrow censoriousness, all the more so because of the activities of the Women's Liberal Federation, which contained leading 'purity' crusaders like Laura Ormiston Chant – for example, in 1888 the Federation came out strenuously against the attempted rehabilitation of Charles Dilke, whose career had recently been wrecked by sexual scandal.[47] No wonder that Liberalism gave many outsiders during the 1890s the impression of being 'a Crotchet Castle, from which dreary teetotaling Dissenters launched raids on pubs, music halls, and politicians cited in divorce cases'.[48] The strength of working-class Conservatism lay in its willing acceptance of working men for who they were and its celebration of a popular culture of 'cakes and ales' which prissy, censorious Liberals seemed to be threatening.[49] The pressure put on Gladstone and Morley to disown Parnell in 1890, even before his fellow Irish Nationalists had had time to discuss his suitability as a political leader, is an example of the way in which the puritanical fervour of the Dissenters could some-times get in the way of what would have been a more expedient course of political action.[50] The narrow zeal of many Dissenters also damaged the Liberal leaders in other ways. Many backbench MPs who objected to Rosebery's emergence as Gladstone's successor in 1894, for example, did so on the ground that he owned a racing stud! Such protests sprang from the Dissenters' conviction that 'immorality' disqualified a man from political leadership.

Asquith, with his smart, society-loving wife, Margot, later fell foul of the same prejudices. His private secretary, Edwin Montagu, felt obliged to warn his 'Chief' in 1908 that the presence at a Prime Ministerial garden party of the 'risqué' dancer, Maud Allan, had occasioned much dissatisfaction, although, as Montagu noted, it was 'characteristic of our Party that so many Members who object to meeting the lady were able apparently to recognise her'. 'There is no getting away from the fact that ours is a Nonconformist Party, with Nonconformist susceptibilities and Nonconformist prejudices', Asquith was told.[51] It was a warning that no Liberal leader could afford to ignore. How Lloyd George's adulteries did not ruin his career is something of a mystery; probably many of his Dissenting admirers simply refused to give credence to the rumours that were circulating about their hero's peccadilloes.

Was it wise for the Liberal Party to have allowed itself to be so closely tied to Nonconformity? Certainly there are signs from the late 1880s onwards that within large metropolitan areas like London secularisation was depriving the old sectarian issues of their former importance. Even in Wales the evangelical fervour of the early years of the century soon spent itself: by 1914 the chapels were reporting a steady stream of defections. In South Wales many young working men deserted the chapel for trade unionism and the socialist societies, leaving the older generation of Welsh Liberal politicians looking decidedly old-fashioned. Even where socialism was not making progress, the growth of a new commercial entertainments industry was eroding the social and cultural importance of the chapel in the eyes of those who had traditionally been most loyal to the Liberal Party. Whatever the explanation, most of the Nonconformist sects reached a peak of membership around 1905–8, but then rapidly declined.[52]

On the other hand, it is easy to exaggerate the speed with which these developments were undermining traditional political culture. London, for example, was atypical of urban Britain – still less of the country as a whole.[53] The election as Liberal MP for Ipswich in January 1910 of the famous Congregationalist divine, the Reverend Silvester Horne, marked a high point in the political enthusiasm of Dissent. In Norwich the old chapel networks retained their social and political vitality until well into the 1920s.[54] Neither, as D. W. Bebbington has argued, should all Nonconformist 'desertions' from the Liberal Party be seen as symptoms of creeping secularisation, since this development was caused, not just by religious indifference, but also, in some cases, by a reawakening of anti-Catholicism. Religion had not yet lost its capacity to shape political allegiance.[55]

The Nonconformists may well have damaged *themselves* in the early twentieth century by getting too involved with the secular work of the Liberal Party. Ministers of religion who cancelled their services in order to speak at Liberal rallies were behaving in a way that was likely, sooner or later, to provoke a strong reaction. Indeed, by 1910 'political Dissent' had reached something of an impasse. Its metropolitan leaders, through close association with the Liberal ministry, were beginning to drift apart from their laity. The Conservative-minded resented the way in which the Chapel was being committed to party politics of the most partisan kind; at the same time, paradoxically, rank-and-file militants often rejected the compromises, like those over the education problem, into which their leaders were being drawn. The suicide of Thomas Law in 1910 (he drowned himself at Brighton, after being seen to wander listlessly about the seafront, his breath smelling of spirits) ushered in a more politically quiescent phase in the work of the Free Church Council.[56]

But for the Liberal Party itself the relationship with Nonconformity brought many benefits. First, it kept many of its traditional supporters loyal to Liberalism. It was essential for Liberals to devise a balanced pro-gramme which would retain middle-class enthusiasm (and money), while also appealing to the material self-interest of the poorer sectors of the electorate.[57] A single-minded concentration on social policy, to the exclusion of older concerns, would have narrowed the party's social base and weakened its electoral appeal.[58]

Nonconformity also strengthened the party by giving it a sense of moral purpose. To quote a phrase usually applied to the Labour Party, the Liberal Party was a moral crusade or it was nothing. In protesting against injustice in Ireland, denouncing the evils of Chinese Labour, and pressing for reforms in the issue of licensed premises, Liberals believed that they had God on their side – that they were engaged in a campaign against class selfishness, materialism and evil. Finally, at the local level Dissenters often provided the bulk of the party activists, the local officers and the Liberal representatives on elected bodies.[59] In short, Nonconformity was probably on balance an asset to the Liberal cause.

Land reform was also a powerful generator of Liberal energy, though here perhaps the balance sheet was less favourable. For, despite their enthusiasm, Liberal land reformers were divided over exactly what they wanted to achieve. All could agree on removing the fiscal privileges enjoyed by landowners – something partly effected in Harcourt's 1894 Budget, which imposed graduated taxes on all estates, real as well as personal. A common commitment to site value rating (and its prerequis-ite, land valuation) also drew the various groups of reformers together. But there agreement ended. Some Radicals subscribed to the nostrum of the American, Henry George, and wanted a 'single tax' to be imposed on land; others favoured land nationalisation. Some wanted to give power to local authorities to purchase land which could be leased in the form of allotments and smallholdings; others (joined by many Conservatives) favoured a system of state-aided land purchase, as in Ire-land, to create a class of peasant *proprietors*. In other words, a primary division existed between those who wanted to diffuse landownership and those who wanted to abolish it (or subject it to stringent public controls). In addition, whereas some Radicals saw 'land colonisation' as a remedy for specifically *urban* problems like unemployment and overcrowding, others were interested in the regeneration of rural life for its own sake.[60]

Moreover, as Chamberlain and Collings had found in 1885, help for the farm labourer risked estranging the farmers, whom the Liberals were also trying to attract with promises of a measure to strengthen tenant right. Here was a dilemma which was to reappear in Lloyd George's Land Campaign of 1912–14. The Radical 'solution', of course, was to unite farmer and labourer in an assault on the privileges of the landowners. This stratagem worked well enough in areas like rural Wales where farmers and labourers enjoyed close social and economic ties and both felt alienated from an 'Anglican' landed elite. But elsewhere the project was replete with difficulties. Over much of England, in fact, farmers were now gravitating towards the Conservative Party.[61] Paradoxically, after 1906 it took a large landowner, Lord Carrington (one of a declining band), to convert land reform into a practical programme. Even then, little was done to satisfy the somewhat utopian expectations that surrounded the issue.[62]

Yet, when all is said and done, sectarian politics, land reform and similar attempts to prise the government of the country out of the grasp of the landed classes had not lost their relevance. It is tempting to contrast the Liberal Party, rooted in the past, with the socialist societies and the Labour Movement which represented the 'future'. Yet most socialists and trade unionists strongly backed these traditional Radical causes. For example, nearly all Labour MPs favoured land nationalisation (as did many Liberals). Leading socialists, like Keir Hardie and Philip Snowden, and pillars of trade unionism, like Arthur Henderson, were also zealous temperance reformers.[63] And Nonconformity accounted for an even higher percentage of Labour than it did of Liberal MPs.[64] Moreover, the entire Labour Movement could join the Radicals in calling for House of Lords reform, the only difference between the two groups being that Labour tended to favour the abolition of the Upper House, not just the replacement of its 'absolute' by a 'temporary' veto. As for the moralising strains in militant Nonconformity, these, too, were obtrusively present in the ranks of the early Labour politicians, who, in their eagerness to change the lives of the poor, all too often gave the impression of disapproving of their character and behaviour – an electorally damaging impression to have given.[65]

In short, even in the Edwardian period much work had still to be done in dismantling the 'aristocratic state', and the Radical–Liberals cannot be accused of living in the past when they reminded the country of its necessity. These preoccupations would only have been damaging had they led the Liberals into a total disregard of other social problems – problems to which traditional Radicalism had given insufficient weight.

Perhaps the greatest danger to the Liberal Party was that it might degenerate, under Radical pressure, into a mere party of protest. In the 1890s, when the Liberals spent most of their time on the Opposition benches, unsympathetic critics claimed that Liberalism was becoming a bundle of fads and crotchets and a congenial home for an assorted band of 'Antis'.[66] The party gave many the impression of being the vehicle through which social outsiders expressed their hostility towards the 'Establishment', the peripheries (including the 'Celtic Fringe') protested against control by the Metropolis, and 'Little Englanders' inveighed against the Empire. It was perhaps fitting that the party should have been briefly led by the utterly negative Harcourt, who behaved like an Opposition politician even when in office: 'I am not a supporter of the present Government', he said in 1894, while serving as Chancellor of the Exchequer![67]

Doomed to spend a long period in opposition, the Liberal Party frittered away much of its energy in the 1890s and during the opening years of the new century on internecine strife. Moreover, Gladstone's deliberate failure to groom a successor landed the Liberals in a leadership struggle which debilitated the party for the best part of a decade. Lord Rosebery, who eventually filled that post, never succeeded in imposing his will on MPs, and his ministry ended after only a year when it was brought down by a revolt of its own Welsh supporters. The next leader, Harcourt, lasted little longer, just over two years, before the amiable but ineffectual Campbell-Bannerman took over – soon to be disowned by a substantial section of his own party.

Liberal divisions came to a climax during the course of the Second Boer War (1899–1902).[68] Nearly all Liberals thought Chamberlain's blustering diplomacy at least partly responsible for the outbreak of hostilities, but the leadership had little alternative but to give general support to the Unionist government, once the Transvaal had initiated the war by invading British territory. Nevertheless, Liberal opinion sharply divided over the way in which the fighting should be conducted and over the terms of the eventual settlement. Such uncertainty played into the hands of the government, which called an early election in the late summer of 1900, from which the Unionists returned with their large majority all but intact.

Campbell-Bannerman's attempts to maintain party unity in the face of 'pro-Boer' sniping, on one wing, and the disaffected Liberal Imperialists, loosely led by Rosebery, on the other, came to grief in the summer of 1901 when his reference to 'methods of barbarism' in South Africa brought the latter out in open revolt. In 1901 and early 1902 the Liberal Party seemed on the verge of disintegration, as the Liberal Imperialists founded their own organisations in an apparent bid to force Campbell-Bannerman out. Virtual civil war raged in Scotland, where many of the rival leaders had their base.[69] Only Rosebery's chronic indecision and the ending of the Boer War in the summer of 1902 saved the party from further humiliation.

Although foreign affairs provided the basis for most of the Liberal Party's internal squabbles, these were sharpened by personal animosities. At a deeper level the divisions also reflected the problems which the Liberals were having in developing a set of coherent and *constructive* social policies. What were the factors that had contributed to this particular situation?

4

THE 'PROBLEM OF LABOUR', 1886–1905

The New Electoral System

There was a particular reason why the Liberals should take social politics seriously. For in 1884 Parliament had passed the Third Reform Act, which for the first time gave Britain a popular, though not a democratic, electoral system. The extension of the household franchise from the boroughs to the counties meant that some 76 per cent of the adult male population would be able to vote in parliamentary elections. (Gladstone used his authority to crush a woman's suffrage amendment – with fateful long-term consequences).[1]

Accompanying the Third Reform Act was a measure of seat redistribution which also had a large impact on the older parties. In a way the latter turned out to be the more important of the two measures. As a result of redistribution the single-member constituency became the norm both in counties and in boroughs. Whereas previously the large industrial cities formed two-member, or in the case of the very large boroughs (Manchester, Birmingham, Leeds, etc.), three-member constituencies, they were now divided up into single-member constituencies of *approximately* equal size along lines which recognised the social and economic characteristics of specific urban areas. And so Manchester now had six parliamentary constituencies, all but one of which was either definitely working-class or middle-class in composition. Instead of representing, say, Manchester as a whole, an MP returned for a wealthy residential area of Manchester would be likely to identify, not with other parts of his own city, but with similar districts in other big cities. This process tended to promote the development of a class-based electoral system very different from the one in which the old Liberal Party had flourished.[2]

However, contemporaries showed greater interest in the implications of franchise extension. Were they right to do so? Historians once believed that the 'democratic' potential of the Third Reform Act had been much exaggerated. Even after 1884, they argued, the electoral system continued to discriminate against the poorer members of society: while many of the well-to-do benefited from the survival of plural voting, certain categories of working-class males were excluded entirely, among them paupers, domestic servants, and soldiers living in barracks. A lodger vote did exist, but few were able to meet its complex requirements, as a result of which (to take one example) many unmarried men living in the parental home were not allowed to vote in parliamentary or municipal elections, even though they might well be politically conscious trade-unionists. It has been argued that Labour's inability to make its own way before 1918 owed much to the class bias in the franchise.[3]

More recent work has shaken this interpretation.[4] It has been shown that the main 'class bias' in the electoral system was provided by plural voting.[5] But those who were totally denied the vote hardly formed a separate 'class', since most of them were the sons of existing voters. In fact, the defective lodger vote had the effect of discriminating against the young and the mobile. Such groups, mainly unmarried men living in lodgings or in the parental home, were by no means *all* working-class.[6] Contemporaries were thus right to assume that a 'mass' electorate had recently been created and that this had massive implications for the older political parties.

How did the Liberals react to these electoral changes? Some were unconvinced of the need to make any drastic innovations aimed at wooing the new working-class voters. Even greater anxieties, they remembered, had been stirred up during the Reform Crisis of 1866–7 which had preceded Disraeli's famous 'leap in the dark' – anxieties which in retrospect looked groundless. Sporadic attempts to create independent working-class organisations during succeeding decades had come to nothing. Between 1867 and 1885 'Labour' amounted to little more than a pressure group, one of many encompassed within the wider Liberal Party.[7] Why should the equalisation of the suffrage (between borough and county) be any more revolutionary?

Not all Liberals, however, shared this complacency. True, some traditional Radicals continued to believe that class attacks from working men against 'capitalists' proceeded from a kind of 'false consciousness':

after all, employer and employee, they argued, had a common interest in breaking the landed monopoly and in extending the realm of 'freedom'. But such an approach was discredited by the Liberals' electoral failure in the two decades following the passing of the Third Reform Act – a failure all the more poignant when compared with the situation during the preceding half-century, when the Liberals had functioned as the 'natural' party of government.

In the 1885 election, held just before Gladstone's 'conversion' to Home Rule, the Liberals had secured a majority of eighty-six over the Conservatives – which exactly matched the size of the Irish Nationalist Party, which held the balance of seats in the Commons. But that result was the best that the Liberal Party achieved until the landslide victory of 1906. In 1892 they won forty-one fewer seats than the combined Unionist Parties – which again left them dependent on the good offices of the Irish when forming their 'minority' administration. As for the general elections of 1886, 1895 and 1900, these all resulted in resounding Liberal defeats.

By and large it was not socialist or independent Labour candidates who inflicted the main damage on the Liberals. True, in some industrial parts of the country, particularly the West Riding, the newly founded Independent Labour Party (ILP) was winning seats on local authorities in the 1890s – often after bitter clashes with the established employer-dominated local elites. But in the 1895 election every ILP candidate came bottom of the poll. The Liberals' discomfiture resulted, rather, from *Unionist* success.

It was in the big cities, the working-class constituencies included, where the Liberal performance was most disappointing. In the seven major cities of London, Glasgow, Birmingham, Manchester, Liverpool, Leeds and Sheffield, the Liberals won only seventeen of the available ninety-eight seats in the 1895 election and still fewer, thirteen, in 1900; all the rest were captured by the Unionists (with the sole exception of the 'Scotland' division of Liverpool, which consistently returned an Irish Nationalist). This reflected the weakness of Liberal organisation, which was partly the result of financial difficulties following the defections of 1886. But it also suggested that the Liberal Party lacked popular appeal. Although, with some notable exceptions (for example, Birmingham and Liverpool), working-class areas tended to support the Liberals and middle-class areas the Unionists, the latter were considerably more successful in attracting their 'natural' constituents.[8] What was to be done? Two obvious remedies suggested themselves: first, a change in policy and, second, a determined effort to field more working-class candidates.

Liberalism and Social Policy

The party schism over Home Rule prevented Chamberlain from developing the ideas which had been outlined in the *Radical Programme* when he was still a Liberal, but he remained convinced that it would be imprudent to ignore the 'social question'. Chamberlain was soon trying to win his new Conservative allies over to this point of view, and, as a Cabinet Minister in Salisbury's last administration, he was able to put some of his principles into practice when he steered through the Commons an important measure of workman's compensation – provision for which had already been established in Germany, whose social insurance schemes aroused the keen interest of Chamberlain and many of his contemporaries. Significantly Chamberlain had been the first politician of importance to come out (in April 1891) in favour of state-organised old-age pensions. These, too, he worked hard to get the Unionist administration to adopt. Indeed, it was not entirely out of the question that Chamberlain would succeed in his ambition of converting 'Unionism' from a narrowly defensive creed, centred on Ireland, into a heady concoction which combined social reform at home with imperialism abroad. This certainly had many demagogic possibilities.[9] Why, then, was the Liberal Party so slow to see the dangers of allowing Chamberlain to make the running as a social reformer?

To be fair to the Liberals, there was a group of younger MPs who, while accepting the case for Irish Home Rule, worried about the party's lack of a domestic programme and tried to provide it with a more constructive, 'governmental' ethos than was likely to emanate from old-style Radicalism. Between 1886 and 1892 this group organised itself around the so-called 'Thirty-Nine Articles Club'. One of its most active members, R. B. Haldane, a friend of Sidney Webb, provided a line of communication with the Fabian Society, and some hard thinking on social policy resulted. In 1892 two of the leaders of the coterie forced their way through sheer ability into the Cabinet: Asquith as Home Secretary and Arthur Acland as Vice-President of the Council with responsibility for education. Unfortunately, these young MPs lacked support at the highest levels of the party. John Morley encouraged them in private but disowned them in public; Rosebery's patronage later proved to be only slightly more fruitful.[10]

In the early and mid-1890s it was the obsession with Home Rule which proved the major obstacle to the Liberal social reformers. Not that Gladstone's fourth ministry did nothing in the field of social legislation: Asquith devoted much time to an Employers' Liability Bill (which eventually came to grief in the Lords). And in the President of the Board of Trade, A. J. Mundella, the Liberals had one of their few senior politicians with a proven track record as a social reformer. Under his auspices a Labour Department was set up and the groundwork laid for what eventually became the 1896 Conciliation Act. Certain categories of workers also benefited from the period of Liberal rule. Employees in the royal ordnance factories and the dockyards were promised trade-union wage rates and granted an eight-hour day, and railwaymen were brought under the protection of the 1893 Railway Servants (Hours of Labour) Act (though this piece of legislation was primarily intended to safeguard the travelling public). All these innovations suggested that the Liberal Party was beginning to develop a new set of policy interests.[11] All the same, to make an electoral impact, social reform needed to be placed towards the top of the legislative agenda and vigorously promoted. This was never going to happen as long as Gladstone controlled the party.

Gladstone's retirement in 1894 and the temporary eclipse of the Irish Question did little to improve the situation. We have already seen how the resulting leadership squabbles sharpened differences amongst the Liberal front bench over foreign and imperial policy, but they also had the effect of inhibiting the party from developing a positive domestic programme, as can be seen from the following two examples.

In 1894 Harcourt produced an innovative Budget which sharply increased the incidence of death duties on larger estates. Though this measure was welcomed by many traditional Radicals as a long overdue assault on landed privilege, it also has the appearance, particularly in retrospect, of an important step towards a more 'progressive' fiscal system, i.e. one in which wealth was deliberately redistributed by Treasury policy from richer to poorer people. Yet the Budget reached the statute book only after bitter protests from Rosebery – a slightly surprising development since Rosebery had acted as Chairman of the London County Council since 1889, where he had come into contact with 'Progressive Councillors', some of them Fabians. Indeed, Rosebery had earlier seemed to be making a conscious effort to identify himself with those groups in the Liberal Party to whom a bold policy of social reform deeply mattered. Of course, it may be that Rosebery's professions of concern for social questions amounted to little more than rhetoric. But it is also likely that his reactions to the 1894 Budget were coloured by deep personal antipathy to its author.[12] However, Harcourt's own behaviour was only slightly less perverse. Having pointed the Liberal Party in a promising new direction, he then failed to follow up his success. In 1895 he based his own election campaign on the promise of Local Option – and was defeated by his Derby constituents for his pains.[13]

Personal rivalries also damaged the attempts of the Liberal Imperialists to say something fresh and challenging about urban problems. When this group created the Liberal League in January 1902, sympathisers, like the Fabian, Sidney Webb, attached themselves to the organisation. In the interests of 'National Efficiency', attempts were made to develop a range of social policies. But, again, this part of their campaign quickly petered out. Some of the Liberal Imperialist MPs clearly did not believe seriously in social reform at all, their main concern being to testify to their 'responsible' attitude to Empire and national defence and to put distance between themselves and Home Rule. Indeed, some, like Robert Perks, came from that wing of the party to which redress of Nonconformist grievances was the only kind of reform that mattered. Contempt for Campbell-Bannerman and a hope that he might be replaced eclipsed serious thinking about housing, unemployment, and the like.[14]

But the Liberal Party's domestic problems can be explained, not simply by the distractions from which it suffered, but also by the kind of party that it was. Here we come to a major source of disagreement among historians. At one extreme, there are those who believe that the Home Rule schism alienated from Liberalism most of its wealthy business supporters (as well as most landlords), leaving it a much more 'democratic organisation'. The starting point of such interpretations is a famous utterance made by Gladstone to his Midlothian electors in 1886: 'On the side adverse to the Government are found . . . in profuse abundance station, title, wealth, social influence, the professions, or a majority of them – in a word, the spirit and power of Class.' Faced by problems of fundraising, the Whips in the 1890s were talking in a very similar way.[15] But the corollary of this, some historians argue, was the Liberals' growing dependence upon the working-class electorate.

In total contrast is the interpretation offered by Professor Lubenow, who insists that the crisis of 1886 polarised the House of Commons 'along ideological and regional lines rather than social lines'.[16] After all, business families, like the Quaker Peases of Darlington, split, some members following Gladstone, others becoming Unionists. Moreover, the voting on the Home Rule Bill divided Liberal business MPs in almost exactly the same proportion as it did the Liberal parliamentary party as a whole (about sixty-three to thirty-seven).

Yet attitudes towards Home Rule were not entirely divorced from wider social and political beliefs. Lubenow's own statistics show that Liberal MPs with 'right-wing' views fell from 21 per cent before the 'Great Separation' to only 8 per cent – which suggests that Liberalism had indeed been 'radicalised' by the Irish issue.[17]

It is undoubtedly true that the Home Rule schism resulted in the final defection from official Liberalism of the big railway interests, which had been restless for some time.[18] And if we look at the behaviour of the *electorate*, it seems that the events of 1886 led to an exodus from the Liberal Party amongst prosperous middle-class voters – although, again, this probably accelerated a trend that had already become established. Professor Blewett, for example, has convincingly argued that Liberal Unionism's importance was that it offered a stepping-stone to the right amongst wealthy men who still thought of themselves as being anti-Conservative but had, over many years, been losing confidence in Gladstonian Liberalism. These defections, he points out, occurred in particularly large numbers in London and the Home Counties. In such areas voting was heavily class-based from 1886 onwards, perhaps earlier.[19]

Why should 'villa Toryism' have been so strong in southern England? W. D. Rubinstein contends that the divisions within the middle class over Irish Home Rule were by no means arbitrary. Rather, they reflected a deep fissure within the middle class between, on the one hand, commercial and financial centres, such as Greater London and Merseyside, and, on the other, the industrial/manufacturing cities. Bankers and the larger merchants, suggests Rubinstein, had always been closer, socially and culturally, to the world of the landed estate than had northern industrialists (many of whom were Dissenters); if so, it is hardly surprising that the former should have aligned themselves with the Conservative Party during the decade after 1886, while the latter did not move decisively in this direction until the 1920s.[20] This, in turn, explains the accentuation after 1886 of a pronounced North/South political divide, with the Liberal Party's centre of gravity lying north of a line stretching from the Bristol Channel to the Humber.[21]

This thesis needs to be qualified and refined. For example, two of the areas which broke most decisively with Gladstonian Liberalism in 1886 were the West Midlands (Chamberlain's fiefdom) and, obviously, the Belfast region (where Home Rule polarised the population between Irish Nationalism and Unionism). Nevertheless, it remains broadly true that in *most* manufacturing districts, such as the West Riding, the northeast, and south Wales, business Liberalism retained its strength until 1908 and perhaps later still. Even middle-class constituencies in these areas tended to stay loyal to the Liberal Party.[22]

Businessmen, particularly in the coalfields and the heavy industrial areas, continued, therefore, to play a crucial role in Liberal politics throughout the 1890s. They dominated the party organisation: the powerful President of the NLF after 1886, James Kitson, was a wealthy Leeds railway engineer. They supplied Liberalism with many of its local councillors: over 40 per cent of Liberal councillors and executive members in Leeds, Leicester and Norwich were businessmen, mainly manufacturers (the figure excludes the large shopkeeping element).[23] Liberal 'millocrats' were especially prominent in the towns of the West Riding.[24] At Westminster, too, the Liberal benches contained many 'captains of industry', in particular textile manufacturers and coal owners. And, finally, by the early twentieth century eighteen of the twenty-seven wealthy individuals on whom it had come to depend for its central funding were businessmen, most of them major Scottish and Northern industrialists.[25]

Now, it was amongst these key supporters that opposition to legislation which raised taxation and interfered with 'industrial freedom' tended to be particularly fierce. Indeed, the complaints of Liberal businessmen in the early 1890s that employers' liability legislation threatened to 'cripple, if not destroy' the staple industries of the country greatly worried the Whips, who foresaw a loss of much-needed financial backing. Similarly, on the eve of the Newcastle Conference, Liberal MPs were hearing sentiments about 'the relation of capital and labour analogous to the sentiments of Tory squires on the relation of squire and labourer', as one of them put it.[26] Alfred Illingworth, a Bradford wool manufacturer, actually announced his retirement from Parliament in protest at the Government's sympathy for a Miners' Eight-Hour Day Bill.[27]

Liberal MPs who happened to be major employers of labour involved in bitter industrial disputes, such as C. H. Wilson, the Hull shipowner, had additional reasons for their aversion to any 'concessions' to Labour. So long as these powerful businessmen remained within the Liberal

Party, relations with the trade union movement were likely to be tense. Significantly, the one industrial dispute of this period in which prominent Liberals came unequivocally to the support of strikers was the Penrhyn slate workers' dispute at Bethesda in North Wales, where the employer was a landowning Conservative peer.[28] More typical was the West Riding, where working men active in the Labour and socialist movement not infrequently found themselves victimised by their 'Liberal' employers.[29] Business Liberalism, in short, was by no means destroyed by the great schism of 1886. Indeed, after 1903 it actually enjoyed a new lease of life in reaction to Joseph Chamberlain's ill-fated Tariff Reform campaign.

The purpose of Tariff Reform was threefold: to bind the self-governing countries of the Empire more closely together through a system of 'Imperial Preferences': to protect native industry against 'unfair' foreign competition: and to broaden the basis of taxation in order to meet growing demands for public expenditure, both for defence and for the provision of social services. But the very suggestion of tampering with Free Trade, the central component of the Liberal creed ever since the 1840s, was bound to galvanise the Liberal Party. Its working-class followers were alarmed at the prospect of dearer bread ('The Little Loaf'), which the imposition of a corn duty seemed likely to produce. At the same time, many businessmen, too, were dismayed at the probable consequences of any return to Protection. They feared a trade war which would threaten their sources of supply (e.g. raw cotton for the textile industry) or their foreign markets (which were considerably larger than the Empire markets, upon which the Tariff Reformers pinned their hopes). Moreover, wage increases resulting from food price rises might well have blunted the competitive edge of British manufacturers in world markets. Businessmen in industries with thriving export markets had a rational economic case for favouring the fiscal status quo, and hence working for the establishment of a Liberal government.

Tariff Reform, then, helped to revive what some historians have called 'economic liberalism',[30] strengthening many businessmen in their allegiance to the Liberal Party. Free Trade also won back some of the faint hearts who had deserted it in the depressing 1890s. This particularly happened in Scotland, where the *Glasgow Herald*, organ of the business community, was staunchly free-trade. Two Scottish Unionist MPs, both businessmen, crossed the floor of the House in protest at

Chamberlain's démarche.[31] As a result, in 1906, even more than in 1886, the Liberal Party was a party in which, especially at parliamentary level, the role of great capitalists was very visible. This, in itself, put a break on any attempt to create an advanced programme of social reform.

But Tariff Reform hindered the social reformers in another sense. Already by 1903 party unity had been largely restored. The divisive war in South Africa formally ended in the summer of 1902. The Balfour Education Act then drove nearly all Liberals together in opposition to this affront to their principles. Finally, confronted by Tariff Reform, Liberals of all shapes and sizes could unite in defence of Free Trade, secure in the knowledge that they now had an issue ('cheap bread') on which, barring accidents, they would sooner or later be swept back into office.

This meant, however, that a social programme was no longer so necessary. It is even doubtful whether the Liberals would have agreed to the Lib-Lab Pact (discussed below) but for the fact that the negotiations with Labour had acquired an unstoppable momentum by the time that the significance of Chamberlain's activities had been fully appreciated. As the increasingly accident-prone Balfour ministry stumbled to defeat, senior Liberals concluded that they need do little more than sit tight and wait for power to fall into their laps.

What this cautious approach entailed in practice can be illustrated by a telling vignette. In the autumn of 1904, with the economy in recession once more, Herbert Gladstone produced a memorandum on the unemployment problem, designed to provoke his colleagues into doing more than attack Chamberlain, but the discussion he initiated soon petered out.[32] On the eve of the formation of his ministry, Campbell-Bannerman reported his discovery from meetings which he had addressed in Glasgow that 'much mischief was being done by the notion that we had little or nothing to say about the unemployed. So I risked one foot upon that ice, but was very guarded and only spoke of enquiry and experiment.'[33] By the time of the 1906 general election, serious thinking on social policy had *still* not advanced very far.

Surface appearances, however, were somewhat deceptive. Away from the world of 'High Politics', Liberalism was changing. This came about in part because interest in the plight of the 'people of the abyss' had never entirely disappeared, even after the economic and social crisis which had originally brought it to prominence had abated. Throughout the 1880s and early 1890s a motley crowd of middle-class investigators and philanthropists descended on the slum areas of the great cities, in particular the East End of London, to study the problems of social deprivation, to demonstrate their 'neighbourliness' with their poorer fellow-citizens, and to search for remedies for the ills which they had uncovered. Most were young men (but young women, too, were caught up in these activities), often graduates from Oxford and Cambridge. Their conscience aroused by having had their attention drawn to the gap between their own living conditions and those that prevailed in the inner-city slums, these middle-class 'do-gooders' were activated by a mixture of feelings, in which guilt, curiosity and fear all played a part. Toynbee Hall and other 'Settlements' acted as magnets for these young social explorers and investigators; in time they also served as bases from which serious social 'fieldwork' could be organised.

Not all of those caught up in the Settlement Movement and similar activities were Liberals. Indeed, in the early 1890s a commitment to the serious study of social problems was widely thought to be something quite apart from 'politics' – an indication of how little these concerns had as yet impinged on Westminster and Whitehall. But perhaps a majority of such people felt a vague sympathy with the Liberal Party, if only because Liberalism favoured the achievement of social progress through the exercise of benevolence and the application of rationality. In any case, the loose-jointed Liberal Party had always extended a welcome to a variety of reforming pressure groups – and social reformers were as welcome, say, as temperance workers.

A good example of a person involving himself in Liberal politics in this way is Charles Masterman.[34] On graduating from Cambridge, where he had been deeply influenced by Canon Scott Holland of the Christian Social Union, a High Church pressure group interested in social reform, Masterman took up residence in working-class lodgings in Camberwell. Soon he was using his personal knowledge of the London poor in contributions to the Radical newspapers and in his various books (of which the most famous, *The Condition of England*, was published in 1909). When in 1906 Masterman first entered Parliament, it was the start of an important political career.

Other like-minded young men followed a similar path. The 1906 election saw the return to Parliament, on the Liberal side of the House, of several former residents of the Settlement Movement, men who could speak with authority about urban problems in a way which, say, the leading Liberal Imperialist politicians could never possibly do. As the most talented of these young MPs began to establish their Commons reputations, the agenda of Liberal politics was likely to change.

What these social investigators learned through their encounters with urban poverty succeeded, in time, in modifying what Liberalism meant. But before this could happen, more was needed than a growth of empirical social knowledge and understanding. For Liberals also had to reassure themselves (as a prelude to reassuring others) that social reform did not mean an abandonment of the principles which their party had traditionally followed. It was not just inertia and the distraction of other issues which had made the Liberal Parliamentary Party hesitant to embrace new proposals like old-age pensions; there were also formidable ideological obstacles that had first to be surmounted.

Traditionally, most Liberals had started off with a presumption that state intervention in the working of the market was both futile and wrong. This particularly applied to projects of social reform involving public expenditure. Gladstone had believed that money was best left to 'fructify' in the pockets of the taxpayer. To overcome this inherited prejudice would not be easy. It was all the more difficult in that, in the municipal arena, Liberal councillors were often closely allied with – or even coterminous with – ratepayer protection groups.

But there was also a more general suspicion of state activities: nothing should be done that would interfere with the operation of the market, damage work incentives or weaken contractual obligations. By the 1880s many exceptions had been made to these general rules, but usually in the interests of those who were unable to look after their own interests or make binding contracts (like children, minors, and – though this was more controversial – women). Liberal political thought was essentially individualistic, concerned with the protection of citizens' rights and the removal of 'trammels' on individual freedom. Before it was possible to add to the attainment of individual rights the pursuit of social justice, as most social reformers wanted, Liberals would have to demonstrate that the new departure was really a logical development of their principles, not an abandonment of them.

The trouble with much of the pioneering work of Radical social reformers was that, not being couched in a Liberal idiom, it was prone to be rejected as a deviation from the true faith. That was even true of the youthful Joe Chamberlain and his friends in the early 1880s. The doctrine of 'ransom', constant invocations of the will of the majority, and talk of the need to pursue the 'greatest happiness of the greatest number', set many Liberals' teeth on edge. Chamberlain seemed to be a dangerous 'Jacobin', a latter-day disciple of Jean-Jacques Rousseau.

This revolutionary French approach was not something with which mainstream British Radicals felt comfortable.[35]

A similar difficulty faced the 'Thirty-Nine Articles' group, who seemed too closely tied to the Fabian Socialists for most Liberals' liking. Later in the 1890s the attempt by the Liberal Imperialists to float a social policy on the back of the 'National Efficiency' movement also faltered, in part because the rhetoric of efficiency had no recognised place in Liberal ideology. Even when at their least provocative, the 'efficiency group' gave the impression of being mainly motivated by a desire to occupy the 'centre ground' of politics. On other occasions, its spokesmen displayed an authoritarian temper, pouring scorn on party and advocating a 'Germanic' kind of bureaucratic centralism, totally foreign to the Liberal tradition. This made it easy for their enemies within the party to castigate them as heretics.[36]

All of this was important. A party easily loses electoral credibility if it gives the impression that, in its eagerness to win power, it is prepared to jettison all that it supposedly stands for. Moreover, late Victorian Liberalism assigned primary importance to ideas – which were thought to provide the basis upon which policy could later be erected. John Stuart Mill was typical of Liberals in his insistence that 'ideas' were primary, 'interest' secondary. Could Liberalism, then, be 'modernised' so as to encompass issues of social policy without the whole ideological tradition being called into question? What answer could Liberals give to old-fashioned Radical MPs like Labouchere and Bradlaugh, who opposed social legislation as 'immoral' because it 'would strike a blow at the self-reliance of the individual'?[37]

Many leading Nonconformists, from John Clifford to Hugh Price Hughes, attempted to rise to the challenge. Like leading churchmen of other denominations, they became involved in a discussion of the 'social question', took part in the 'exploration' of 'unknown London', and ran settlement houses in the city slums. The Congregationalists' Browning Hall Settlement, for example, played an exceedingly important part in the later old-age pensions campaign.

But, left to their own devices, few Dissenters would have made much progress in the field of social reform. For a start, they were less shocked by poverty as such than by the existence of the kind of destitution likely to lead to 'sin'. For example, overcrowding, as revealed by Mearns (himself a Congregationalist minister), arrested their attention because of its supposed links with incest. But few Dissenters (again, Mearns well illustrates the point) had either the time or the knowledge to devote themselves to the elucidation of difficult social problems. Hence, with a few notable exceptions, Dissenters often drifted off into innocuous platitudes, speaking of the desirability of arbitration and urging the need to see that women and children did not suffer during strikes (in fairness, one should add that their Anglican counterparts were usually no better). Alternatively, they simplified complex issues, as when they attributed a range of social evils to a single moral failing, for example, drunkenness or gambling. Moreover, like the Radical businessmen (they were often the same people, of course), most Dissenters were nervous of doing anything that would undermine family obligation or the individual's sense of responsibility. Finally, even the most advanced 'social reformers' among the Dissenters tended to attach less significance to these issues than they did to the old sectarian causes.[38]

It therefore needed the secular intelligentsia to work out a considered rationale for social reform. This was the task tackled by those who have come to be known as the 'New Liberals'.[39] The two most important figures in this movement were L. T. Hobhouse, sociologist and leader writer for the *Manchester Guardian*, and J. A. Hobson, the heterodox economist. The 'two Hobs' did much to convince influential Liberals that their creed was a living, not a static, thing. Their views were disseminated, not just through their books, but also through a variety of newspapers, both national (the *Daily News*) and provincial (the *Manchester Guardian*), as well as through small-circulation but prestigious periodicals, like the weekly *Nation*, whose editor H. W. Massingham was another key player in the movement. Significantly, almost the entire *Daily News* team entered the Commons in 1906, strengthening the social reform elements on the Liberal benches.[40]

In setting out to revise the Liberal ideology, the 'reformers' found that the 'Manchester School' Liberalism of Cobden and Bright, still a source of inspiration to many traditional Radicals, was worse than useless. They were able to make much greater use of the writings of John Stuart Mill, whose linkage of 'liberty' with the idea of the 'realisation of personality' was capable of drastic extensions. These it received, particularly at the hands of Hobhouse, who added elements from the German 'Idealists' (filtered through the writings of T. H. Green), and from the conception of society as an 'organism', popularised by the Social Darwinists. 'New Liberalism' was necessarily an eclectic affair. Its advocates even exchanged ideas with congenial souls within the Fabian Society and with ILPers like Ramsay MacDonald through such organisations as the 'Rainbow Circle', a dining club which was founded in 1894 and carried on until the late 1920s. (Ten of the twenty-five members of the Circle were elected to Parliament in 1906.[41]) But the Liberal intellectuals almost certainly influenced their socialist friends rather than vice versa, and 'New Liberalism', despite the fact that it amounted, in Peter Clarke's view, to a kind of 'social democracy',[42] remained an authentically 'liberal' ideology, not a raid on other political traditions.

What the 'New Liberals', were, in fact, doing was persuasively arguing that the all-important concept of freedom had to be defined in more sophisticated ways. It was too simple to contrast 'freedom' and 'coercion'. What mattered was to draw a distinction between the freedom which stimulated and the freedom which cramped the development of personality. 'New Liberals' also contended that (in Hobhouse's famous words) 'liberty without equality is a name of noble sound and squalid result'.[43] Freedom of contract, in other words, was not freedom at all if one side to the bargain was constrained by poverty or in some other way impeded from a rational prosecution of his own best interests. 'New Liberals' also insisted that since property rights had a 'social' as well as an 'individual' dimension, there would be situations in which the community was entitled to intervene: property rights, in other words, should not be treated as absolute.

It was equally necessary to develop an entirely new fiscal strategy. The Liberals had inherited from Gladstone a strong commitment to 'economy' as a good in itself, along with the belief that taxation should be 'proportionate', i.e. that taxes should not be graduated in order to benefit any particular class. It took bitter experience to convince Liberals that 'economy' was simply not reconcilable with social reform. The move away from 'proportionality' (an axiom strongly endorsed by Mill) required even more of an intellectual revolution.

However, from the 1890s onwards, the notion of 'social value' helped the Liberals to escape from the straitjacket of orthodox economic theory. Liberals initially emphasised the ways in which social spending could raise production by stimulating effective demand (Hobson's theory of underconsumption was important here); later they argued that redistribution of wealth was important in its own right. But the important point is that from the 1890s onwards Liberals were beginning to view the budget as a possible instrument of social policy – an important break with the past.[44]

Now, even this bald summary of the 'New Liberal' creed demonstrates that a theoretical justification was being advanced of quite far-reaching interferences in the market, resting on principles that could be invoked, not just in support of all the welfare initiatives which the Liberals were to take in the Edwardian years, but to justify policies which proved too radical even for later Labour administrations: for example, Hobhouse and others were prepared to countenance minimum-wage legislation as a necessary condition for the realisation of their particular concept of 'freedom'.

Nevertheless, there were also important limitations in the 'New Liberalism', which it shared with Liberalism as a whole. The purpose of progress was adjudged to be the attainment of 'social harmony' through a collective exercise of rationality. In consequence, Hobhouse specifically rejected the idea that a just society could only come into existence by a process of class conflict. The people he labels 'mechanical socialists' (i.e. the Marxists) receive very rough treatment at his hands. 'Class', indeed, was a phenomenon which could find no legitimate place in this style of political philosophy. Social reform was seen as an enlightened stratagem for promoting the 'common interest', not as a way of carrying out the will of the majority, still less as a way of advancing a sectional interest.

This made even the most advanced of Liberal thinkers view trade unionism with considerable suspicion. As mechanisms for helping the poor and disadvantaged to assert their true needs, trade unions had a useful role to play; as agencies for schooling their members in the duties of citizenship they were wholly admirable. But 'New Liberals' recoiled in horror at the thought that they might also develop into 'armies' that could wage war on employers or on capitalism itself. Indeed, most of them took the employers' side, in the sense that they tended to emphasise the interdependence of the interests of capital and labour, rather as employers themselves did.

Moreover, although the willing co-operation of the working class was necessary to the achievement of 'social harmony', the 'New Liberals', by implication at least, assigned the key role of defining the 'common good' to their own intelligentsia – to men like the two 'Hobs'. As one historian has put it, 'the New Liberals were so intent on preserving their policies from the "taint of sectionalism" that they failed to see that it was as a sectional interest that Labour felt most threatened'.[45] Nor, arguably, did Labour want 'collectivism', if this meant, for example, the regulation of industrial relations. As Chiozza Money argued in 1906, there may well have been more 'collectivists' amongst the Liberals than in the Labour Party.[46] But this merely indicates that the 'New Liberals' were anxious to 'do things for' the working class, while the Labour

Movement was seeking to control its own destiny. This was to be the source of much misunderstanding in the future.

We will return in a later chapter to the vexed question of what contribution, if any, was made by the 'New Liberalism' to the social legislation which the Liberal governments enacted between 1908 and 1914. But three questions can immediately be posed. First, how successfully did 'New Liberalism' harmonise old philosophical traditions with new social needs? In other words, was this ideology coherent and persuasive? Second, how widely did these ideas circulate? Did they make a significant impression on the Liberal politicians who held power at central and local levels, or were they ingenious intellectual constructions which largely ministered to the amusement of the 'chattering classes' of Hampstead and the leafy suburbs of Manchester, the natural habitat of the Liberal intelligentsia? And, third, would this particular concept of social reform be acceptable to politically conscious working men and women, or would it be seen (if encountered at all) as paternalistic or patronising?[47] Much would depend on what Liberals were doing to increase working-class representation on elective bodies.

Working-Class Representation

Unfortunately one of the Liberals' greatest failures was in not matching their solicitude over obtaining working-class votes with a willingness to sponsor working-class candidates. There was no shortage of influential voices urging local constituency parties to adopt manual workers. For example, the Secretary of the NLF, Schnadhorst, sent out a warning letter to this effect in 1890;[48] other party leaders echoed his advice. Yet little was done. Only in some coal-mining districts, where so high a proportion of the electorate consisted of miners that the local lodges could impose their own favoured candidates upon the middle-class Liberals in their locality, were these difficulties overcome. Almost one half of the dozen or so 'Lib-Lab' MPs were miners – men who consulted the interests of their trade union in industrial matters but were otherwise happy to take the Liberal Whip.[49] The most prominent of all the Lib-Labers, the former socialist, John Burns, an engineer by trade, managed to create in Battersea his own 'Labour' organisation with the help of which he was able to win and retain this poor working-class seat – but his was an unusual accomplishment.[50]

For where Liberalism was already well organised, its local managers were usually loath to put up working men for winnable constituencies, and, since the local parties enjoyed autonomy in the matter of candidate selection, there was little that party headquarters could do to coerce them. Perhaps nothing more alienated politically ambitious working men from the Liberal Party. Many of Labour's pioneers came to accept the need for a new working-class party only after they had suffered personal rebuffs at Liberal hands. To take a famous example, Keir Hardie was turned down by the Mid-Lanarkshire Association in 1888 (he eventually stood as an Independent Labour candidate, coming a humiliating bottom of the poll). A similar fate befell Ramsay MacDonald in Southampton six years later.[51]

The future careers of Hardie and MacDonald perhaps suggest that the local Liberal organisers who spurned them had good grounds for so doing. But many Liberal trade unionists found themselves similarly baulked at the last moment of a prize to which they felt that their services to the party entitled them. For example, Arthur Henderson (the later Labour leader) was rejected in 1895 by the Newcastle Liberal 'One Thousand', in opposition to their executive's advice, despite the fact that he held orthodox Liberal views on 90 per cent of the political issues which currently dominated national politics.[52] Middle-class prejudice was even more blatantly displayed when Bradford's Liberal Executive Council refused in 1885 to allow the President of the local Trades Council, a lifelong Liberal, to stand as a candidate in the School Board elections, and when Fred Mappin, the leader of the local Liberal caucus, blocked attempts to run a working-class candidate in the Sheffield (Attercliffe) by-election in 1894.[53]

Why did Liberal management committees display so little vision? In some cases, it seems, they hesitated to put forward manual workers because they believed that lack of education and social standing were a disqualification from performing an MP's role. To put it another way, working-class Liberals were hampered in their political careers by considerable social prejudice. But there were also practical considerations. Not until 1912 did MPs receive a salary. They (or their backers) were also obliged before 1918 to pay the returning officer's expenses, as well, of course, as meeting the costs of the election campaign itself. Finally, to win all but the safest seats, a candidate was expected, before the campaign formally opened and restrictions on legal spending began to operate, to show generosity to a variety of local clubs and associations. The outlay could be daunting. In Lancashire it cost a parliamentary candidate between £500 and £1000 to fight a borough and twice as much to fight a county division.[54] Little wonder that constituency associations tended to select wealthy men who could entirely or largely pay their own way.

The Liberals' parliamentary leaders were obviously aware of the importance of helping into the House able men of limited financial means. Some of the money accumulated by the party's Chief Whip was used to subsidise such people. However, it seems that most beneficiaries were impecunious young professionals, like Masterman, rather than manual workers.[55]

In any case, the party's Central Fund was raised by means of donations from wealthy supporters and sympathisers (some of them on the look-out for 'honours'). With the departure of so many of its landed members in 1886, this meant that the party was falling dependent on a relatively small number of very wealthy businessmen. Some of these men, like the cocoa manufacturer, George Cadbury, were 'advanced Radicals' who genuinely wanted to see more working men in the House. But most were not. Moreover, in the long run it proved damaging to the Liberals that, despite their claim to be a 'democratic' party, they rested on such a plutocratic financial base. So long as this situation persisted, it was unlikely that the Liberals were ever going to put up working men in significant numbers.[56]

A partial resolution of this difficulty eventually came about, but in a very unlikely way. Angered by the Taff Vale Judgement, which put at risk the very existence of independent trade unionism, union leaders and socialists came together in 1900 to form the Labour Representation Committee (LRC), the forerunner of the modern Labour Party. When it became apparent that this new body, unlike earlier attempts to establish independent Labour associations, would probably survive as an effective force, most Liberal politicians expressed anxiety and disapproval. Even Lloyd George, speaking in 1904, called the decision to 'go in for anything like independent class representation' 'a mistake' which working men themselves would 'sooner or later' regret.[57]

Yet the Liberal organisers also realised that, given their failure to put up their own working-class candidates, there might be advantages in running them by proxy, as it were. An electoral pact with the LRC would not only avoid a splitting of the anti-Unionist vote, it would also align Liberalism with an authentic working-class organisation, thereby adding to its own popular electoral appeal. This formed the background to the signing of the Lib–Lab Pact in 1903, negotiated between Herbert

Gladstone, the Liberal Chief Whip, and his assistant, Jesse Herbert, on the one hand, and Ramsay MacDonald, secretary of the LRC, on the other.[58] It was an informal understanding, which neither side could publicly proclaim. Although the two sets of leaders could exercise influence over their own constituency parties with the aim of avoiding electoral clashes, the pact therefore largely rested upon the willingness of local activists to co-operate with one another.

In England and Wales such co-operation was indeed forthcoming. In the 1906 election, the LRC sponsored fifty candidates, of whom twenty-nine were successful; but of these, all but five were elected either in a straight fight against a Unionist or as single candidates running in harness with one Liberal in a two-member constituency (in Merthyr Tydfil Hardie was elected against the opposition of two Liberals, but no Conservatives, in a two-member seat). This set the pattern for subsequent Liberal-Labour co-operation (some call it the 'Progressive Alliance'), which survived, more or less intact, until the outbreak of the First World War.

But was it wise for the Liberals to have entered such an arrangement? Even at the time there were provincial notables who, suspecting what was afoot, warned of 'nursing into life a serpent which will sting [the] Party to death'.[59] In Scotland, where Liberalism was strong and anti-Labour feeling among its activists ran high, the pact did not operate at all. Even in the North-East of England nineteen out of the twenty-three Presidents of Liberal constituency organisations opposed such an arrangement, while in the West Riding, firmly in the grip of wealthy industrialists, reactions were similar.[60]

The case against the 'Lib-Lab Pact' ran as follows. According to the critics, the Liberals should never have given a helping hand to this new party, which threatened in time to become a formidable rival. It was all the more dangerous in that, though the leaders of the LRC might find it expedient to present their party as a kind of working-class Liberal association, in reality it was very much more than that: for the LRC was a federation of affiliated trade unions and socialist societies, and, although most trade unionists may indeed have been 'sound' on the major political issues of the day, the same could not be said about ILP members like Keir Hardie, Bruce Glasier and Philip Snowden, who, true socialists that they were, viewed both the 'capitalist' parties with contempt. In areas like Bradford, where the ILP had for many years been challenging the Liberals in local elections, such objections were frequently raised.

In retrospect, it can also be argued that the sacrifice of seats to the LRC was totally unnecessary. The LRC leaders were merely bluffing when they claimed to control one million working-class votes; most trade union members had always voted Liberal in the past and would probably continue to do so. Conversely, the result of the 1906 election seemed to confirm that the Liberals were strong enough to go it alone; LRC candidates had shown their utter incapacity to win seats through their own unaided efforts. The pact was therefore a one-sided affair, from which the Liberals had secured little advantage.

But the arguments on the other side are equally strong. The danger of splitting the anti-Unionist vote really did exist, and this would have been a tragedy, given that there was so much common ground between the LRC and the Radical wing of the Party. From this viewpoint one cannot easily call the pact a 'betrayal' of the Liberal creed. Indeed, in 1900 Labour and the Radical 'Little Englander' wing of the party were so close to one another in their hostility towards the Boer War that Keir Hardie actually suggested that Labour put itself under the leadership of John Morley – a declaration all the more startling, coming, as it did, from an avowed socialist.[61]

Over the next few years, on the most important issues of the day, education, licensing, and the tariff, little separated the Liberal Party from most Labour politicians.[62] Ever since the establishment of the London County Council in 1889 Sidney Webb, the Fabian, and a handful of working-class candidates had worked harmoniously with the dominant Radical–Liberal group (which in the capital called itself the 'Progressive Party'). That such co-operation could be extended to parliamentary politics seemed proven by the outcome of the Woolwich by-election of March 1903, when the Cockney Will Crooks was triumphantly returned as an LRC candidate – with a sympathetic Liberal Party forbearing to put forward a candidate of its own.[63] Even 'socialists', like Hardie, Snowden and (pre-eminently) MacDonald, took the Liberal side against the Unionists on almost every live political issue that counted. Campbell-Bannerman therefore had good reason to proclaim that Liberalism and Labour 'were both elements in the progressive forces of the country' who 'were going together nine-tenths of the way'.[64]

Moreover, even granted that 'socialism' posed a *long-term* challenge, the pact could be defended as a cunning way of 'containing' its advance. For the LRC, as we have seen, was a federal organisation, linking the trade unions to the important socialist societies. The Liberals, through this informal alliance, could strengthen the 'moderate' trade unionists

at the expense of the socialists, with their anti-capitalist rhetoric, since an electoral understanding, from which the LRC had much to gain, would encourage it to emphasise those things which it had in common with the Liberal Party. 'Socialism' (in which most members of the LRC anyhow disbelieved and which was not so much as mentioned in the party's Constitution) would become nothing more than a misty aspiration.

There were also more tangible advantages to be gained. If an informal pact with the new party could be negotiated, the Liberals, still hard-pressed for money, would, as Jesse Herbert of Liberal Central Office noted in March 1903, save £15 000 by leaving certain constituencies to be contested by their junior allies.[65] Nor was this all. In those parts of the country, particularly Lancashire, where the Liberal Party was weak and working-class Conservatism strong, the LRC with its class appeal might succeed in taking votes away from the Unionists, as Liberal candidates were unlikely to do. Indeed, almost all the seats where Liberal candidates stood down in 1906 were seats which the Liberals had been unable to win in 1900 and could not be sure of capturing the next time round: surely not much of a concession to the new party.[66] Finally, in return for ceding such difficult seats to Labour, the LRC would be obliged to recommend its working-class sympathisers, in constituencies where Labour was not standing, to support the Liberals. The Liberal vote must have been swollen in 1906 by the adhesion of thousands of working men who perceived the Liberals to be the allies of Labour. For a party concerned to maximise its working-class appeal, this was a powerful recommendation.

In the short run the advantages of the pact undoubtedly outweighed its disadvantages, so far as the Liberal Party was concerned. Its authors cannot, in any case, reasonably be criticised for misfortunes which befell Liberalism over ten years later in circumstances wildly different from anything that could have been envisaged in 1903. Indeed, the 'understanding' with Labour worked so well that, appropriately modified, it also operated in the two elections of 1910, and, but for the war, might have continued still longer. So great was the swing towards the Liberals in 1906 that, with the wisdom of hindsight, it seems that the pact contributed little to the party's victory of that year. However, it was quite different during the close-run contests of 1910, when Liberal-Labour clashes could easily have tipped the balance in favour of the Unionists. Moreover, the very benefits which Labour gained from the pact indirectly helped the Liberals by cramping the smaller party's freedom of manoeuvre. True, Labour MPs occupied benches on the Opposition side of the House following the Liberals' landslide victory of 1906. But, where else could they comfortably have sat? Largely returned on the strength of Liberal votes as many of them were, Labour MPs found it difficult after 1906 to behave as members of the truly independent party which they still claimed to be.

Nevertheless the 'Progressive Alliance', even if it was the best that the Liberals could hope for under the circumstances, fell short of the ideal. As one historian argues, it conceded the formal independence of a separate working-class party and was thus 'a setback rather than a victory for the New Liberal point of view'.[67] Moreover, the pact had only come into existence because of the Liberals' failure to put up enough working-class candidates of their own. Finally, when the Miners Federation of Great Britain (MFGB) finally decided to affiliate to the Labour Party in 1908, the last big industrial union to do so, most of the miners in the House transferred their allegiance from the Liberal Party and took the Labour Whip, so depriving the Liberals of almost all their working-class MPs.

It is true, as we shall see, that the Liberal governments of 1905–14 showed an acute concern for the problems of the poorer members of society. But 'doing good' in this way was never an adequate substitute for helping (or allowing) working men and women to take charge of their own lives.

Admittedly, the whole issue of working-class 'representation' was rather more complicated than historians once made it appear. Almost by definition, pioneering Labour politicians (to say nothing of their successors!) were atypical of those they claimed to represent, many of them being strongly pro-temperance as well as having a vision of social betterment which set them apart from the urban poor they wanted to uplift. In Wolverhampton over 85 per cent of Labour activists lived in the largely suburban areas of the town, not in its poverty-stricken wards.[68] In any case, representation could take more than one form. Because he articulated their emotional needs, Gladstone, to the end of his life, 'remained the unparallelled leader of the British working classes', as one historian puts it.[69]

However, although putting up working-class candidates certainly did not guarantee electoral success, it helped if an ostensibly 'democratic' party was prepared to do this. It is ironic that even the urban Radicals, who had never been happy with the notion of entrusting their welfare to 'enlightened' aristocrats, should not have seen that politically conscious working men would similarly resent a political system which did not allow people of *their* order a place of dignity and influence in the running of the country.

5

THE RADICALS IN OFFICE, 1905–14

So long as the Liberals were in opposition, or held office in precarious circumstances (as between 1892 and 1895), what strategy Liberals should adopt was largely a matter for *debate*. It was quite otherwise with the formation of Campbell-Bannerman's ministry in 1905. For the next decade the Liberals held power. What use were they going to make of it?

To understand how the Liberals faced up to this dilemma one must take account of the rather odd circumstances in which the Liberals displaced their Unionist opponents. The reversal of party fortunes between 1900 and 1905 was both sharp and unexpected. So demoralised had the Liberals been in the 1900 ('Khaki') election that they had left 152 constituencies on mainland Britain uncontested (more even than in the disastrous year of 1895, when the figure had been 117); the outcome had therefore been decided even before the polling booths opened. Then, over the next eighteen months, Liberal fortunes reached the lowest point that they had yet touched, as faction fighting enveloped the party. It seemed as though the Unionists would remain in office for the foreseeable future.

Yet even in the highly disadvantageous circumstances of 1900 – a war in progress, weak leadership, deep divisions at all levels of the party – the Liberal vote had stood up reasonably well, amounting to 48.2 per cent in contested seats (44.6 per cent overall). The Liberals' performance was most disappointing in the densely populated constituencies, which generally experienced low turnouts. This suggests apathy among many of their potential working-class supporters – a situation that was remediable.[1]

Moreover, the relationship between the different wings of the Unionist Alliance was a fragile one. Once the 'danger' of Home Rule had been seen off, it was no longer clear quite what 'Unionism' stood for. Tension steadily increased between Radical Unionists, like Chamberlain, and more traditional Conservatives. The climax came with Chamberlain's launching of the Tariff Reform Campaign in 1903, in which he announced that Free Trade had outlived its usefulness and should be replaced by a system of 'Imperial Preference'. Such an attack on one of the most sacred Liberal tenets quickly reunited the Opposition party.

There followed a series of ministerial mishaps and blunders, all of which played straight into Liberal hands. In December 1905 Balfour resigned as Prime Minister. Campbell-Bannerman, having quickly quelled a half-hearted mutiny from his Liberal Imperialist adversaries,[2] was able to form an extremely strong government, one which contained three future Prime Ministers, Asquith (Chancellor of the Exchequer), Lloyd George (President of the Board of Trade) and Winston Churchill (Under-Secretary at the Colonial Office), as well as Edward Grey (Foreign Secretary), Haldane (War Secretary) and John Morley (Indian Secretary).

Early in 1906 Parliament was dissolved, and the Liberals were confirmed in office with the third biggest landslide achieved in any twentieth-century election (after 1931 and 1997). The Unionists were reduced to a rump of 157 MPs, while Liberals won many apparently 'safe' Conservative seats, like Bath, Salisbury and Exeter.[3] In the excitement of the moment many Liberals struggled to make sense of what had happened, but enthusiastic Radicals sensed that a new age of rationalism and enlightenment had dawned. Disappointment was bound to follow.

Parties, it is often said, never win elections, though they sometimes lose them. That adage applies very well to 1906. Not only did Tariff Reform tear the Unionists into antagonistic factions. The Unionists had also managed to alienate almost every conceivable interest group in the land. The Nonconformists were furious over the 1902 Education Act, and their anger deepened with the passing of a licensing measure in 1904 which could plausibly be denounced as a sell-out to the drink trade. Organised Labour was aggrieved over the government's refusal to reverse the Taff Vale Judgement and at its employment of indentured 'Chinese Labour' in the South African gold mines. Even natural supporters of the government were disheartened when they looked back on the bungling, incompetence and inadequate preparations which had marked the military campaigns in the recent South African war. In these circumstances, the Liberals did not need to formulate an alternative programme or even an alternative strategy.

Admittedly, some have claimed that the Liberal victory of 1906 represented a popular mandate for sweeping measures of social reform. But there is very little truth in this. The landslide victory swept into Parliament a motley crowd of enthusiastic reformers, among whom can be identified a group of 'Social Radicals' who had made a serious study of urban social problems, between twenty-five and forty in number.[4] On the other hand, the frontbenchers were ominously non-committal about social reform, even about old-age pensions, which had been on the political agenda for nearly twenty years. The emphasis fell upon retrenchment and economy, not on a programme of state-aided welfare that was bound to be expensive. As George Bernard Shaw correctly observed, the 1906 election was a triumph for conservatism with a small 'c'.[5] It was quite clear what the Liberals were *against*. They were against Tariff Reform, against high arms expenditure, against Chinese 'slavery', against the 1902 Education Act, and so on. The Liberals had even promised not to introduce a Home Rule Bill within the lifetime of the forthcoming Parliament: a promise which probably reassured the nervous and destroyed Balfour's frenzied attempts to frighten the electorate with his last-minute claims that the Union was in danger. But what were the Liberals *for*?

Certainly, there was a mood of expectancy in 1906. But no detailed commitments had been made. Nor is it easy to extract a class meaning from the 1906 election results. Undoubtedly, the majority of working men cast their votes for the Liberals – though many must have supported the recently formed Labour Representation Committee, which, as we have seen, was linked to the Liberal Party through an informal electoral alliance. At the same time, the Unionist government's affront to Nonconformist sensibilities and the attack on Free Trade had between them driven a large bloc of middle-class voters, including businessmen, into the Liberal camp.

In 1906, then, the Liberals enjoyed popularity with electors from a wide variety of social backgrounds. But it soon became apparent that the Liberal triumph had been brought about by an unusual combination of circumstances that was unlikely to recur. Moreover, the Liberals, having won power, had to make up their minds what they were going to do with it. The rather spurious sense of 'national unity' seemed likely to evaporate, once such a decision had been reached.

With Campbell-Bannerman failing to give a firm lead, the Liberal ministry drifted aimlessly for its first couple of years. Important commitments were made in foreign affairs, but in domestic politics no clear pattern emerged. In 1906 Campbell-Bannerman threw over his own law officers and, with the Trades Disputes Act, gave trade unionists what they had been demanding ever since the passing of the Taff Vale Judgement: an unconditional restoration of their immunities in the event of a strike. This perhaps denoted an eagerness to propitiate the Labour Movement both inside and outside the House. The same might be said of the 1906 Workmen's Compensation Act, which extended Chamberlain's 1897 measure. The Liberals also took over a private Bill introduced by a Labour backbench MP which permitted local authorities to provide meals for necessitous schoolchildren, using a rate subsidy if necessary.

But the main legislative priority, if indeed there was one at all, seemed to involve the paying off of political debts to the Liberals' Nonconformist followers. 'We have been put into power by the Nonconformists', Campbell-Bannerman is alleged to have said.[6] An Education Bill aimed at ending the 'obnoxious' features of the Balfour Bill was the principal government measure of the 1906 session.[7] But when, to no one's surprise, the House of Lords obstructed the passage of the Education Bill, the Liberals declined to dissolve Parliament, fearing to jeopardise their majority over an issue which, they suspected, aroused little popular enthusiasm in the country at large. Moreover, this Bill (through its Clause 4) had made provision for the public funding of church schools in urban areas, should four-fifths of the parents petition for it – a clear attempt to curry favour with the Irish Nationalist Party, which damaged the Bill in Dissenters' estimation. Thereafter, the educational grievance was given low priority, and the Dissenters soon found themselves powerless to pressurise the government into changing its mind. Nonconformity's later disillusionment with Liberalism can be traced back to this initial failure.[8]

Other government bills, such as the 1906 Plural Voting Bill, made no better progress, coming up, as they did, against the Opposition veto in the Upper House. The Liberals also suffered a humiliating setback over their Irish Council Bill of 1907, a botched attempt to extend Irish local government without going the length of Home Rule; the measure had to be withdrawn in the face of furious protests from the Nationalist leaders.[9] Such events badly undermined the morale of Liberal backbenchers, and by the spring of 1908 the fortunes of the party were at a low ebb.

But there was another reason for this. In 1907 the economy had started to go sour. A cyclical depression, originating in America, was producing bankruptcies, falling profit margins and mounting unemployment. Contemporaries called it 'the Rich Man's Panic'. By 1908 unemployment among trade unionists had gone up to nearly 8 per cent, its highest point since 1886. This development had immediate political consequences. The government started to lose a string of by-elections: three seats fell to the Opposition in early 1908 on swings of between 3.5 and 6.5 per cent. There were another two by-elections in which an independent socialist did the damage,[10] but the real threat to the Liberal position in 1907 and 1908 came from the Unionists. Now recovered from their stunning defeat in 1906, the Tariff Reformers saw that the recession gave them a golden opportunity. They began to take control of the Opposition party, with Balfour's grudging acquiescence, shrilly blaming high unemployment on the Free Trade system. Tariff Reform, they promised, meant work for all.[11]

At just this moment, in April 1908, the dying Campbell-Bannerman submitted his resignation. Asquith, as expected, succeeded to the premiership. The Cabinet reshuffle which followed saw Lloyd George promoted from the Board of Trade to the Treasury and his close friend, Winston Churchill, enter the Cabinet for the first time, in Lloyd George's old post. The period of drift and uncertainty was over. The Radical crusade was about to resume.

In the new Asquith government the drive was increasingly provided by Lloyd George himself, a complex figure who arouses among historians, as he did among his contemporaries, feelings both of admiration and disgust.[12] Faced with a rejuvenated Opposition fighting for Tariff Reform, Lloyd George did at least have the imagination to see that a negative defence of Free Trade would not suffice. Instead, he decided to pick up the gauntlet thrown down by the House of Lords and renew the assault on aristocratic privilege, while, at the same time, seeking to broaden the Liberals' electoral appeal by a constructive policy of social reform.

Lloyd George's own background and personality partly explain why he determined to combine these two campaigns. Although by no means a typical product of the Dissenting communities of rural North Wales, Lloyd George instinctively felt that the Liberal mission was to undermine the Anglican establishment, destroy the remnants of the pre-industrial aristocratic order – or 'feudalism', as he liked to call it – and to create a society in which there would be equality of opportunity, and men and women would be valued for their intrinsic qualities without reference to their ancestry or social status.

An insensitive observer, listening to Lloyd George's emotional and demagogic platform orations, might suppose that he was an egalitarian. The Welshman certainly hated, with fierce hatred, what he called 'privilege', and boasted that he was better qualified than most politicians to speak for 'the People', since he was one of the children of the People. Like a number of left-wing politicians, Lloyd George invented, as he grew older, an almost entirely spurious childhood, supposedly marked by poverty and suffering. Having got to the top, he boasted, with pardonable but childish pride, of the dizzy social ascent he had had to make. In fact, Lloyd George's background can best be described as 'petit bourgeois'. He started life as a small-town solicitor. By no conceivable stretch of the imagination can Lloyd George be called working-class. In fact, growing up in the area around Criccieth, the Welshman seldom came into contact with the proletariat proper, and some historians would say that he never really understood the psychology of the unionised industrial worker.

It is perhaps worth remembering at this point that Lloyd George, though his speeches were soaked in class feeling and often lifted his audience into a state of great emotional excitement and anger, never used the language of class in its *modern* sense. As with so many nineteenth-century Radicals before him, he saw himself as leading 'the People', with a capital 'P', against the forces of privilege. His bogies were landlords, peers, brewers, publicans, priests. But he had no quarrel with capital. Providing that businessmen, bankers and shareholders acknowledged their social responsibilities, he was happy to defend their role as a necessary and beneficial one, and he did not begrudge them very large incomes if these had been earned by a contribution to the production of wealth. Essentially, Lloyd George was trying to create a unity of the so-called 'productive classes', by which he meant the industrial workforce, and capitalists, entrepreneurs, managers and shareholders. This pan-class alliance he then wanted to lead in a fight against parasitic monopolists and idlers, notably the landlords, who battened on the country's wealth, but did nothing to create it. In a way Lloyd George was therefore picking up the Radical Programme which Chamberlain had dropped in 1886, when his attention had been distracted by Ireland.

Lloyd George had first achieved national prominence by the zeal with which he had led the Welsh Nonconformists in their impassioned protests against the Balfour Education Act, and he retained strong links with the Chapels. Listening to sermons and hymn-singing remained one of his favourite pastimes. The great Baptist preacher, Dr John Clifford, was so impressed by this aspect of Lloyd George's character that he assured a political rally in 1910 that 'Lloyd George was in politics as Mr Gladstone was in politics, that he might serve God in politics.'[13]

Even had he wanted to break free from his chapel connections, Lloyd George would have found it difficult to do so. But he had no such wish. Apart from anything else, Lloyd George knew that pushing forward Nonconformist demands helped to preserve the *balance* in the Liberal programme, which was necessary if its traditional middle-class supporters were to be kept loyal to the Party[14] – something which, on both practical and ideological grounds, was indispensable to Liberalism's survival.

But Lloyd George also saw that sectarian issues by themselves were not enough – the events of 1906–8 had proved that. Without ever quite renouncing the causes which had brought him into politics in the first place, Lloyd George outgrew them to some extent. If the Liberal Party were to have a future, it needed to move in a Radical direction, and its Radicalism would have to acquire a social, as well as a political, conscience.

What was true of Lloyd George was broadly true of the Edwardian Liberal Party as a whole. And so the years between 1908 and 1914 saw two parallel campaigns: the final assault on 'feudalism', and an earnest attempt to tackle the 'social problem', along the broad lines already laid down by the 'New Liberal' intelligentsia. The two campaigns sometimes intersected. Lloyd George's famous 'People's Budget',[15] for example, exasperated the landed interest but caused corresponding delight to the party's traditional Radical supporters by including, not only a number of land taxes, but also provision for the valuation of all land. Increased duties on tobacco and spirits could be counted upon to please the Dissenting teetotallers, as could provisions for increasing the cost of licences issued to publicans (a provision partly taken from the government's 1908 Licensing Bill, which the House of Lords had earlier rejected). Yet, if these proposals seem to look back to a nineteenth-century conception of Radicalism, the introduction of a 'super-tax' of sixpence in the pound on incomes over £5000 and the move towards a more sharply graduated income-tax system seem to point to the future, as does the establishment of the Development Commission.[16] A similar ambiguity surrounded the later Land Campaign and another of Lloyd George's highly innovative budgets, that of 1914.[17]

Edwardian Liberalism, in short, was 'Janus-faced': it looked back to the great Radical tradition of Cobden and Bright, but it also looked forward to the social democratic policies promulgated by later twentieth-century governments. At the risk of some simplification, it seems sensible to take these two aspects of Liberalism one by one, starting with the final 'assault on feudalism'.

The Assault on Feudalism

The assault began in earnest in 1909 with the first of Lloyd George's eight budgets. This 1909 Budget, the so-called 'People's Budget', contained, along with other controversial proposals, a group of land taxes and a scheme of land valuation. The Radical backbenchers were delighted; the Conservative Party predictably enraged. The land taxes themselves were moderate enough; in fact, they were later repealed by the post-war coalition government, of which Lloyd George was the head, on the ground that the revenue which they generated did not warrant the administrative costs involved in their collection. But it was the provision for land valuation which caused all the furore; for once valuation had been completed, a Radical government had a number of extreme options available to it, including land nationalisation, which was actually backed by nearly 130 MPs, most of them Liberals.[18] Characteristically, Lloyd George, though by temperament and conviction an ardent land reformer, had only the haziest idea exactly what sort of reform he wanted. Equally characteristically, he concealed his imprecision under a flood of emotional rhetoric. Here many landlords played into the government's hands by the extravagance and bad temper with which they attempted to justify their traditional privileges. Their outspokenness enabled Lloyd George to reply with a platform invective which, even over the years, still gives off a charge of violence and excitement.

The fight over the Budget had an important, but not entirely planned, outcome. The House of Lords, with the blessings of the Conservative leadership, broke a constitutional convention of nearly 200 years' standing by rejecting the Budget. An earlier view that Lloyd George cunningly framed the Budget in order to provoke this response now finds little favour. But the Lords' decision greatly pleased most members of the Liberal Party, and no one was more pleased than Lloyd George himself.

The Constitutional Crisis which followed is one of the most familiar episodes in British political history.[19] Summarised baldly, the defeat of the Budget forced Asquith to dissolve Parliament. The Liberals came back from the January 1910 general election in roughly equal numbers to the Unionists, with Labour and the Irish Nationalists, who held the balance of seats, keeping Asquith in power. The Budget, now that it had received a popular endorsement, soon became law. But Asquith's freedom to move against the House of Lords was hampered by the insistence of the King that *another* election must take place before he would use his prerogative to create enough Liberal peers to swamp the Opposition in the Upper House when – as would inevitably happen – their Lordships refused to consent to their own emasculation. Following the death of Edward VII in May, a constitutional conference was held in an attempt to break the deadlock. The conference failed, and Asquith promptly asked for a dissolution and also for an advance promise ('the contingent guarantees') that the royal prerogative would be used for a mass creation of Liberal peers if and when the need arose.

The result of the second 1910 election closely followed the first. The government introduced its Parliament Bill; the Unionist Opposition objected, but, informed at the last minute of the King's promise, prudently gave way – though only after an internal party dispute which cost Balfour the Conservative leadership. In August 1911 the Parliament Bill became law. Under its terms the Lords' right to throw out Bills passed by the Commons was replaced by a suspensory veto; the immunity of Finance Bills from interference by the Lords was formally affirmed; and the life of Parliaments was reduced from seven to five years.

While the Constitutional Crisis was in progress, Lloyd George, at least in public, gave the impression of greatly enjoying himself. Some of his sallies against the landed aristocracy and against the Upper House have become legendary. He and other Radicals could also take satisfaction from the final outcome of the struggle. The curbing of the powers of the House of Lords had been something which all nineteenth-century Radicals had thirsted to achieve. To have brought it off was something of a triumph for 'the People'. Moreover, the Lords' loss of its absolute veto enabled the Liberal government to promote legislation which would otherwise have been doomed. In 1912 a measure for the disestablishment and disendowment of the Church in Wales was introduced. It was rejected by the Lords, but under the terms of the Parliament Act a measure which passed through the Commons in three successive sessions automatically became law. The Bill accordingly received the royal assent in September 1914, though its operation was suspended due to the recent outbreak of war.[20]

At the same time Lloyd George was pressing forward with his Land Campaign, an ambitious attempt to revolutionise the countryside. Abandoning the old Radical obsession with the creation of smallholdings, Lloyd George concentrated upon improving the lot of the downtrodden agricultural labourers, who were promised a minimum wage, to be fixed by local statutory wage boards. Rent courts, as well as providing security of tenure (a pledge which went down particularly well in the West Country), would reduce farmers' rents to offset their higher wages bills. Thus the main cost of reform would fall on the landowners – a most satisfactory outcome, from the Liberal point of view.[21]

The Land Campaign posed a serious electoral threat to the Unionist Party since, although the Opposition had won about two-thirds of all English rural constituencies in December 1910, its leaders felt that their hold on many of these seats was precarious.[22] A delighted Masterman was writing to Lloyd George in 1913, 'Create an organisation to spread the "Virus" in every village, even the neighbourhood of Hatfield [Lord Salisbury's residence], and we will at least stir things a bit before we die!!'[23] The prospect of harassing the aristocrats in the heart of their great estates was a highly pleasing one to the Radicals. Indeed, there is evidence that the proposals generally went down well in England, though in Scotland, where economic and political circumstances were quite different, necessitating a separate Report, the Liberal campaign had not yet been launched when war broke out.[24] In addition, together with slightly improved agricultural conditions, these anti-landlord agitations had the effect of encouraging landowners to put part of their estates on to the market. By late 1914 some 800 000 acres of English land had changed hands – a sign of the loss of confidence felt by many great aristocrats in the future of landed property.[25]

Nevertheless, something had gone wrong with the Radical crusade. For the 'destruction of feudalism', if that is what it was, did not, at least in the short run, seem to be doing much to boost the Liberal Party's fortunes.

There are broadly two reasons for this. The first is that the Liberals were only able to reduce the powers of the Lords with the help of the Irish Nationalists, and the Irish, in return for their help, exacted an assurance that Home Rule would again be brought out of cold storage. When the first of the two general elections of 1910 left Redmond, the Irish leader, holding the balance of seats in the Commons, the Liberals found that they had fallen dependent upon the Irish, a situation which many of them resented. Indeed, the Constitutional Crisis, almost from the start, became overshadowed by the Irish issue. In early 1910, for example, a number of ministers, among them Grey, the Foreign Secretary, announced that they did not want to reduce the *powers* of the Upper House but preferred to alter its *composition*. This might mean anything or nothing, but the Irish reckoned that even a 'reformed' Lords would probably be hostile to Home Rule, and held out for a removal of the Lords' veto. Indeed, Redmond threatened Asquith that if the government reneged on this policy, his followers would refuse to vote for the 'People's Budget' when it was reintroduced into the Commons. The unpopularity of the Budget in Nationalist Ireland gave this threat plausibility. There was even a brief moment in the spring of 1910 when it seemed possible that the Asquith ministry might fall, to be replaced by a minority Conservative administration enjoying temporary Irish support.

Although on this issue the Liberal Cabinet gave way and secured the passage of the Budget by a public commitment to the policy of veto, the constitutional conference of the summer saw them once more trying to back away from the strategy to which Redmond and the Irish were trying to pin them. No Irish MP was invited to the constitutional conference, which was ominous in itself. In their absence, and quite unbeknown to the wider public, the delegations from the two major parties sat down to discuss the so-called 'Ripon Plan', a scheme for resolving deadlocks between the two Houses by special 'joint sessions'. The Liberals were even prepared to debate an Opposition proposal that 'organic' (or 'constitutional') Bills, which might possibly include a Home Rule Bill, should be accorded special treatment by being first referred to the judgement of the people in the form of a referendum. The Liberals turned down this suggestion – not surprisingly, for to have done otherwise would undoubtedly have brought their alliance with the Irish Nationalists to an abrupt end.[26]

But before the conference had finally collapsed, Lloyd George had secretly approached Balfour with the proposal that a 'National Government' be set up to dispose of all the outstanding issues of the day. This episode, like so many of Lloyd George's escapades, is surrounded to this very day by ambiguity and confusion. But what is not in doubt is that Lloyd George had floated the possibility that the Irish Question be resolved within a larger measure of 'Home Rule All Round' or 'Devolution' – that is to say, that other parts of the United Kingdom as well as

Ireland be given subordinate assemblies, prior perhaps to an attempt to federate the entire Empire.[27] Such an arrangement, even if practical, would have proved entirely unacceptable to the Irish Nationalists, who, facing opposition within their own country from separatists and physical force nationalists, could not afford to be too accommodating. But, of course, if a coalition of the two main parties had been formed, the Irish could have been left to 'stew in their own juice', as Lloyd George remarked to one delighted Conservative MP who was 'in the know'.[28]

The Secret Coalition talks petered out after some desultory discussion. The parties returned to their battle stations. But, as many Liberals had predicted, Asquith's Third Home Rule Bill, first introduced in 1912, brought the ministry nothing but trouble. In the north-east of Ireland there took place what amounted to a pan-class rebellion of Protestant Loyalists. Indeed, between 1912 and 1914 the threat of civil war in Ulster overshadowed all other political issues. It was in vain that Lloyd George launched his Land Campaign in October 1913. His speeches received disappointing coverage in the press. People were not interested in the plight of tenant farmers whose crops of mangel-wurzels had been destroyed by pheasants, when Carson's men were drilling in Belfast and angry Conservatives were openly advertising for strong and willing men prepared to cross the Irish Sea and join the Ulster Loyalists in armed rebellion to Home Rule.

On several occasions the Liberal ministry almost broke up under the strain of the Irish Crisis, as its members hunted desperately for a compromise solution to the difficulty which they could recommend to their supporters without too much loss of face. Lloyd George showed himself to be particularly eager to devise an expedient which might meet the anxieties of the Ulster Protestants, even if this mean watering down the original Home Rule measure.[29]

For it remained a fact that Irish Home Rule did not command widespread support on mainland Britain. The stubborn refusal of Asquith even to contemplate a national referendum on the question may in part reflect his lawyer-like antipathy towards constitutional innovation, but it also suggests that, like his colleagues, he was not prepared to risk the future of his government on what he thought was a vote loser. In any case, even some people within his own party sympathised with the plight of Ulster Protestants fighting for the retention of what they considered to be their 'civil and religious liberties'. The backbencher who first publicly suggested that the predominantly Protestant counties of Ulster should be allowed to opt out of a Home Rule settlement was, significantly, the Liberal MP for Mid-Cornwall, Agar-Robartes, who had many Nonconformists in his constituency. To use armed force against the 'Loyalists' would have been politically hazardous, perhaps suicidal. Yet to defy the wishes of Redmond and the Irish, who naturally insisted that Ireland be treated as a unity, might involve the Liberals' ejection from office, since the government depended very largely on Irish Nationalist votes.

It falls outside the scope of this book to describe how the Cabinet twisted and squirmed as it attempted to grapple with this dilemma and how it attempted to manoeuvre its Irish Allies into accepting at least some measure of *temporary* partition. An earlier generation of historians had scathing things to say about the government's floundering over Ireland between 1911 and 1914, citing it as proof of the 'failure of Liberalism'. But subsequent governments have enjoyed no greater success in reconciling the divergent claims of Irish Nationalists and Ulster Unionists. Perhaps the Asquith ministry was more unfortunate than culpable in its handling of the Irish Crisis before 1914.

However, in the short run, Ireland damaged the Liberal Party, taking the shine off its recent triumph over the House of Lords. Since at precisely this time ministers were facing trouble from militant strikers and suffragette outrages, an impression was perhaps being given that the country had become ungovernable on traditional Liberal lines. So, at least, argues George Dangerfield in his famous book, *Strange Death of Liberal England*.[30] Unfortunately, Liberal policies also aroused nationalist feeling in both Scotland and Wales, which the government then failed to satisfy.

But this leads on to the second reason for the relative failure of the Radical assault on feudalism. Both in the Constitutional Crisis, and in the struggle over Ireland which followed, the Radicals found that the forces which opposed them were surprisingly strong and self-confident. To some extent Lloyd George had made the mistake, common among politicians, of taking his own rhetoric too seriously. In his great platform speeches he had portrayed landowners and peers as an anachronistic and useless caste, whose attempts to obstruct reform could no longer be tolerated by 'the People'. But, as the general elections of 1910 showed, the electorate did not altogether share this view. True, the Liberals, with their Labour and Irish allies, managed to win a conditional victory in both elections, which was better than they could have hoped for in 1908, but their success was far from overwhelming. Why?

The question can be answered on a number of levels. But it does seem clear that the social forces represented by the House of Lords were, oddly enough, stronger in 1911 than they had been in the 1880s. For in the intervening period a silent but important social transformation had occurred. One historian has called it 'the Gentleman's Revolution'. Despite the continuing depression in agriculture, the large landowners had *not* gone under. On the contrary, with remarkable resilience they had adapted to their straitened circumstances and, after a fashion, come to terms with the modern world. Many landowners, overcoming their instinctive aversion to self-made men and financiers, made a prudent accommodation with the new wealth. For example, some sold off parcels of land and invested the capital in stocks and shares. Others exploited the many lucrative offers that came their way and served as guinea-pig directors on company boards. In short, landed society became fused with financial wealth to form a new governing class – the plutocracy. The aristocracy underwent a profound change. But it was, to some extent, strengthened by that change and acquired important new allies.[31]

Finally, there is one respect in which the great landed families remained true to the traditions of their class. They were nearly all involved, in one way or another, in military or naval life. Some had distinguished service records; most had sons or relatives serving in the officer corps. A high proportion enlisted in Haldane's Territorial Army, the new home defence force. Indeed, about three-quarters of all landed Unionist MPs during the Edwardian period were connected, directly or indirectly, with the armed services. Landowners were also the life and soul of local rifle clubs and of other organisations designed to promote the martial virtues. For the British aristocracy was, first and foremost, a *military* caste, as it showed in its passion for blood sports. The Radicals were appalled by such displays of 'militarism': how horrible, they lamented, that in an advanced civilisation like that of industrial Britain well-educated gentlemen should devote so much of their time, money and energy to slaughter.[32]

Lloyd George himself often derided the aristocracy in precisely these terms. But surely in doing so he was getting dangerously out of touch with the spirit of the age and indeed with much of public opinion. For in 1912, 1913 and 1914 professional soldiers, Territorial officers and the like did not strike most Britons as comic, anachronistic or sinister, rather the contrary. For these years saw a resurgence of patriotism in the face of the German challenge. From 1908 or 1909 onwards, if not before, the newspapers were full of the threatening international situation and of the risk of war. Invasion scare stories poured off the presses, and readers thrilled as they read fictional accounts of German armies jackbooting their way through Surrey or the eastern counties. There were outbreaks of mass neurosis; the excitable and suggestible reported sightings of Zeppelins hovering mysteriously over the English countryside. Right-wing editors worried over the presence of German waiters and musicians in British holiday towns, suspecting them of being an embryonic fifth column.[33]

Most of this was hysterical nonsense. Nevertheless, in 1911 Britain came close to being involved in war with Germany at the time of the Agadir Crisis, when, interestingly enough, one of the most hawkish ministers was Lloyd George, a recent but ardent convert to the view that German expansion threatened the very existence of the British Empire. Was this quite the right moment to pillory and attack a social class – the landed aristocracy – which would inevitably provide the country with leadership in war, if and when the long-awaited clash with Germany finally occurred? The 'Diehard Peers' had no doubt about their own importance. In fighting against the Parliament Act of 1911 and in resisting Home Rule, these men did not see themselves as defending, in a spirit of selfish obstinacy, a social order whose usefulness had passed. They believed – and with some reason – that they occupied an important position of trust in national life, that upon their shoulders rested, in large part, the security, and hence the prosperity, of the entire Empire. They hated Liberals, not least because they thought the political ambitions of these men were leading them into actions prejudicial to vital national interests.[34]

What particularly angered the Diehards were the activities of the Radical backbenchers in attempting to force their leaders to adopt policies more likely to avoid the horrors of war (only a small minority, mostly Quakers, were doctrinaire pacifists). This was also a constant source of embarrassment to the pre-war Liberal cabinets, not least because some ministers sympathised with the backbenchers' complaints or, like Lloyd George, found it politically expedient to pretend that they did so. In 1909 and again in 1914 the party was honeycombed with disaffection at all levels, as 'economists' and peacemongers tried to stop the escalating naval arms race with Germany. In fact, most Radicals strongly believed in the desirability of Britain's continuing naval supremacy; they simply did not believe the claims of Admiralty and Opposition that the country's supremacy was in serious jeopardy. Nor did they feel happy about Grey's anti-German foreign policy, which involved the consolidation of the French Entente (through the military talks of 1906) and the 1907 rapprochement with tsarist Russia (a development that nearly all Radicals found morally obnoxious).[35]

In practice, the 'anti-war' Radicals achieved few, if any, of their objectives. But these disagreements had two regrettable consequences for the
Liberal Party. First, with the connivance of Campbell-Bannerman and
then of Asquith, Grey avoided having his foreign policy challenged by
not bringing what he was doing to the attention of the Cabinet. Notori-
ously the military conversations with France were kept secret until they
were revealed at a 'packed' meeting of the Committee of Imperial
Defence in August 1911, in the wake of the Agadir Crisis. Thereafter,
Grey's ministerial critics, of whom Loulou Harcourt, the Colonial Secretary, was the most persistent, belatedly insisted on the Cabinet's
involvement. Yet Grey still found ways of evading external interference.
This meant that the ambiguities and dangers inherent in British foreign
policy did not receive the sustained criticism and scrutiny they required.
The Foreign Office's evasiveness may also have prevented the government from sending out sufficiently strong warning signals to the
Germans, thereby contributing to the set of misunderstandings which
culminated in 1914 in a general European war.[36]

Second, once war had indeed broken out, Opposition critics were able
to claim that the Asquith government had been paralysed in its dealings
with the German threat by the 'Potsdam Party' within its own ranks.
A sense that the patriotism of the Liberals was in doubt and that the
party could not be trusted with the defence of the Empire, however
unfair it may have been, undoubtedly seriously damaged it after 1914,
but it also encouraged open displays of disaffection from many members
of the Opposition even before hostilities commenced.[37]

Against this background, many of the great landlords and their
dependants, confident about their own indispensability and convinced
of the righteousness of their cause, came out in revolt against the authority of the elected government in 1913 and 1914, ostensibly over Home
Rule, but more fundamentally to mark their contempt for parliamentary institutions and radical demagoguery. The prospect of civil war
breaking out in Ireland and spilling over on to the mainland frightened
some right-wing peers and landlords, but others welcomed the drift to violence as a refreshing contrast to the cant and hypocrisy of party politics.[38]

But this 'Revolt of the Right' was not confined to aristocrats, army
officers and other traditional members of the country's ruling elite. It
cannot, therefore, truly be characterised as 'the politics of paranoia' or as
the death throes of an obsolete social order.[39] For associated with landowners like Willoughby de Broke in his challenge to the Liberal government were angry patriots from other social backgrounds and different

political traditions. Together these people formed what has recently been called the 'Radical Right': 'a collection of super-patriots unable for one reason or another to identify with their "natural" party': 'a movement of rootless nationalists who felt alienated to a lesser or greater extent from *all* the major political organisations of the day'.[40]

The Liberal government and Liberal values generally proved to be resilient enough to survive the 'Revolt of the Right' in Edwardian Britain. But, momentarily, Liberalism was weakened by the strength of the reaction which it had provoked. Meanwhile, how was the Asquith ministry faring in its attempt to consolidate the relationship between the Liberal Party and the working-class electorate?

6

LIBERALISM, LABOUR AND SOCIAL REFORM, 1905–14

The landed aristocracy did not topple over, politically, when attacked, as perhaps some Radicals had intended. But there was at least this satisfaction to be derived from the situation. Organised Labour – and the clear majority of working-class voters – sided with the Radicals. The assault on feudalism, though it led to complications aplenty, at least helped Lloyd George in his attempts to win over the working man. For the Constitutional Crisis raised issues of fundamental importance to ordinary working people. After all, it was very much in the interests of Labour that Radicalism should prevail. The Labour Movement, for example, had a vested interest in securing a reduction in the powers of the House of Lords. Many Labour MPs would have preferred the total abolition of the Upper House, but they saw a removal of its absolute veto as a step in the right direction. Irish Home Rule was viewed with greater ambivalence. Labour supported Home Rule, but one senses a certain weariness with the everlasting complaints of relatively prosperous Irish tenant farmers. Perhaps what most brought the British Labour Movement out in warm support of Asquith's Home Rule Bill between 1912 and 1914 was the unconstitutional nature of the opposition which it encountered.

For, although, as we will see, Labour was throwing up from its own ranks rebels against the parliamentary system on the eve of the First World War, the leadership, including nearly all Labour MPs, were parliamentarians to the core. They hated violence and illegality of any sort. So, in a way, we have in these years an odd reversal of roles. The Conservatives were in open defiance of the parliamentary system, proclaiming the need for revolutionary action, while decent, dull trade union officials and socialist journalists (all manual workers by background) showed a thoroughly bourgeois sense of social and constitutional propriety. Violent parliamentary scenes like the shouting-down of Asquith by Conservative backbenchers in July 1911 (the House had to be adjourned in disorder) simply made Labour politicians aware of how deeply attached they were to constitutionalism and to Liberal values generally, and this in turn helped to cement the alliance between Liberals and Labour. In other words, the 'Revolt from the Right' provided them with a common enemy which, as progressives, they could combine to fight.

But this, by itself, would not ensure that the Liberal Party remained the 'people's party', to which the working-class electorate would instinctively turn for protection. For all his commitment to land reform, even Lloyd George seems to have sensed that, if Liberalism were to enjoy a secure future, it would have to prove its legitimacy in the eyes of the working man by showing an entirely new kind of sensitivity to the problems thrown up by *industrial* society.[1] This was one of the principal sources of the social legislation which characterised the 1908–12 period. In rapid succession the Liberal ministry carried old-age pensions (1908), the establishment of labour exchanges (1909) and of trade boards (1909), an ambitious National Insurance scheme covering sickness, invalidity and unemployment (1911), and a Miners' Minimum Wages Act (1912), to mention only the most important initiatives.[2] The tax system also changed, with the introduction of differentiation between earned and unearned income (1907) and steeper graduation, while the percentage of income derived from direct taxes increased sharply: from 44 per cent to 60 per cent between 1888 and 1914, mainly, though not entirely, as a result of Liberal policies.[3]

But did these reforms fulfil their main purpose? In other words, were the Liberals able to demonstrate that a Radical party, enjoying mass support but under a progressive middle-class leadership, could be a viable proposition by the early twentieth century? And did welfare legislation really slow down the advance of socialism?

At first sight the answer would appear to be an unqualified 'Yes'. Historians who have studied the 1910 elections are generally agreed that, although the Liberals lost ground in the south of England in predominantly rural and suburban constituencies, the party held its own very well in working-class areas, especially those in the industrial north. The fact that in December 1910 plural voting seems to have given the Unionists some thirty seats which they would not otherwise have picked up provides further evidence that Britain's political system was becoming more 'class-based' – or so, at least, many historians believe.[4]

Yet these developments, it has been claimed, proved highly beneficial to the Unionist Opposition, which rallied to its support middle-class groups frightened by the 'predatory socialism' of the government. Tariff Reform, so decisively rejected in 1906, enjoyed a new lease of life in 1908–9. Its attraction was that it provided a way of raising additional revenue which promised to shield the rich from any personal discomfort or inconvenience. Unionists contrasted the painless strategy of 'making the foreigner pay' with the horrors of the People's Budget, which had raised income tax to what many contemporaries thought the punitive level of 1s 2d (6p) in the pound, as well as introducing surtax – the City had been particularly angered by this.[5] The almost equally radical Budget of 1914 (originally planned to be 1s 4d in the pound on earned incomes over £2500, with surtax on the highest incomes)[6] merely confirmed these fears. In fact, according to some historians, what was happening in the years after 1908 was a polarisation of society along class lines, with the Conservatives and Unionists increasing their appeal to the middle-class electorate and becoming more than ever the party of property: all property, landed, commercial and industrial. The Liberals' abandonment of the ideology of retrenchment and their reduced emphasis upon the paying-off of the National Debt also contributed to this realignment.[7]

Yet, interestingly enough, in a political system where class allegiance was becoming more important, the main working-class party in 1910 was not the Labour Party, which ran only fifty-six candidates in December 1910 – in all but eleven cases with Liberal support. Instead, most manual workers who had the parliamentary vote still supported the Liberals. It seemed as if the combination of social reform plus the commitment to mildly redistributive fiscal policies was making Liberalism the popular cause. Indeed, so successful was Lloyd-Georgian Radicalism that some Labour candidates in 1910 found it difficult to carve out a distinctive niche for themselves. Many were driven into claiming credit for popular measures, like old-age pensions, which the Liberal government had recently passed; as one historian has noted, there were some constituencies in which an ignorant observer might have supposed from the election literature put out by the Labour candidate that *Labour* had been in office for the previous four years![8]

It would be churlish to deny that the Liberals had achieved a considerable success. But how durable and significant was it likely to prove? Here historians differ dramatically. Some (the 'revisionists') argue that the Liberals had converted themselves by 1914 into a kind of 'social demo-cratic' party, with strong popular support. From this they draw the deduction that the eventual Liberal collapse did not have profound socio-economic causes since the Liberals, far from being destroyed by the advent of class, had successfully adapted themselves to its require-ments. Such an interpretation leads logically on to the claim that only the 'accident' of the Great War brought about the Liberals' eventual downfall.[9]

On the other hand, there are historians who admit the importance of the Great War, but insist that it merely speeded up a Liberal disintegra-tion of which there were already abundant signs *before* 1914. The debate, which is nicely poised, seems unlikely ever to be resolved to everyone's satisfaction, since much depends upon guessing what course British politics would have taken if the First World War had not broken out when it did. But all can agree that the Liberals were grappling with two kinds of challenge before 1914. First, could they hold on to a modicum of middle-class support, at the same time as wooing the working-class electorate with a policy of social reform? Second, would the working classes continue to be satisfied with the kind of reforms which Liberal ministries were likely to produce? In the words of a leading Liberal, Herbert Samuel, it was 'the abiding problem of Liberal statesmanship to raise the enthusiasm of the working class without frightening the middle classes'.[10] Had the Liberals carried off this difficult trick?

Holding on to some middle-class support was clearly essential to the long-term survival of the Liberal Party. But it also posed serious problems. After 1906 a plethora of middle-class defence groups came into existence, such as 'the Middle-Class Defence Organisation', the 'Income-Tax Reduction Society', and the 'Anti-Socialist League', all of them avowedly anti-Liberal in their politics. Some traditional middle-class Liberal supporters, especially in London, were bound to be unset-tled by the activities of these bodies and by reading articles such as 'The Bitter Cry of the Middle Classes', which a Liberal paper, *The Tribune*, was publishing in July 1906.[11] Significantly, the Progressive Party, which had controlled the LCC since its establishment, suffered a heavy defeat in 1907 at the hands of opponents campaigning on the slogan, 'It's Your Money WE Want'.

Partly with a view to countering these complaints and to rallying the faithful, ministers took up the Nonconformists' various grievances.

Indeed, the assault on the House of Lords during the Constitutional Crisis vividly recalled to many Liberal activists, the Dissenters especially, the struggles of their ancestors against the tyranny of Strafford and Laud – in language which also tapped into the democratic rhetoric of plebeian Radicalism.[12]

But even as early as 1910 this strategy was running into difficulty. Some leading Dissenters began to express alarm over Radical demagoguery and the contents of Radical social legislation. A straw in the wind was the formation in 1909 of the Nonconformist Anti-Socialist Union, organised and financed by wealthy Methodist businessmen, among them Robert Perks (leading to Lloyd George's public taunt that he wished that Sir Robert 'would not always talk as if the Nonconformist conscience were locked up in his City safe'[13]). Even some Congregationalists and Baptists, the sects closest to Liberalism, were losing the enthusiasm which had brought them on to the hustings in support of Liberal candidates four years earlier. In fact, by 1910 Nonconformist clergymen who abused the pulpit by indulging in party political propaganda sometimes had the disconcerting experience of seeing wealthy laymen rise to their feet and march out of the chapel in protest. On the other hand, Primitive Methodism, which had a strong working-class following among groups like north-eastern coal miners and Norfolk farm labourers, was starting to align itself with the Labour Party. To generalise broadly, on the eve of the Great War issues of class were supplanting the old Church/Chapel rivalry – a development that spelled long-term trouble for the Liberal Party.[14]

Yet very few of the Radical MPs concerned with social legislation were themselves trade unionists or manual workers by origins. At parliamentary level, the Liberal Party was overwhelmingly middle-class. Only one Cabinet minister came from a working-class background: the reactionary and inefficient President of the Local Government Board, John Burns, about whom it was unkindly remarked that he did at least drop his 'aitches' and so was regarded by Asquith as the authentic voice of Labour.[15] Despite some democratisation at local level, particularly in areas where Liberalism had traditionally been weak, for example, the East End of London, the Liberal Party gives the impression of being an overwhelmingly middle-class organisation.

With what section of society, then, was Liberal social reform especially associated? Historians are generally agreed that the impetus behind the 'New Liberalism' came from the *professional* middle class: from journalists, writers and lecturers, plus lawyers and doctors with a social conscience. The picture they conjure up is one of high-minded intellectuals, living in spacious but draughty houses in Hampstead or the Manchester suburbs (fresh air was valued as a stimulus to progressive thought), eating raw fruit, and thinking ruthlessly about the political problems of their age.[16] There were men of this ilk in the parliamentary party as well, mainly on the social-reform side of the party – for example, C. F. G. Masterman, the close friend and ally of Lloyd George, who did much of the preparatory work on the National Health Insurance Scheme, for which he eventually became the government's parliamentary spokesman.[17] Some historians go so far as to claim that the New Liberalism was the ideology of the professional middle class and that social reform brought both emotional satisfaction and enhanced career prospects to that particular segment of British society. Though an exaggeration, this claim has some validity.[18]

The involvement in Liberal politics of 'caring' professional men and women undoubtedly gave the party its intellectual vitality; all suggestions that Edwardian Liberalism was an obsolete or bankrupt creed must be summarily rejected. But could, in the long run, the viewpoint of the progressive intelligentsia be harmonised with the class needs of the business community upon which the Liberal Party had historically depended?

The Liberal Party and Business

This is an issue on which historians wildly disagree. Roy Hay, in an important essay, has argued that 'social reform' in some respects met the requirements of capitalism, serving as an instrument of 'social control': it helped stabilise the social system at a time of considerable class tension, as well as integrating certain groups of manual workers into the existing economic system. Indeed, says Hay, many Edwardian businessmen had, for that very reason, become converted to the necessity of social welfare (of the kind pioneered by Bismarckian Germany), to the implementation of which they made a positive contribution.[19]

However, most of the businessmen who admired the Bismarckian project were Unionists, not Liberals. And although certain Radical businessmen did endorse social reform,[20] it is much easier to find contrary examples. The Employers' Parliamentary Association (EPA), for example, was set up in 1911 to resist further social legislation, the costs of which, it claimed, were burdening British industry. Significantly, the

EPA drew much of its support from the Lancashire textile industry, which had traditionally enjoyed strong links with the Liberal Party.[21]

Moreover, within the House of Commons itself some businessmen soon began to display their restlessness over social reform. Prominent in this group was the wealthy Liverpool shipowner, Richard Holt, who participated in a series of successful revolts which forced Lloyd George to amend his path-breaking 1914 Budget, for example, by reducing the top rate of income tax from 1s 4d to 1s 3d. Admittedly, the 'cave' of malcontents who were giving the Ministry this grief were a disparate bunch, not all of whom had a fundamental quarrel to pick with the New Liberalism: indeed nineteen out of the forty-odd rebels actually supported land nationalization or were ardent land taxers. The Chancellor, who had mishandled the complex relationship between his proposed new tax rates and his expenditure plans, had only himself to blame for his parliamentary defeats. Yet contemporaries could not help but notice that about 66 per cent of the Liberal rebels were businessmen, at least some of whom feared that their own government was destroying business confidence and frightening capital out of the country.[22] There is reason, then, for supposing that social radicalism was drifting apart from what passed for common sense among many of the Party's business backers.

But historians who take this view are divided over its significance. According to H. V. Emy, social reform both reflected and contributed to a drift of businessmen out of the Liberal Party. Safe Liberal seats in northern England, he says, tended, once the businessmen representing them had retired, to pass into the hands of professional men. But although this development strengthened 'Social Radicalism', it still further alienated businessmen from Liberalism and boded no good to the party; traditional wealthy supporters were lost, while the working-class votes thereby gained could not be relied upon, since Social Radicalism could only make an electoral appeal to manual workers for as long as a distinct Labour machine failed to emerge.[23]

Some of this analysis is shared by the arch-revisionist, Peter Clarke, but Clarke goes even further. The years after 1908, he claims, saw a fundamental class realignment in British politics. 'Economic Liberalism' collapsed as businessmen abandoned the party for the security offered by the Conservatives and Unionists. Indeed, so disaffected were these deserters from Liberalism that they were ready to embrace Tariff Reform, since they were now thinking, not in terms of the well-being of the industries that employed them, but in terms of their personal class needs. And, faced by an apparent choice between, on the one hand, Free Trade plus social reform (which many of them equated with socialism), and, on the other, protection and economic individualism (which in practical terms meant low taxation), many opted for the latter combination.

But Clarke's originality is to argue that this development was a sign of *health*, not a symptom of decline, since the loss of these businessmen was a necessary outcome of the Liberal Party's transformation into a modern 'social democratic party'. Only the mishaps which befell it during the First World War prevented the Liberals from playing the sort of role in twentieth-century politics that the Labour Party played after 1945.[24]

The Emy–Clarke disagreement largely revolves around the question of whether Liberal social reform did in fact attract the working-class electorate for which it was designed. To that question we will shortly turn. But before doing so, it is worth questioning whether the larger claims which both historians are making stand up to close examination. Two specific questions must be asked. Did businessmen, as voters, really switch over from Liberalism to Unionism? And did the proportion of businessmen within the parliamentary party really fall?

In the absence of opinion polls, the first question is difficult to answer. Certainly the 1910 elections reveal a well above-average swing against the Liberal Party in middle-class suburban areas in southern England, particularly in London, the cathedral cities and the seaside resorts. But in the northern manufacturing districts Liberalism fared relatively well in *all* types of constituency. Clarke attaches great significance to the Liberals' loss, in by-elections in April 1908 and August 1912, of the Manchester North-West constituency, the business heart of the city which, more than any other, had become closely identified with the Free Trade cause. Yet both defeats occurred in mid-term, when the Liberal government was temporarily unpopular. In the two general elections of 1910 the seat reverted to the Liberals; indeed, in the second of these elections, the Liberal candidate, Sir George Kemp, a local cotton spinner, succeeded in beating off a strong challenge from one of the Unionist Party's most prominent figures, Andrew Bonar Law, soon to become its Leader.

Moreover, although Kemp was a reluctant candidate and retired from politics in 1912, his retirement by no means formed part of a decisive trend. True, some Liberal business MPs declined to stand again in January 1910 because they disliked the tone and contents of recent government legislation: proportionately twice as many Liberal as Unionist MPs took this option.[25] Yet well-to-do businessmen had been deserting the

Liberal Party ever since the party had been founded, without dramatic consequences (just as ambitious working-class politicians have often abandoned the Labour Movement as they have risen in the world). In any case, the Liberal Party had no difficulty in finding new candidates from business backgrounds to replace the defectors. An analysis of the parliamentary party indicates that its social balance was almost static. MPs who had earlier pursued a business career continued to make up nearly 40 per cent of the parliamentary party (compared with little over 23 per cent of Unionist MPs).[26] At local level, too, councillors and activists were often businessmen of one sort or another, especially in the West Riding (though there is some evidence of their being displaced in the immediate pre-war years).[27]

What animated these business Liberals remains slightly unclear. Radical social policy is unlikely to have proved the *attraction*. Probably many of those who had traditionally supported the Liberal Party continued to do so, either because they set high store by Free Trade (which the Unionists were threatening in 1910) or because they perceived the Unionist Party as 'alien': which to most Dissenters, and many Scotsmen, Welshmen and Jews, for example, it long continued to be.[28]

Far from being damaged because of its increasing detachment from the business community, perhaps the Liberal Party on the eve of the War suffered from being too unhealthily close to individual business-men. Even Lloyd George, despite his Radicalism, spent much of his leisure time in the company of self-made millionaires. This was important inasmuch as such social activities laid Lloyd George wide open to the charge of hypocrisy. It was all very well for him to extol the simple lives of the poor and to preach the need for a reduction in the inequalities which disfigured society. But these words sounded strange in the mouth of a man who spent so much time in the company of his newly acquired plutocratic friends. The Conservative press mercilessly pilloried Lloyd George (or £loyd George) and his £iberal friends for their resort to double standards.[29]

The Opposition similarly seized with delight on the Marconi Scandal which broke in 1912–13. Three leading Liberal ministers (Lloyd George; Rufus Isaacs, the Attorney-General; and the Master of Elibank, the former Chief Whip) were exposed, not just as deeply implicated in the buccaneering world of Edwardian capitalism, but also for benefiting from the tips of their business friends – using 'inside' information to have a flutter on the Stock Exchange. This behaviour, if not corrupt, was highly improper.[30]

But it was not just *individual* ministers who relied on business support of one kind or another to keep them in the comfort to which they had grown accustomed. Some constituency parties were making a determined effort during the Edwardian decade to broaden their social base. But at central level, the Liberal Party was still largely funded by wealthy businessmen. The impressive election campaigns of 1910 were only possible because of heavy donations from this quarter – from the 'Radical plutocrats' and 'cosmopolitan millionaires', as the Opposition dubbed them. Moreover, a high proportion of these subscribers subsequently featured in the Honours Lists – as knights, baronets, and, indeed, as privy councillors and peers of the realm. By 1913 even loyal backbenchers and sympathetic pressmen could hardly deny that the government was cynically exchanging titles and honours for cash – and doing so more brazenly and on a much larger scale than any previous ministry. On the eve of the war, the Liberal government, rocked by the Marconi Scandal and plagued by complaints about honours trafficking, was becoming associated in the public mind with scandal and corruption.[31]

The Liberals could ill afford to generate this sort of publicity, given their claim to be the party of public purity and morality. The Nonconformists were especially upset. But, more importantly, perhaps, any suggestion that the Liberal Party was entangled in the seamy side of capitalism threatened to weaken the 'Progressive Alliance' and shake the confidence of the working-class electorate. Left-wing socialists, who had always disapproved of the Lib-Lab Pact, were quick to exploit an episode like the Marconi Scandal because it beautifully illustrated their contention that the Liberal Party was a capitalist party, and a corrupt one at that.

This leads on logically to the second part of the enquiry. What about the workers? Would Labour consent, for ever and a day, to have its interests represented by its Liberal 'friends', or would working men, sooner or later, insist on taking full control of their own destinies?

The New Liberalism, Social Policy and the Labour Movement

The answer to these questions depends, in part, upon whether one believes that the nature of the Liberal Party really had been transformed in the years immediately preceding the outbreak of the First World War. Without in any way denigrating the importance of the welfare legislation passed by the Asquith government, several aspects of contemporary

Liberal politics give one cause to doubt the validity of the wider claims that have been made by the 'revisionists'.

First, the government, as a whole, does not seem to have been that committed to the welfare reforms. Nearly all the great welfare measures originated with Lloyd George and Winston Churchill, helped by Masterman and a few other junior ministers. These Bills were obviously endorsed by the Prime Minister and the Cabinet. But, significantly, the People's Budget had encountered fierce initial criticism (in private) from more 'traditional' Liberals, like Runciman, Loreburn and Morley.[32] Moreover, as one historian has noted, it is a little startling that welfare initiatives should have been discussed so seldom in the correspondence of most Cabinet ministers: 'The men who ran the Edwardian party show in their private archives virtually no sign of progressive motivation.'[33] This may partly explain why no coherent welfare strategy developed in these years. Indeed the Liberal ministry lacked a reform programme as such: what it was sponsoring was a patchwork quilt of *ad hoc* measures, based on no single principle or philosophy, and sometimes colliding with one another. The desperate plight in which the party had found itself in 1908 allowed ministers who wanted to address these social problems to do so; meanwhile other ministers, with different priorities, like Burns at the Local Government Board, went their separate ways. Hence, the failure of Poor Law Reform, which would have required co-ordinated action across a range of Whitehall departments.

Moreover, in the first of the two 1910 elections the government focused on the constitutional outrage which the peers had committed in rejecting the Budget; in the second election the main plank in its campaign was a call for a mandate to curb the powers of the Upper House.[34] Indeed, once the 1911 National Insurance Act had been carried, the impetus behind social reform considerably slackened. For although in June 1914 Asquith did give his support to the idea of a minimum wage, as recommended by Lloyd George's committee into the problems of urban land, it is unclear whether this would have featured prominently in the Liberal programme had war not broken out when it did.

True, with the encouragement of the Whips' Office, social radicals were entering Parliament on the Liberal side in greater numbers after 1908, especially in Scotland.[35] But even revisionists concede that the position of the 'New Liberals' was precarious in the sense that they lacked an institutional power base and depended far too heavily upon personal contacts and the attractiveness of their ideas.[36] All of this perhaps goes some way to explaining the sudden disappearance of welfare politics from the party's agenda during and immediately after the war – a development which otherwise seems rather mysterious.

At the local level, the impression is still more strongly conveyed that the New Liberalism had done little to break the traditional political mould. Many local Liberal newspapers and party activists were far more solidly committed to the old sectarian objectives than to old-age pensions – to say nothing of labour exchanges and the promise of Social Insurance. In February 1909 the *Leicester Daily Mercury* could still list the issues which required immediate attention as follows: 'monopolies in land, in liquor, in ecclesiasticism, in electoral machinery, and in the House of Lords, which is the very holy of holies of monopoly'.[37] In Wales, too, the New Liberalism made comparatively little impact. Lloyd George, it has been claimed, was 'a new liberal in England, an old liberal in Wales'.[38] Even a radical pressure group like the Young Scots attached as much importance to temperance as to all other social issues combined, if their speakers' lists of 1911–12 are any guide, while in Devon and Cornwall it was as though the New Liberalism had never happened.[39]

Nationwide generalisations are hazardous. The Liberal Party was a shifting coalition, varying in character from one region to another. Where Liberalism had been traditionally weak, the East End of London, for example, New Liberalism seems to have been making progress in the immediate pre-war years. But in most of the Liberal heartlands there was no pressure from below in support of new welfare initiatives. On the contrary, judging from the stance taken by a famous Liberal organ of opinion like the *Leeds Mercury*, social reform was deeply unpopular with many of the party faithful.[40]

This leads on logically to a further point. Whereas the Lib-Lab Pact was reactivated for the *parliamentary* contests of 1910 (and never more successfully than in the December 1910 election), at *municipal* level it was more common for the Liberal and Labour parties to fight one another. This happened even in a city like Norwich, a two-member constituency where the 'Progressive Alliance' worked well in the parliamentary arena, but where the ILP's attack on the Liberals' failure to municipalise essential services, as advocated in its own 1903 programme, triggered off a fierce electoral battle.[41] In Leicester, too, the local Liberal dignitaries were divided, and 'socialism' proved to be a highly divisive issue. Let them 'have no more talk about "two wings of a Progressive party"', declared Councillor Kemp, a hosiery manufacturer, in April 1907: if his fellow Liberals did not fight the socialists, he warned, 'they would be wiped out'. Even sympathetic Liberals envisaged a subordinate position for Labour, which they tended to address as though it were a child unable to understand its own best interests.[42] This generated predictable conflict. Moreover, in the matter of municipal contests, Labour had few inhibitions about going it alone, perhaps because many council wards were socially homogeneous and contained concentrations of groups like railwaymen and dockers, who were its 'natural supporters', whereas in parliamentary constituencies a broader appeal was needed for success.[43]

Admittedly, one can find other towns (Wigan and Gloucester, for example) where a municipal electoral alliance between Liberals and Labour was successfully operated.[44] On the other hand, an anxiety to hold down the rates and keep Labour at bay led in many parts of the country (notably Bradford, Leeds, large areas of London, and Glasgow) to informal electoral understandings between the Liberals and the *Conservatives*.[45] The Labour press alleged that such anti-Labour alliances had existed at one time or another in no fewer than thirty-two different municipalities in England and Wales – to say nothing of Scotland.[46] Some of these arrangements, as in Glasgow, were of long standing, but others came about as a response to the heightened social and industrial tension of the immediate pre-war years and seem to foreshadow the Anti-Labour Alliances that sprang up all over the country in the wake of Labour's advance in the 1919 municipal elections.

All of this raises two fundamental questions. How long would it be before the 'class' issues which were creating animosities in local government elections spilled over into the parliamentary arena? Secondly, does not the story of municipal politics suggest that the Labour Party's co-operation with the Liberal government at national level owed less to their shared commitment to the creed of 'Progressivism' based upon welfare reform than to a common interest in triumphing over the House of Lords and safeguarding Free Trade?

This, in turn, leads on to the issue of how popular social reform was anyway amongst the working-class electors whom the Liberals were trying to attract. The first thing to note is that the Liberals did not do quite as well in working-class constituencies in January 1910 as the revisionist thesis might lead one to suppose. In many ways all that happened in that general election was a reversion to a more 'normal' pattern of behaviour; nearly all the middle-class seats which the Liberals had won for the first time in the 'freak' contest of 1906 returned to their former Unionist allegiance, while the Liberals held on to constituencies where they had earlier been strong. In fact, the outcome of the two 1910 elections quite closely echoed that of 1892. It can be argued, in other words, that, in so far as pre-war politics had become class-based at all, this had occurred in the immediate aftermath of the Home Rule schism, long before the New Liberalism could have had any serious impact on the party's policy agenda. Nor was the New Liberalism of any help to the Liberals, at any time before 1914, in breaking the traditional hold of the Conservatives in the working-class constituencies of Liverpool and of the Liberal Unionists in working-class areas of Birmingham.[47]

Is there even any evidence that sizeable numbers of working-class voters *were* attracted by social reform? This is a tricky issue. Old-age pensions (although Labour politicians criticised them for being nig-gardly) proved to be immensely popular. Significantly, the normally unflappable Balfour became quite agitated when a junior Liberal minister alleged in the run-up to the first 1910 election that a future Unionist government would repeal the Old-Age Pension Act: a 'frigid lie', Balfour called it. But even Asquith privately admitted in November that there could 'be no doubt that the Insurance Bill [was] (to say the least) not an electioneering asset'.[48] Lecturers had to be paid to tour the country to 'explain' the measure and expound its merits. The main reason for this popular antipathy was that, whereas old-age pensions had been financed out of general taxation, National Insurance involved contributions from insured workers, as well as from employers and the state, and the resulting deductions from the weekly pay packet came as an unpleasant surprise. Many trade unionists, too, harboured deep suspicions about labour exchanges as strike-breaking organisations – suspicions which ministers tried hard but not entirely successfully to allay.[49]

The ministers involved in their formulation had certainly started off with the *belief* that the welfare reforms would be attractive to the work-ing-class electorate, even if they also had other aims in view (promoting national efficiency, pure humanitarianism, etc.). Lloyd George privately commented to his brother in May 1908, apropos of old-age pensions, that it was time that something was done that 'appealed straight to the people' and would 'help to stop the electoral rot'. Churchill was writing to Asquith at the same time in similar vein.[50] But had Liberal ministers, in their benevolent aloofness from the lives of the urban poor, miscalcu-lated? All that can be said with any confidence is that working people seem not to have had any particular view about social reform as such, judging specific measures by whether they thought they would personally gain or suffer from them. Trade unions took the same pragmatic approach.[51]

But what is equally clear is that the greater security in everyday life provided by the Asquith ministry's welfare legislation mattered less than the preservation of living standards, which were determined by the level of real wages. So much became apparent when, only a year after their 1910 electoral successes, the Liberals found themselves enveloped in what has gone down in the history books as the 'Great Labour Unrest'. Over the next two and a half years strikes and lockouts affected large swathes of industry. Historians have offered different explanations for this working-class militancy, but undoubtedly the most important cause was declining real wages at a time of inflation; moreover, given the low level of unemployment, union leaders knew that in bringing their men out on strike they were running fewer risks than usual.

Some of the resulting industrial disputes were conducted in a mood of intense class bitterness. The Merseyside dock strike of August 1911, for example, spread panic and confusion. At the request of the Mayors of Liverpool and Birkenhead the government despatched a warship to the Mersey. Lord Derby wrote personally to Churchill, the Home Secretary, complaining that people in London did not realise that this was no ordinary strike riot, but that 'a revolution' was in progress. In August 1911 200 people were injured in the disturbances, two of them fatally.[52]

Dock strikes were traditionally violent affairs. But the railwaymen also became drawn into serious rioting, especially in South Wales, where the miners were also simmering with anger. Indeed, in 1912 there was a nationwide coal strike which, though largely free from violent incidents, had a devastating impact on the economy, throwing thousands of men from other industries out of work. Even more alarmingly, in 1913 moves were made for co-ordinated strike action between railwaymen, miners and transport workers, who linked up in the so-called Triple Alliance. Meanwhile the syndicalists, a revolutionary socialist sect, were calling for the overthrow of capitalism by means of a 'general strike' and its replacement by a workers' state.

For the government this was a disturbing development. When Lloyd George, Churchill and Masterman had made their bid to secure the working-class vote, they had not expected to be faced with this kind of assault from below. Concessionary social reform, it seemed, was not working.

How did this affect the relations between the Liberal and Labour Parties? It did so in many different ways. Most obviously, the class tension of the 1910–14 period weakened the Liberal Party by creating antagonisms in many parts of the country between Liberals and Labour. At parliamentary level the moderate and dispirited group of Labour MPs, led after 1911 by the cautious Ramsay MacDonald, might still cling to the Progressive Alliance, but in many coalfields, for example, industrial tension was undermining the position of union moderates and promoting the rise of militant socialists.[53]

Moreover, not even left-wing Radicals were likely to welcome working-class militancy, especially when this was expressed in the language of syndicalism, with calls for 'Direct Action' and 'Workers' Control', accompanied by vague threats to overturn the capitalist system by means of a general strike. Faced with such declarations of class war, the most 'advanced' Liberal politicians and intellectuals recoiled in horror. For example, L. T. Hobhouse, philosopher of the New Liberalism, who found himself on the receiving end of a piece of working-class militancy from the London coal porters, an experience he did not enjoy, angrily dismissed the views of those who argued that nothing could be gained except by fighting: 'The moment you convince me of this', he wrote in a private letter, 'I shall shut up shop as a radical or socialist or anything reforming, for I shall be convinced that human nature is hopeless, and that the effort to improve society had better be left alone.'[54] Hobhouse was a reformer, but he wanted orderly, constitutional change, based upon rational debate. He emphatically did not approve of assertions of working-class power.

But Hobhouse's discomfiture was nothing compared with the embarrassment of the Liberal government, which found itself being drawn willy-nilly into industrial conflicts where it had to take sides – which, in practice, often meant offering resistance to the striking men. Most governments flounder, confronted by such situations, and the Asquith administration was no exception. It was especially unfortunate, from the Liberal point of view, that the Home Secretary in the crucial years of 1910 and 1911 was Winston Churchill, who took an obvious and rather childish delight at moving troops about the country to enforce law and order in troubled areas. His Napoleonic moods and gestures made the worst possible impression on the Labour Movement, leading to harsh criticisms of his conduct during the Tonypandy Riots of November 1910 which, despite their inaccuracy, clung to him for the rest of his career.[55] Even MacDonald turned angrily upon Churchill in the House of Commons and reminded him that he was not the Tsar of Russia.

The effect of the labour unrest was to increase the militancy of the Labour Party. For example, in areas like South Wales, miners began to ask themselves whether it made sense to go on co-operating politically with a Liberal Party whose local leaders were often coal owners (among them, the hated Lord Rhondda, head of the Cambrian Combine, who, as D. A. Thomas, had recently been the Liberal MP for Merthyr).[56] Moreover, industrial unrest tended to increase the influence of left-wing socialists within Labour's affiliated organisations and gave rank-and-file members in the constituencies the confidence to take on all-comers.

How far had this challenge to the party leadership gone by 1914? On this historians disagree. Some believe that the Lib-Lab Pact was disintegrating in the by-elections of 1912, 1913 and 1914. In five of the seats lost to the Unionists in these years, a Labour candidate, intervening for the first time, secured more votes than the margin of victory – a sign of how damaging this development was to the Liberal Party. True, in all these by-elections Labour came bottom of the poll. But, in Ross McKibbin's view, since many of these contests took place in the Midlands coal-mining belt, which was untypical in many ways, this does not conclusively prove that Labour's level of support in the country as a whole was low. Arguably, these Labour candidates did quite well considering that they were contesting their particular constituencies for the first time. In any case, the important feature of these contests, to historians like McKibbin, is the fact that Labour were even *willing* to make a dash for 'independence'.[57]

Meanwhile, at grass-roots level the Labour Party's membership was being swollen by trade union expansion, which was important since, following the enactment of the 1913 Trade Union Act, all affiliated members paid a 'political levy' to the Labour Party unless they specifically 'contracted out'. The extra income which this generated encouraged Labour to extend its organisation in the country: many unified local Labour Parties date their origins to this period, including the London Labour Party, set up in May 1914. And this, in turn, increased the probability of Labour's mounting many more candidates than the paltry fifty-six which had stood in December 1910. Had a general election been held in 1915, alleges McKibbin, Labour would probably have fielded between 120 and 150 candidates, many of whom would have had to face sitting Liberal MPs, so forcing the Liberals to retaliate.[58] In short, it is arguable that the pattern of Progressive politics was at last breaking up.

But Duncan Tanner challenges this interpretation. By-election conflict between Liberals and Labour, he argues, was no more of a problem in 1911–14 than it had been during the corresponding period of the previous Parliament.[59] Moreover, most Labour 'interventions' had been sanctioned by MacDonald and the NEC of the Labour Party in a calculated bid to put pressure on the Liberal organisers, with the aim of securing a more favourable allocation of seats at the next general election. Tanner's meticulous examination of electoral arrangements at constituency level leads him to the conclusion that, after a process of negotiation and 'pruning', Labour would probably have fielded no more than the sixty-five candidates already sanctioned once Parliament was dissolved – certainly nothing like McKibbin's figure.[60] This would have permitted the perpetuation of the Lib-Lab Pact – albeit on terms slightly more advantageous to Labour. Militant socialists might well have grumbled at this outcome, but, Tanner believes, the anti-MacDonaldites did not control the Labour Movement, besides which most activists realised that the party was still nowhere near ready for a total breach with Liberalism at the level of national politics. Indeed, despite its organisational reforms, Labour still had no significant presence over much of the country, and where it *was* active it too often gave an impression of incoherence and factionalism.[61] (Nor was Labour's performance in local authority elections anything other than disappointing, even in industrial areas where it had hoped to do very well.[62])

Meanwhile the PLP, as so often, was split over what strategy to pursue – and the rank and file even more so. Most ILPers wanted Labour to behave with total 'independence'. But MacDonald and the bulk of the trade union MPs knew how risky this would be. Given the fact that in December 1910 none of its forty-two MPs had been returned in a genuine triangular contest (though two had had straight fights against a Liberal), all-out war against the Liberals in a general election threatened the PLP with annihilation. Ever since 1910, when Labour had found itself, along with the Irish, holding the balance of seats, it had given general support to the Asquith ministry. Symbolically, Labour MPs now sat on the government side of the House. Consequently, MacDonald's ploy was, on the one hand, to maintain his party's organisational independence, coming down hard on trade union mavericks who failed to toe the line, while at the same time buying favours from the government: for example, payment of MPs and the 1913 Trade Union Act (both made necessary by the 'Osborne Judgement') as a reward for supporting the National Insurance Act.[63]

It was an adroit balancing act. But for how much longer could it have been carried on? By 1914 Labour had probably reached the point where it either had to move closer to the Liberal government or disentangle itself completely from the 'Progressive Alliance'. Significantly, some Liberal leaders were thinking in the same way. Twice in 1912 and again in 1914 ministers put out 'feelers' as to the willingness of certain senior Labour politicians to join the Asquith ministry. MacDonald was tempted by the third of these overtures, made in March 1914, but Keir Hardie had it killed off.[64] Yet simultaneously MacDonald was coming under pressure from some of the rank and file who wanted to go it alone. Such moves towards greater independence were further encouraged from 1912 onwards by the decision of the National Union of Women's Suffrage Societies to help Labour candidates challenge the Liberal machine.[65] So MacDonald faced a considerable dilemma, the resolution of which would have fateful consequences, not only for the future of his own organisation, but for that of the Liberal Party as well.

Tantalisingly, the war then broke out, transforming the entire political landscape. Inevitably, confusion and uncertainty still surround the question of how strong the Liberal Party still was in 1914 and whether it would have 'survived' but for the war. Even the result of the general election, due to be held by the end of 1915, at the latest, cannot be predicted with any certainty. The Liberals (and their Labour allies) had done badly in by-elections between 1912 and 1914, even where triangular contests had not occurred. But something similar had happened in the middle of the 1906 Parliament, and the Liberals had then gone on to secure their qualified 'win' in January 1910.[66] The same might have happened again. Nor would the loss of the election in itself necessarily have proved fatal. On the contrary, the creation of a new Unionist administration might well have shocked the two 'parties of progress' into re-creating, or strengthening, their former alliance. Alas, all this cannot be other than speculation.

However, a few concluding remarks may be hazarded. It now seems likely that, even though the outcome of the 1915 election must remain wreathed in mystery, the Lib-Lab Pact, in some form or another, would still have operated. But the perpetuation of the pact does not, as most historians assume, have any very great bearing on the question of the success or otherwise of the New Liberalism. After all, MacDonald and Herbert Gladstone had reached their 'understanding' in 1903 at a time when the Liberal agenda was still heavily dominated by the old issues: the need to rectify Nonconformist grievances and to defend Free Trade. The Liberal Government's subsequent espousal of social reform may have facilitated co-operation with Labour, though even this is unclear.

Far more important to the pact's survival was the mutual recognition that each party needed the other (Labour's need, of course, being much the greater) if the Tories were to be defeated.

In fact, the co-operation between the two parties operated smoothly at national (though not at local) level precisely because each complemented the other so well. Labour was able to make progress in the former Tory strongholds and in many working-class areas where the Liberals stood little chance of success. Conversely, the Liberal Party continued to appeal to groups like middle-class Nonconformists whom Labour was unlikely to reach.[67] Even on the eve of the war the Liberals still derived almost one-quarter of their English seats from heavily rural constituencies, mostly in East Anglia, Lincolnshire and Cornwall, which later proved to be unrewarding territory for Labour, while national sentiment gave Liberalism a popularity in Scotland and Wales which often overrode the class factor; indeed, in January 1910 the Liberals managed to win all but ten of the seventy Scottish seats, a better result than they had achieved in 1906.

In short, the Edwardian Liberal Party cannot easily be portrayed as a precursor of the late twentieth-century Labour Party. It operated from a different social base (especially in municipal elections[68]) and was making a rather different electoral appeal. In the short run, this did not matter. Indeed, as with the Liberal–Irish Nationalist alliance, the two 'parties of progress' worked together reasonably well because they were *not* direct rivals. Paradoxically, the Lib-Lab Pact might have been less effective if New Liberal ideas had achieved a greater centrality in the Liberal Party's thinking.

But the long-term prospects of Liberalism were more problematic. Social reforms like old-age pensions and the National Insurance Act were important measures in their own right, but it is questionable whether they did the Liberals much good in narrowly party terms. Their introduction frightened off some former middle-class adherents, including Dissenters whose support was essential to the Liberals' self-image as a 'national party'. Yet Edwardian Liberalism still had deep roots in the business world and, at least at central level, depended financially on a handful of rich business backers. Meanwhile, by 1914 social reform – distrusted by many middle-class Liberals – was not proving to be the antidote to the growth of the Labour Party which it had promised to be between 1908 and 1910.

Finally, although there are few signs that the Liberals were on the point of supersession in 1914, two developments within the Labour

Party were taking place which threatened Liberalism's long-term future. First, there was the danger that the party's formal adoption of socialism (something which did not, in fact, take place until 1918) would turn Labour from being uneasy allies into overt enemies. But more immediately worrying was evidence that the Labour militants were attacking the Asquith government, not so much for what it was *doing*, but rather for what it *was*. As McKibbin puts it, what fuelled the Labour Movement in these years was the working man's intuitive belief that he wanted to have a government of his own.[69] This was ominous for the Liberals because, whereas they could have settled policy differences with Labour through discussion and negotiation, they could do little about such class antagonisms – antagonisms which, on the evidence of the Liberal organisers themselves, were particularly to be found among young manual workers who currently lacked the vote but would, in the fullness of time, gain it.[70] Thus did the earlier failure of the Liberal Party to match its enthusiasm for working-class votes with a willingness to put up working-class candidates return to haunt it.

7

THE LIBERALS, WOMEN'S
SUFFRAGE AND THE WOMEN'S
VOTE

In June 1912 the left-wing Labour MP, George Lansbury, lost his temper with Asquith over the government's treatment of hunger-striking Suffragettes. Defying all efforts to restrain him, Lansbury marched up to the despatch box, waving his arms and shaking his fist in Asquith's face: 'You will go down to history as the man who tortured innocent women', he shouted, 'that's what you'll go down to history as.'[1] Lansbury was ordered from the House and suspended for 'grossly disorderly conduct', but he had made a telling point: the reputation, not just of Asquith, but of the Liberal Party as a whole did indeed suffer damage as a result of the government's treatment of the Suffragettes. Indeed, one participant in these events later claimed that the Liberals' later decline was 'largely attributable to the fast-and-loose methods that they adopted in dealing with ... woman suffrage'.[2]

Liberalism and Feminism

That things should have come to such a pass surprised and distressed most Liberals. For giving women the parliamentary vote seemed a logical extension of the Liberal reforming mission. After all, the bible of the women's suffrage societies was John Stuart Mill's tract, *The Subjection of Women* (1869), and their campaigners, male and female, invariably

105

deployed the Liberal rhetoric of citizenship, extolling justice and 'reason' over custom and brute force.[3] Mrs Wynford Phillips, addressing the Annual Council Meeting of the Women's Liberal Federation (WLF) in 1891, made it quite explicit where her political sympathies lay: Votes for Women, she argued, was based on 'the true Liberal principle that taxation and representation must go together', and she added: 'I am a strong suffragist because I am a strong Liberal. . . . I learned my Liberalism from Gladstone and Bright.'[4]

If Liberals seemed to have a natural affinity with the cause of women's emancipation, most women, or at least most middle-class women, seemed to be the natural allies of the Liberals. The pioneering Victorian feminists had worked industriously, and with some success, to change the married women's property laws and to extend girls' secondary and higher education – both causes that drew the support of Liberal MPs and appealed strongly to the Liberal mind. More fundamentally, the whole tone of Liberalism, with its emphasis upon peace, conciliation and reform, was widely regarded as evidence of the growing feminisation of public life. An additional bond of sympathy was forged with the eruption of the fiscal controversy in 1903, when the Liberal Party staked out a strong claim to be the protector of the consumer from the depredation of 'producer interests' – in other words, to be the prudent housewife's friend. The Women's Free Trade Union was only one of several organisations which campaigned vigorously on the Liberals' behalf in the run-up to the 1906 general election – labelled by some contemporaries the first 'women's election'.[5]

It therefore seemed highly likely that the Liberal Party would, sooner rather than later, give women full political rights. In 1869 Jacob Bright, John Bright's younger brother, slipped through an amendment to the Municipal Franchise Bill, under which ratepaying spinsters and widows were allowed to vote in municipal elections – a concession that was later extended to other areas of local government.[6] Admittedly, this development gave new life to the traditional concept of 'separate spheres', suggesting to some contemporaries (of both sexes) that women's public role was best confined to the work of 'municipal housekeeping' and 'compulsory philanthropy', leaving men to decide those issues of peace and war which fell under the control of Westminster and Whitehall.[7] But as Parliament, partly under Liberal pressure, increasingly involved itself in social issues such as the welfare of mother and child, the boundary between the worlds of local and central government became ever more nebulous and problematic.

Moreover, all the early promoters of women's suffrage came from the Liberal side of the House: John Stuart Mill, the mover of the original motion in May 1867, was succeeded by Jacob Bright, Leonard Courtney, and Henry Fawcett, Gladstone's blind Postmaster-General – today better known as the husband of Millicent, soon to emerge as leader of the largest women's suffrage society. In 17 divisions on suffrage bills and motions between 1867 and 1904 the Liberal MPs contributed on average 59.7% of the support, the Conservatives only 33.8%.[8]

Because the progress of women's suffrage was so closely bound up with the fortunes of the Liberal Party, the Liberals' decline during the twenty years following the Home Rule schism inevitably set back the women's prospects of success, at least temporarily. But the suffragists still had grounds for optimism. For the creation of an enlarged electorate after 1884, combined with much tighter limits on electoral expenditure, meant that both major parties required the support of an army of volunteers. Women, with time at their disposal, soon proved extremely efficient as canvassers, fund-raisers and electoral organisers – even, in some cases, as public speakers. Perhaps surprisingly, the Conservative Party was the quicker to exploit this resource through the Primrose League, some branches ('habitations') of which were all-female.[9] But the Liberal Party soon followed suit with the establishment in 1886–7 of the WLF, under the presidency of Catherine Gladstone, the 'Grand Old Man's' daughter. Despite secessions, by the turn of the century the WLF boasted 60 000 members, distributed between nearly 500 branches.[10]

Many prominent members of the WLF were the wives, sisters and daughters of Liberal MPs: for example, the energetic Eva McLaren was the wife of Walter McLaren (Jacob Bright's son-in-law). But few Liberal women were content to follow the example of their counterparts in the Primrose League by confining themselves to the task of helping their husbands. Instead they tended to import into the Liberal Party their own particular enthusiasms (peace, temperance, social purity, and the kind of welfare issues that many of them were pursuing at the level of local government), thereby helping to modify the party's agenda.[11] The WLF also wanted women, generally, to involve themselves actively – an objective it pursued, not by challenging head-on traditional notions of femininity, but by redefining femininity in such a way as to promote an enlarged conception of family life – one that would embrace the 'wider family' of the disadvantaged.[12]

A turning point in the history of the WLF came in 1892, when its 'Progressive' wing, led by Lady Carlisle, managed to commit the organisation officially to women's suffrage, thereby provoking a schism. Catherine Gladstone stepped down as President, and a minority of moderate 'loyalists' broke away to form the Women's National Liberal Federation (WNLF), taking about 10 000 members with them. (The split was not healed until after the women's vote had been achieved, in 1919.[13]) But this left the WLF, much the larger of the two organisations, free to campaign for the vote.

Meanwhile the cause of women's suffrage, initially set back by Gladstone's refusal to countenance the Woodall Amendment in 1884,[14] began to move forwards once more. In 1897 Mrs Fawcett presided over the amalgamation of local suffrage associations into the National Union of Women's Suffrage Societies (NUWSS) – the membership of which significantly overlapped with that of the WLF.[15] By the turn of the century the movement was also spreading outwards and becoming more 'democratic', as it acquired a trade union base. For example, the NUWSS's North of England Society largely consisted of Lancastrian female factory hands.[16] The ILP also took up the cause. Out of this northern milieu there emerged in October 1903 a new society, the Women's Social and Political Union (WSPU), led by Mrs Pankhurst and her daughters Christabel and Sylvia.[17]

Parliament was not unresponsive to the changing situation. In March 1904 the Commons passed a pro-suffrage motion by 184 votes to 70. Then came the Liberal Party's triumph in the 1906 General Election, which greatly strengthened the pro-suffrage forces in Parliament: as many as 400 members of the new House were now claimed as sympathisers.

However, women's suffrage, for all the support which it attracted from Liberals, could never become a straightforward party issue. Several early feminists, like Emily Davies, the founder of Girton College, were, in fact, Conservatives, and there was a sizeable minority faction inside the Conservative Party which favoured a moderate suffrage bill, a minority which included, for example, many members of the powerful Cecil family. Moreover, on several occasions after 1886 the National Union of Conservative and Unionist Associations endorsed suffrage motions at its annual conference.[18] Significantly, too, Mrs Fawcett (widowed since 1884) broke with Gladstone over Home Rule for Ireland, as did some male sympathisers with the women's cause, such as her ally Leonard Courtney.[19]

But just as not all suffragists were Liberals, the converse also applied. As Brian Harrison notes, 'in only six of the 24 woman suffrage divisions before 1914 did the Liberals and Radicals contribute less than a third of the anti-suffrage vote'.[20] These Liberal 'antis' acted from a variety of motives. The elderly Gladstone held to a traditional concept of femininity, believing that 'a permanent and vast difference of type ha[d] been impressed upon women and men respectively by the Maker of both', and fearing that votes for women would bring about the intrusion of the state into the 'sacred' precinct of the family, where it might 'dislocate, or injuriously modify, the relations of domestic life' and 'trespass upon the delicacy, the purity, the refinement, the elevation' of woman's nature.[21] Even a Radical like Chamberlain entertained very similar opinions to these. Some Liberals, including Labouchere, also took fright at the spectacle of women flocking to join the Primrose League and concluded that, because females were so deferential and susceptible to priestly influences, they would, if enfranchised, tend to throw their weight behind the forces of 'reaction'.[22]

These were minority views within Liberalism. Unfortunately the majority which favoured votes for women on principle had their own internal divisions. Should, for example, women's suffrage form part of a larger scheme for the democratisation of the franchise, or should the vote be confined to ratepayers? And was it wise to back schemes which would enfranchise mainly spinsters and widows, as the early suffrage bills would have done? There were MPs in all parties who queried (often in highly offensive language) whether women should be 'rewarded' for their failure to find a husband, thereby fulfilling their biological destiny.

Both Liberal and Labour sympathisers also struggled with the problem of establishing priorities. Few male 'suffragists' thought that the women's claims mattered in the way that, say, Irish Home Rule or social policy mattered. Partly for that reason, the National Liberal Federation did not get round to endorsing women's suffrage until 1905, while in the general election of the following year only 48 Liberal candidates expressed their approval. In the January 1910 election only 51 per cent of Liberal candidates so much as mentioned *any* kind of electoral reform, and in the December 1910 election even fewer (34 per cent) did so.[23]

Indeed, Liberal women activists themselves differed on how far they could reasonably press their demands. In 1902 the pro-suffrage WLF adopted the so-called 'Cambridge Resolution', which forbade central assistance to any Liberal candidate who had failed its 'test questions'. But this policy, understandably, made many of its members uneasy.

Liberal women, in other words, had to ask themselves whether they were women first and Liberals second, or vice versa – a question which many had difficulty in answering.

Given all these uncertainties, little wonder that most Liberal leaders chose to procrastinate. Campbell-Bannerman, a tepid friend, advised a suffrage delegation on 19 May 1906 to go on preaching their cause with patience, but he declined to offer any 'definite statement or pledge on the subject'. His patronising remarks infuriated all the women campaigners. The NUWSS, no longer a genteel debating club-cum-pressure group, rapidly increased its membership, becoming in the process a formidable mass organisation: from a mere 5836 in 1907, it mushroomed to 21 571 three years later. Meanwhile, the much smaller WSPU stepped up its campaign of publicity-catching 'stunts'. During the recent general election the 'Suffragettes', as they were now dubbed, had seldom gone beyond interrupting Liberal meetings. But a turning point came on 23 October 1906 when ten WSPU members were arrested and briefly imprisoned in Holloway after a scuffle outside Parliament.

Why No Liberal Women's Suffrage Measure?

Why did the Liberal Government not make life easy for itself by satisfying the expectations that its advent to office had raised? In a nutshell, it could not sponsor its own legislation because a minority of Cabinet ministers were opposed on principle to women being given the parliamentary vote on any terms whatever. This group, which usually included Loulou Harcourt, Samuel, Pease, C. E. Hobhouse and, increasingly, Churchill, was led by none other than Asquith. The alternative strategy was to proceed via a private members' bill. But, without strong government backing, such a bill was unlikely to get on to the statute book even if it secured a Commons majority.[24]

The pro-suffrage Liberal ministers, who formed a clear majority within the Cabinet, might have imposed their will on the 'antis', if only they could have agreed on how best to proceed. The difficulty was that the suffrage societies were backing an 'equal suffrage' bill which, by simply removing sexual discrimination, would have enfranchised mainly propertied widows and spinsters, numbering little more than a million women – effectively, the local government franchise.[25] The

Conservative suffragists had no quarrel to pick with such a measure, which also proved acceptable, at least as a first instalment, to the likes of Haldane and Grey, who shared Christabel Pankhurst's desire to remove the 'stigma upon womanhood as such'.[26]

But Lloyd George, a half-hearted suffragist, warned the Government Chief Whip in September 1911 against the Conciliation Bill then before the House, which rested upon just such a basis: it would, he predicted, add, on balance, 'hundreds of thousands of votes throughout the country to the strength of the Tory party'. (He was particularly suspicious of the conservative proclivities of the WSPU leadership, which, after moving to London in 1906, had quickly cut free from the society's northern working-class roots.) The Liberal Party, Lloyd George argued, should therefore 'make up its mind as a whole' either to 'have an extended franchise which would put working men's wives on to the Register as well as spinsters and widows' or to 'have no female franchise at all'.[27] According to the historian, Brian Harrison, 'no Liberal government with life in it could have taken any other course'.[28]

The obvious solution to the dilemma seemed to be for the government to sponsor an Adult Suffrage Bill, leaving women's amendments to be determined by a free vote of the House. This, in fact, was precisely what the Liberal Cabinet eventually decided upon in the autumn of 1911. However, in January 1913 the Speaker ruled, controversially, against the women's suffrage amendments on the ground that they would radically alter the content and purpose of the Franchise and Registration Bill. Asquith was privately amused: 'The Speaker's *coup d'état* has bowled over the Women for this session – a great relief.'[29] But the government, genuinely caught by surprise, felt honour-bound by its earlier promises to the suffrage societies to withdraw the entire Bill – a step which meant that the abolition of plural voting on which the government had long set its heart had to be reintroduced in the form of a separate Bill (which had still not reached the statute book when war broke out).

Though Christabel Pankhurst angrily accused the government of sabotage, it was probably innocent of this offence. Asquith and the relevant ministers (notably Harcourt and Samuel) can more reasonably be criticised for carelessness in not clarifying in advance the exact status of the women's amendments.[30] However, would any of the four suffrage amendments that had been tabled have been carried through the Commons – to say nothing of the Lords, which still retained its delaying powers?

Of these four amendments, the NUWSS had endorsed the one sponsored by the pro-suffrage Liberal backbencher, W. H. Dickinson, which proposed to enfranchise the wives of householders aged twenty-five and over, as well as the householders themselves, some six million women in all. Mrs Fawcett did not entirely like this amendment since it applied to women a test (of marital status) not applicable to men, thereby offending her severe sense of sexual equality, but she calculated that the Dickinson amendment stood the best chance of success because it would be supported by a clear majority of Liberal MPs and by the Labour Party – though Labour preferred Arthur Henderson's adult suffrage amendment.

On the other hand, the Dickinson Amendment, as well as attracting very few Conservative votes, would probably have fallen foul of the Irish Nationalists, who, though broadly sympathetic to the women's cause at the start of the Liberal regime, were in the process of changing sides, stirred up by Churchill and Harcourt, who played upon their fear that 'Votes for Women' was jeopardising Asquith's position and thereby the stability of his government at a time when the prize of Home Rule was finally within their grasp. Ominously, whereas thirty-four Irish MPs had voted for the 1911 Conciliation Bill and only nine against, by 1912 the position had become reversed: only four voted for the new Bill and thirty-five against, this being the most important single factor in its defeat.[31]

Finally, escalating suffragette militancy had become distinctly counter-productive – to the mounting exasperation of Mrs Fawcett, who fumed at the 'criminal violence' of the WSPU and privately called its leaders 'the most powerful allies the antisuffragists have'.[32] Originally confined to the disruption of meetings, the WSPU's campaign had developed into a series of grave assaults on property, accompanied by indiscriminate physical attacks on Cabinet ministers: police at one time feared that an attempt would be made to assassinate Lloyd George. Revulsion at such behaviour partly explains why the third Conciliation Bill, unlike its two predecessors, was defeated in March 1912 (by 208 votes to 222). Many of the 'turncoats', Liberals as well as Conservatives and Irish Nationalists, explained their volte-face as an expression of disapproval of suffragette lawbreaking, an 'explanation' which is significant even if, in some cases, it merely furnished a pretext for a 'U-turn' taken for other, less reputable, motives. In early 1914 Lloyd George frankly told a suffragette deputation that they had 'made it almost impossible for those Liberal leaders who [were] in favour of women's suffrage to address meetings in support of it'.[33]

The Impact of Women's Suffrage on Liberal Party Fortunes

So much for the reasons why the pre-war Liberal ministries failed to promote or to preside over a women's suffrage measure. How, if at all, did this failure affect the long-term prospects of the Liberal Party?

Clearly the government did not handle the issue at all competently, as the debacle over the 1912 Franchise and Registration Bill demonstrates. The Liberal Party was also unlucky to have been led during these years by someone whose views about women in public life were so much at variance with mainstream Liberal opinion: a shy man who froze with embarrassment at any display of political emotion, Asquith was ill-equipped to deal with the suffrage issue – indeed, he and the militants tended to bring out the worst in one another. But it would be unfair to lay all the blame on Asquith personally. More fundamental was the difficulty, by the Edwardian period, of carrying a great reforming measure or resolving a contentious political issue when so many individual MPs held strong conscientious convictions that could not be silenced by the cracking of the whip.

In fairness to the Liberals, it must be stressed that women's suffrage was an exceedingly tricky issue to handle because it raised the competing claims of class and gender. Even Labour, the most sympathetic of all the parties to the women's cause, found it difficult to balance the evil of sex subordination against that of class exploitation.[34] Eventually, in 1912 Labour plumped for the democratic option – that is to say, it urged the conferral of the parliamentary vote on all adults, both men and women, as advocated by the People's Suffrage Movement. But the drawback to 'adult suffrage' was that those of a conservative disposition shrank from enfranchising the poor and ignorant, while many suffragists feared that such a 'solution' might, in practice, merely lead to the establishment of adult *male* suffrage and that women's enfranchisement would accordingly be set back by decades – which is exactly what happened in Switzerland.[35] In any case, was it sensible to move, in one stride, from an electorate which excluded women from the parliamentary franchise entirely to one in which women (for demographic reasons) formed the majority?[36]

The Liberals were therefore not alone in their indecision over the issue of 'Votes for Women'. Indeed, the situation of the Conservatives provided in many ways a reverse image of theirs, since the Conservative Leaders, Balfour and Bonar Law, favoured a (moderate) extension of the franchise to women but were in a minority within their own party. However, the Conservatives, being in Opposition, did not have to formulate legislation on the subject and could survive their disagreements without too much pain. The Liberals, being in office, did not enjoy this luxury.

Where the government seems to have found itself in a quandary that was quintessentially Liberal was in responding to the Suffragette disturbances. What happened in 1908 proved a foretaste of the trouble to come. Three militants, including Christabel Pankhurst, were summoned to appear before the magistrates' court for breach of the peace. Pankhurst, the holder of a law degree, personally conducted the defence, during which she cross-examined Lloyd George and Herbert Gladstone, the Home Secretary, and made a brilliant speech which indicted the government for having 'practically torn up' Magna Carta. She also attempted to show that violence had historically been a legitimate form of protest against injustice, and asked why different standards were being applied to women and to the rebellious Ulstermen – a critique which became ever more cogent over the next few years.[37]

Soon afterwards the WSPU began deliberately committing criminal offences, such as breaking windows, leading to their imprisonment, and then, when in prison, going on hunger strike – a potent political weapon of which the British government had not had any previous experience. In late 1909 Herbert Gladstone reluctantly sanctioned the introduction of force-feeding. But this response seemed, like the administration of the Contagious Diseases Acts a quarter of a century earlier, to involve male officials violating the female body – a situation ably exploited by the WSPU, which was only too happy to appeal to men's chivalric sentiments when it suited their convenience. The Liberals found themselves accused, and not just by the militants, of perpetrating 'brutal outrages upon defenceless women', even of judicial 'torture'.

In 1913 the Liberal government tried a different tack, with its 'Prisoners' Temporary Discharge for Ill-Health Bill', better known as the 'Cat and Mouse Act', which allowed the authorities to release a prisoner on hunger strike if her health was endangered and then to arrest her again if she reoffended. The government's critics denounced this measure, too, as a worrying departure from the accepted canons of British justice.

And so the Liberal ministry found itself in a dilemma not wholly unlike the one thrown up by events in Ireland: it disliked resorting to force, but felt that it had no option but to administer the law of the land. Liberals, in other words, were loath to concede that a crime became political simply because it had been committed by a politician. Yet this had been precisely the line which 'Bloody Balfour' had taken with Irish lawbreakers during the 'Plan of Campaign' in the 1880s – only to be denounced by Gladstone for his inhumanity in words which now came back to haunt the Liberals. Ironically, it had been revulsion against the Unionists' coercion in Ireland between 1887 and 1892 which had galvanised into life so many of the Liberal women's associations and fostered in their members a sense of themselves as custodians of the party's moral conscience.[38]

Many other lifelong Liberals, male as well as female, were similarly disheartened by what they saw as the government's cruel conduct. On the eve of the January 1910 election two of the party's most famous journalists, H. W. Nevinson and H. N. Brailsford, resigned from the *Daily News* in protest at their paper's refusal to condemn forcible feeding. But it was the WLF which was most destabilised by the government's conduct.

In June 1914 that organisation for the first time demanded a Government Bill on Women's Suffrage and only narrowly defeated a motion that its members should refuse to work for the re-election of Liberal anti-suffragist candidates at the next election. The militant minority split away to form the Liberal Women's Suffrage Union, composed of some 5000 members.[39] As a result of such disagreements, the WLF's membership, which had risen from 66 000 to 133 215 between 1904 and 1912, then dropped back: by 1915 there were only 749 branches with a membership of 106 997, 68 local associations having withdrawn or collapsed between 1912 and 1914. Many well-to-do activists of long standing, like Catherine Marshall, resigned from the WLF and threw in their lot with the NUWSS.[40]

How did the suffrage societies themselves react? The Pankhursts had from an early stage grasped a fundamental truth which Mrs Fawcett took much longer to accept: that, in modern political conditions, no private MP could carry a Bill on a subject like women's suffrage. In the WSPU's eyes, this put the onus on the Liberal government to meet the women's demands, and its failure to do so convinced them that the ministry was fundamentally hostile – a stance for which it should be punished until it repented the errors of its ways or acknowledged the expediency of surrender. But the WSPU pursued the logic of its position to extremes by not only declaring war on the entire Liberal Party but by also demanding that the minor parties that were sustaining the Asquith ministry in power, the Irish Nationalists and the Labour Party, should vote against all government measures until the vote was won – a quite impossible demand.[41] From her exile in Paris, Christabel Pankhurst also stepped up the campaign of militancy, which now extended to arson – this kind of extremism leading to a significant exodus of members.[42]

But by this time much the greater threat to the Asquith ministry came from an angry and radicalised NUWSS. In January 1912 Labour had resolved at its Conference (over the objections of the miners) to support no franchise measure which did not give women the vote. The NUWSS responded by committing itself to help Labour run candidates against the Liberals (with exemptions being made only for a handful of 'tried friends'). An Election Fighting Fund (EFF) was established to implement this new policy.

Many long-time members of the NUWSS, who had spent all their lives within the Liberal Party, were upset; a few defected – notably Eleanor Acland, who was also a member of the WLF's executive.[43] On the other hand, some NUWSS campaigners enthusiastically embraced the new initiative: a suffrage–Labour alliance, they argued, was desirable for its own sake since the sex barrier and the class barrier were both expressions of monopoly and privilege.[44] This conviction particularly took root among a group of youngish middle-class women, which included the Society's Secretary, Kathleen Courtney, Helen Swanswick, and Catherine Marshall (the ex-Liberal, now serving as NUWSS's parliamentary secretary). Prominent places were also found in the EFF for hardened working-class activists like Ada Chew Nield. Although still middle-class in ethos, the NUWSS thus began to acquire a genuine industrial base: by August 1914 it had enrolled 46 000 working-class supporters as Friends of Women's Suffrage. Once suspicious working-class groups like the miners revised their views, and in September 1913 the TUC passed an unequivocally pro-suffrage motion.[45]

What practical consequences did the establishment of the EFF have? MacDonald was initially hesitant about accepting help and money from the NUWSS, fearing that this would compromise his party's independence and complicate his already delicate relationship with the Liberals. However, a deal was eventually struck, and by the outbreak of war Labour had been encouraged by the offer of support from the EFF to contest four by-elections where they might otherwise have left the Liberals a free run against the Conservatives. This resulted in perhaps two Liberal defeats. The NUWSS also encouraged Labour to put up candidates for the forthcoming general election against a number of hated Liberal 'antis', all of them ministers: Hobhouse at East Bristol, McKenna at North Monmouth, Harold Baker at Accrington, Harcourt

at Rossendale and Pease at Rotherham: joint Labour–suffragist committees sprang up in these constituencies, regardless of MacDonald's
hesitations.[46] Labour was thus helped to build up its organisational
infrastructure and its members were encouraged to show a spirit of
independence, at just the moment when the 'Progressive Alliance' was
coming under severe strain for quite other reasons.

The outbreak of war in 1914 brought this interesting political experiment to an abrupt halt. All the suffrage societies suspended their activities for the emergency, and the electoral truce put a stop to further
by-election contests for the time being. This leaves hanging in the air a
very important question: would the developing 'alliance' between
Labour and the NUWSS have maintained its momentum, precipitating
a major party realignment, if the war had not supervened?

On this the evidence is ambiguous. As early as October 1913 a member of the WLF was informing Lloyd George that 'women Liberals' were
'leaving in shoals, and joining the only party honestly pressing women's
suffrage [i.e. Labour]'.[47] On the other hand, there was something
intrinsically unstable in an alliance between 'bourgeois women's right-
ers' (as they had once derisively been called) and a trade union-based
Labour Party seeking to mobilise the (male) working-class electorate. In
fact, Mrs Fawcett herself, who privately called the EFF a 'temporary accident', had no interest whatever in a major political realignment: like
other leading members of the organisation, she simply wanted to
squeeze concessions out of the Liberals by stirring up rebellion among
the latter's working-class supporters in the run-up to the next general
election.

As a tactical ploy, the turn to Labour seemed to be working. Such was
the pressure to which they were being subjected that the Liberals, had
they won the 1915 general election, would probably have introduced
a measure of women's enfranchisement early in the new session of
Parliament – a volte-face to which even Asquith seems to have become
grudgingly reconciled.[48] But, the parliamentary vote once secured,
many NUWSS activists would probably have felt free to return to their
customary allegiances. Even the approach of a general election was
causing some traditional Liberals to drift back in this way.[49]

So no apocalyptic significance should be read into the suffrage question. It raised fierce passions among both sets of partisans, but most
people probably resembled Lord Hugh Cecil and went neither pale
(with apprehension) nor pink (with enthusiasm) when the subject was
broached. Churchill once wrote despairingly that 'it would be appalling

if our strong Government and party, which has made its mark on history, were to go down on petticoat politics'.[50] This slighting reference tells us something about Churchill, who had developed a very personal antipathy to women's suffrage ever since the militants began interrupting his perorations, but his remark also expresses a widespread reluctance (on all points of the political spectrum) to see 'Votes for Women' as the defining issue of the day.

One must also remember that, when (male) candidates stood as independents explicitly on a women's suffrage platform, they received derisory support. True, in Wigan, one such candidate, Thorley Smith, polled well enough in 1906 to push the Liberal into third place, but the three suffrage candidates who engaged in the 1910 contests gathered only 696 votes between them. As for Lansbury, who resigned his East End seat soon after his 1912 outburst, he lost the subsequent by-election in a straight fight against a Conservative opponent, on a 10.5 per cent swing to the Conservatives.

In the absence of opinion polls, it is difficult to say how the majority of the electorate viewed 'Votes for Women'. Some (admittedly prejudiced) observers claimed that only a minority of *women* wanted to participate in national, as distinct from municipal, politics. This claim was endorsed by the Women's National Anti-Suffrage League, founded in July 1908, a body which encouraged famous women to come out and say why it would be inappropriate for them to be given the parliamentary vote. The WLNA, too, insisted that many of its members 'did not want the franchise'.[51]

Antipathy to women's suffrage among men was even more rampant. Significantly it was always the 'antis' who called for a referendum on the subject – a challenge to which the suffrage societies and their supporters signally failed to rise. Mrs Fawcett privately conceded that her supporters would be defeated in a referendum, and, as the 'anti', Lord Curzon, gleefully reported, the suffragists 'shiver[ed] at the very idea'.[52] In short, the Liberals, in failing to remove sexual discrimination from the parliamentary franchise, were not, it seems, blatantly flouting mainstream public opinion.

This was perhaps because by the eve of the war political concern had shifted from the older preoccupation with political rights to a pursuit of social justice – whether through state-sponsored social reform or collective working-class action. The claim that the world would be transformed (either for good or ill) as a result of conferring the vote upon those currently disfranchised carried far less conviction in the early twentieth century than it had done in the 1860s or the 1880s.[53] Hence the difficulty of mobilising vote-less males (a very heterogeneous lot, it is true) behind a campaign for adult manhood suffrage.

Yet, even though the struggle over women's suffrage did not do enormous harm to the Liberal Party, neither had it helped their prospects. The issue poisoned relationships within the party at many levels and seriously strained the Cabinet's unity. The pro-suffrage Grey on more than one occasion threatened Asquith with his resignation. Harcourt, the 'anti', was equally obdurate, sending Grey a letter in December 1911 which declared menacingly: 'Your public appearance on the Suffrage question has reluctantly brought me out into the open and I am now actively organising against you and your pernicious opinions.'[54] Such violent language may have owed something to Harcourt's detestation of Grey's foreign policy. Fortunately for the Liberals, differences over the suffrage usually cut across the normal lines of political cleavage – note Asquith's total separation on this issue from his personal and political friends, Haldane and Grey.

That said, the government's response to the suffrage agitation disheartened and demoralised many of the most loyal of its supporters, men and women alike. It contributed to the destabilisation of the Progressive Alliance. Not least, it prevented the Liberals after 1910 from removing other 'anomalies' in the electoral system such as plural voting and the complicated registration procedures. Since it was a Liberal ministry which had denied women the vote, there is a certain poetic justice in the Liberals having been prevented by women's suffrage from reforming and democratising the franchise in ways from which they would undoubtedly have benefited – even, some historians think, to the extent of shoring up their own position as a major party of government.[55]

Postscript

At the end of the war Lloyd George's coalition government brought forward the Representation of the People Bill. On a free vote, the Commons supported (by 387 to 57) the clause which entitled women to vote in parliamentary elections on reaching the age of thirty if they were householders or wives of householders. The barrier against women sitting as MPs was also removed. Hereafter women constituted just over 40 per cent of the electorate – a proportion which rose to 52.7 per cent once the franchise had been 'equalised' (by lowering the age threshold for women) in 1928.

These momentous changes came about partly because the Prime Minister, Lloyd George, personally backed women's suffrage: partly because the existence of a coalition made possible a broad 'national' settlement of a range of franchise issues: and partly because the absence of militancy meant that the Commons could now enfranchise women without feeling that they were surrendering to violence. The need to 'reward' women for their war work was another argument used (speciously) by MPs of all parties who had prudently changed their position on the suffrage issue – notably by Asquith himself.[56]

In the light of what had happened before 1914, two questions present themselves. Did the Liberals suffer at the hands of the new electorate for having earlier blocked women's suffrage? And did the Liberal Party succeed during the 1920s in making a fresh start by putting together a programme likely to appeal to women?

The first question is easily answered. The MPs who had continued, to the bitter end, to deny women the vote escaped punishment for their obduracy. Of the twelve Liberal MPs who opposed women's enfranchisement on the crucial vote of 19 June 1917, six stood down at next year's general election, three were returned, and three defeated – nothing much out of the ordinary here. Incidentally, in the run-up to the general elections of 1922, 1923 and 1924 the radical feminists of the 'Six Point Group' published a 'blacklist' of MPs they wanted to defeat and a 'whitelist' of those they hoped would keep their seats – but this initiative made little discernible difference.[57]

In any case, of the 57 'bitter enders', 45 were Conservatives, as were 43 of the Six Point Group's 'blacklisted' candidates (which included the names of only two Liberals). Had the new electorate borne the 'antis' a serious grudge, the Conservatives were the party most likely to have been damaged. Yet the Conservatives, of course, were quite the most electorally successful of the three major parties throughout the inter-war period.[58]

There are, admittedly, signs during the 1920s of a continuing Labour–Suffrage 'alliance' – which may in part have been the after-effect of the disillusionment with Asquithian procrastination felt by some progressive women. On the other hand, many constitutional suffragists were quite willing to bury the hatchet once the vote had been secured and to return to the Liberal fold.[59] Five prominent members of the pre-war NUWSS secured election to Parliament during the inter-war years.

Three of these were Labour MPs, but the other two were Margaret Wintringham and Eleanor Rathbone.[60] Wintringham succeeded her husband as Liberal MP for Louth in a by-election in 1921, the second female to take her seat in the Commons – interestingly, as an Asquithian 'loyalist'. Rathbone, the crusader for family allowances who represented the Combined English Universities from 1929 until her death in 1946, was nominally an 'Independent', but came from a staunchly Liberal family (her father, William, had been a Liberal MP), and can perhaps be regarded as an unofficial Liberal. Other former NUWSS members stood as Liberal candidates, but failed to be returned.

Of the latter the most notable was Margery Corbett Ashby, who had once served as secretary of the NUWSS. From 1918 to 1929 inclusive, she fought every single general election as a Liberal, but, although an excellent candidate, was never returned.[61] There were other highly able Liberal women, with feminist interests, whose political ambitions were similarly dragged down by their party's poor electoral performance – Helen Fraser and Mrs Fawcett's friend and close ally, Ray Strachey (nominally an Independent), suffered similarly.

To move on to the second question. How well did the Liberals cope during the 1920s with the presence of female electors? They were fortunate that many well-tried Liberal causes, such as internationalism, temperance and Free Trade, continued to prove popular with many women. This was reflected in the comparative success of the Women's National Liberal Federation (WNLF), as the reunited women's section of the party called itself after 1919. Its membership stood at over 95 000 in 1920, dropped worryingly for a couple of years, but then rose again to over 100 000 by 1928, not far short of the WLF's peak in 1912 – a remarkable achievement, given the decay of so many Liberal constituency parties during this same period.[62]

As in pre-war days, these Liberal women were divided between those who primarily wanted to help the official party and those who hoped, through the Liberal Party, to promote a 'women's agenda'. However, similar divisions also existed in the other two parties. As for the WNLF, far from simply acting as an auxiliary to the parliamentarians, it also set about raising women's political consciousness through educational campaigns and through making what was, by the standards of the time, quite a bold set of demands: its annual conferences during the 1920s passed motions in favour of widows' pensions, equal pay, divorce-law reform, improved separation allowances and family endowment. Moreover, here was a feminist agenda with a distinctly Liberal flavour, emphasising equal rights and citizenship – and, as such, subtly different from the 'social' version being propagated by the Labour women, whose activities, the WNLF thought, were disfigured by class bitterness.[63]

Of course, not all of the WNLF's concerns filtered through into the official Liberal programme. Indeed, critics have argued that Liberal leaders during the 1920s seldom addressed the women electors as women and that their candidates made comparatively little mention of women's issues.[64] In these matters a poor example was set by Asquith, whose 'conversion' to women's suffrage had been skin-deep. Lloyd George, on the other hand, appreciated the importance of mobilising the women's vote and on several occasions went out of his way to woo the National Union of Societies for Equal Citizenship (NUSEC), the non-party organisation which had emerged out of the NUWSS in 1919.

Moreover, just as many energetic women were happy to stay on in the Liberal Party, so the Liberal Party proved not unwilling to sponsor them as parliamentary candidates. Indeed, for the general elections falling between 1918 and 1929, it put up, proportionately, over twice as many women as stood for the Conservatives, though slightly fewer than stood for Labour.[65] Unfortunately, the Liberals notched up only four successes, as against the Conservatives' eleven and Labour's thirteen. This was partly because so many of these candidates had been given hopeless seats. However, getting returned as a Liberal during the 1920s was not easy for anyone, and women's gender was the least of their difficulties.

The Liberal Party's overall record on women's issues was not particularly impressive, but neither was it at all discreditable. However, even if the party had adopted a more positive feminist platform, would this have helped its electoral fortunes? Probably not, since female voters did not behave in a significantly different way in the 1920s from their male counterparts,[66] and, overall, class was far more important than gender, social policy than women's equality, in determining party allegiance throughout the inter-war years – and beyond.

The greatest help that the Liberal Party could have rendered women would have been to carry a measure of proportional representation, since this would almost certainly have encouraged a more balanced slate of candidates, helping women in general and Liberal women in particular.[67] As it was, denied a career at Westminster because of their party's poor electoral performance, a whole generation of forceful Liberal women redirected their energies into other kinds of public work – such as the Women's Institute, the International Women's Suffrage Alliance, the League of Nations Union, and the adult education movement.

(Mrs Ashby herself eventually became president of the NUSEC.) These all happened to be 'causes' with a natural appeal to middle-class women of Liberal sympathies.[68]

So there was no basic incompatibility during the 1920s between Liberalism and feminism – rather the contrary, in fact. The real weakness in the Liberal Party's position was that it could not match Labour's appeal to working-class women, as the membership of the WNLF shows.[69] In short, while sexual politics undoubtedly damaged the Liberals before 1914, this contributed little to the party's later difficulties, for which an explanation must be sought elsewhere, beginning with an examination of the damaging impact of the Great War.

8

LIBERALISM AND THE GREAT WAR

Historians may differ about the prospects of the Liberal Party on the eve of the Great War, but it was in office, as it had been for nearly nine years. In municipal politics Liberalism may have been in retreat.[1] On the other hand, many constituency parties, both in Scotland and in England, were expanding their membership in the immediate pre-war years.[2] Compare this situation with what happened in the election held soon after the signing of the Armistice in December 1918 – an election which, though it took place in somewhat unusual circumstances, did, broadly speaking, establish the main lines of development for the entire inter-war period.

The Conservatives, in alliance with the Lloyd George wing of the Liberal Party, won a crushing victory, and for the next twenty years they remained the dominant group at Westminster. But challenging their primacy for the first time was the Labour Party. True, as a result of having to face a combination of their opponents, Labour won a modest number of seats, 63 in all. But they polled an extraordinary 2 385 472 votes. With 388 candidates in the field (compared with only 56 in December 1910), Labour were projecting a quite different image of themselves from pre-war days. Already the newspapers were speculating about who might be the first Labour Prime Minister.

And Labour's advance had seemingly been achieved at the Liberal Party's expense. The Coupon Election saw the Liberals divided, demoralised and ineffectual. The party's official Leader, Asquith, suffered the ignominy of being rejected by the electors of East Fife, who had regularly returned him to Parliament for the last thirty-two years (though he was also injured by boundary changes).[3] Two former Liberal ministers, Runciman and Samuel, came bottom of the poll. Only twenty-eight

Independent Liberals survived the holocaust. This, too, was a portent of things to come.

In the copious literature dealing with the Liberal Party during the First World War three broad explanations have been advanced for this decline. Some historians are impressed by the play of 'accidental' factors, the mixture of bad luck and poor judgement on the part of certain prominent Liberal politicians which contributed materially to the Party's problems. Others talk about an incompatibility between the Liberal creed itself and the requirements of modern war; this interpretation dates from the seminal study by Professor Trevor Wilson, *The Downfall of the Liberal Party 1914–1935* (first published in 1966). Third, there is a school of thought which gives primacy to the social changes initiated by the war, which allegedly resulted in a class-based political system to which the Liberals never quite succeeded in adapting. Let us take these interpretations one by one.

The Liberals certainly suffered more than their fair share of ill luck between 1914 and 1918. Their central misfortune was to be in the wrong place at the wrong time. Frustrated patriots, who started off with the assumption that the war would quickly be over, directed their rage against the Liberals, who, after all, had been nearly nine years in power and could reasonably be held responsible for the country not being better prepared. Something very similar happened to the Conservative Party in 1939.

Many of the strictures passed on the Asquith ministry by its opponents were unjust. Haldane's creation of the Expeditionary Force, the naval reforms passed in the pre-war years (including the launching of the Dreadnought battleships), the work of the Committee of Imperial Defence in preparing the 'war book', which detailed exactly what each department should do in the event of war, all give the lie to the charge that the Liberals had neglected the country's armed services (though their conduct of foreign policy was more open to challenge). Indeed, Churchill's determination, when at the Admiralty between 1911 and 1914, to maintain Britain's naval superiority over Germany meant that, on the eve of the war (1913), £72 500 000 was being spent on the armed services – unprecedented for peacetime. In 1914 Britain had twenty Dreadnoughts to Germany's thirteen, twenty-six pre-Dreadnought battleships to Germany's twelve, and twice as many cruisers.

In retrospect, it is tempting to compare the hesitant and ineffectual handling of the economy in the opening months of war with the bold planning which characterised the 'war socialism' presided over by Lloyd George in 1917 and 1918. But this, too, is unreasonable. Had Asquith attempted anything of this sort in 1914 or early 1915, he would almost certainly have strained 'national unity' to breaking point.[4] Nor is it at all likely that if the Unionists had taken the country into war, the country would have been any better prepared, either economically or militarily.

Indeed, had the war been the short affair which so many were expecting, the Liberals might well have gained considerable credit from the experience. Asquith, for example, had shown his conciliatory powers to good advantage in holding the Cabinet together in August 1914, with the loss of only two Cabinet ministers (Lord Morley and John Burns).

But the failure to secure a quick and decisive victory – something beyond the reach of any British government – created problems for the Liberals, which Asquith perhaps exacerbated by initially placing too much trust in Lord Kitchener, his War Secretary.[5] Military disappointment intensified the mood of dissatisfaction with the ministry. As early as 15 September 1914 Bonar Law led a walk-out from the Commons of the entire Conservative Party over the decision to put the Home Rule Bill on to the statute book (although its operation was to be suspended for the duration of hostilities). This showed how fragile was the Opposition's offer to provide the government with patriotic support from outside.

In May 1915 the government was rocked by the simultaneous eruption of two crises, one affecting the adequacy of the munitions being supplied to the British Army in France, the other caused by the dramatic resignation of Lord Fisher, the First Sea Lord, over the decision to send further naval reinforcements to take part in the controversial Gallipoli campaign, so weakening the home fleet. The Prime Minister was left with little choice but to invite the Opposition leaders into his government.[6] As a result, many prominent Liberal ministers had to step down to make way for Conservatives. At Conservative insistence, Haldane, the Lord Chancellor, was (most unfairly) forced out of office because of his alleged pro-German sympathies. And Churchill, ironically enough the one senior Liberal to have favoured the creation of a 'National Government' from the moment war broke out, was demoted from the Admiralty – soon afterwards retiring to the backbenches. The Liberal parliamentary party was only narrowly dissuaded from passing a resolution condemning these events.[7] In retrospect, the unhappiness of the Liberal MPs seems well justified. The last purely Liberal ministry had come to an end; there has never been another.

The establishment in May 1915 of the first coalition government over which Asquith presided until December of the following year had two other damaging consequences for the Liberal Party, about which, again, it could have done little. For a start, it brought the alliance with the Irish Nationalists to an end. Redmond, the Nationalist Leader, was offered a post in the government, an offer which the rules of his party prevented him from accepting. But his old enemy, Edward Carson, the Ulster Unionist Leader, entered the coalition as Attorney-General – a galling sight to the Irishmen. The Nationalist Party, all immediate hope of Home Rule having disappeared, was left stranded, and its moderate leaders lost control over nationalist feeling in their own country. This, in turn, contributed to the 1916 Easter Rising and the rapid supersession of the Irish Nationalist Party by Sinn Fein, whose aspirations went well beyond Gladstonian Home Rule.

In some respects release from the Irish commitment came as a relief to the Liberals, to whom the issue had brought little but trouble over the past thirty years. On the other hand, the eclipse of Home Rule deprived the party of a distinctive policy, as well as alienating the Irish Nationalist MPs who, angered by Asquith's botched response to the Easter Rising, began voting *en bloc* against his government, even to the extent of joining Carson during the so-called Nigerian Debate.[8]

The drifting apart of the Liberals and the Irish mattered little for the time being (since the coalition's creation had deprived the Irish of their balancing position in the House), but its long-term consequences were more serious; for in future Irish voters living on mainland Britain would not be urged to vote for the Liberal Party as the only English party that could realistically satisfy Ireland's national aspirations. Indeed, after 1918 most of the working-class Irish vote in areas like Merseyside and Clydeside speedily transferred to Labour: in Glasgow, as one historian has noted, 'Irishmen who had formerly been United Irish League ward bosses resurfaced as Labour councillors.'[9]

Coalition also ended the 'Progressive Alliance'. The wartime electoral truce meant that Liberals and Labour now stood in no need of one another; besides which, the coming together of the two main parties meant that the PLP lost its former leverage over the Asquith government. Yet, unlike the Irish Nationalists, Labour were not left out in the cold. On the contrary, Arthur Henderson, the chairman of the Parliamentary party, was made President of the Board of Education, the first Labour politician to hold office. This was not because Asquith set much store by the PLP. Rather, the war effort required the active participation of the Labour *Movement*, and senior Labour figures from trade union backgrounds were valued because it was thought that they could help preserve the industrial truce and 'sell' necessary but unpopular industrial policies to workers on the factory floor.

This gave Labour an importance and an independent position that it had previously lacked. A revealing incident occurred in the course of the political crisis of December 1916. In its early stages Henderson took counsel with the Asquithian ministers and was treated as though he were actually one of their number. But when the Liberal ministers made a decision that none would serve in a Lloyd George ministry, Henderson announced that he would be guided solely by the wishes of the Labour Movement and by his own particular concept of the national interest. In the event, Labour chose to support Lloyd George's new coalition, and Henderson was promoted by being brought into the new streamlined War Cabinet of five members, which took overall political control of the running of the war.

Experience of office gave Labour a credibility in the post-war years which otherwise it would almost certainly have lacked. Trade unionists and working men had penetrated into the inner recesses of Whitehall, where they had performed with efficiency. This raised their status in the eyes of the electorate. It also gave senior Labour politicians a taste of office and power, which made them more ambitious; never again would they be content with the modest, subordinate role allotted to them in the Edwardian political system. In 1918 Labour felt that it had made a major contribution to allied victory. It now insisted on having a powerful voice in the reshaping of the post-war world. Moreover, Lloyd George's foolish expulsion of Henderson in the so-called 'doormat incident' in August 1917[10] simply made the Labour leaders more determined than ever to build up their organisation to the point where they were not dependent on others. The 'Progressive Alliance' had collapsed and was never to be re-created.

There was yet another way in which a long drawn-out war was bound to damage the Liberal Party. One element in the political truce was an understanding that the 1911 Parliament Act, stipulating quinquennial elections, would have to be suspended for the duration of the emergency, in order to postpone the dissolution which would otherwise have taken place by December 1915 at the latest. But this, in turn, necessitated an annual suspending Bill, which both Houses would have to approve; and since the Lords, in which the Unionists retained a comfortable majority, had not lost their absolute veto but could still hold up legislation, the Liberal ministers were effectively left at the mercy of their Unionist colleagues, who could force a dissolution at any time they chose by opposing the prolongation of Parliament's life.

Yet in all the mishaps which befell the Liberal Party during the war which have so far been discussed, none (except Lloyd George's mishandling of Henderson) resulted from a clear-cut Liberal mistake. Rather, once the country had become embroiled in a long war, events acquired a momentum of their own which the party leadership proved powerless to deflect.

However, the Liberals did also make avoidable errors, so compounding their difficulties. Asquith, for example, was unwise not to have shown more generosity to his erstwhile political opponents (who by May 1915 outnumbered Liberals in the House of Commons). The main posts in his coalition were almost without exception reserved for Liberals (Kitchener at the War Office was, of course, a non-party figure). Only Balfour, the former Conservative Leader, who became First Lord of the Admiralty, was put in a position where he could decisively affect the war effort; his successor, Bonar Law, was fobbed off with the Colonial Office.[11] Asquith was also damaged by his unwillingness or his inability to adapt the machinery of government to the requirements of war. The large Cabinet of twenty-two members could not provide effective overall direction, and smaller bodies like the War Council, the Dardanelles Committee and the War Committee, which might theoretically have performed this function, lacked real authority, since any decision that they reached could always be challenged in full Cabinet.

As a result, many prominent Conservatives felt little loyalty to Asquith's premiership; some actively intrigued to bring it down. Discontent also spread to the ranks of the parliamentary Liberal Party. In January 1916 a patriotic backbench 'ginger group' was set up, the Liberal War Committee. To these Liberals the hero of the day was not Asquith, but Lloyd George, who, put in charge of the new Ministry of Munitions in May 1915, had, by unorthodox methods, successfully organised the economy for war production. By the end of 1915 Lloyd George was even beginning to endear himself to many *Conservatives*, not least because of his alignment with them in a campaign to replace the country's traditional system of voluntary enlistment by conscription. Mainstream Liberals might mutter about 'treachery'. But to many dispassionate observers the former Radical tribune was emerging as a genuinely 'national' leader, able to transcend the petty interests of party in his eagerness for victory.

Lloyd George's growing importance was confirmed in June 1916 when, following Kitchener's death at sea, he became War Secretary. He did so on the eve of the disastrous Somme offensive, an experience which reinforced his belief that strategic command would have to be wrested from the military and transferred to a streamlined civilian administration. Yet such a reform Asquith was neither able, nor perhaps willing, to promote. The rift between the two principal Liberal statesmen began to assume serious proportions. In early May 1916 Lloyd George's henchman, Christopher Addison, helped by David Davies and Frederick Kellaway, initiated a somewhat mysterious sounding-out of Liberal backbench MPs to see how much support there would be for Lloyd George in the event of a breach with the Prime Minister.[12]

The events of the 'Buckingham Palace Plot' of December 1916, which led to Asquith's replacement by Lloyd George, have been subjected to minute examination.[13] This is understandable, for there were several moments during this episode when it seemed as if the disagreement between Asquith and Lloyd George (working with his new allies, Bonar Law and Carson) might be resolved. Provisional agreement had indeed been reached, not, it is true, on personnel, but on the powers of the new War Committee which Lloyd George had been pressing the Prime Minister to establish. But Asquith then went back on the agreement, angered by a mischievous leader published in *The Times* (which Carson had inspired). Edwin Montagu, the Minister of Munitions, a prominent Liberal who liked and admired both Asquith and Lloyd George, spent the crisis running back and forth from one to the other, trying to avert a split which spelled personal tragedy for politicians like himself as well as danger to the party. Unfortunately, the bond of trust between the two senior statesmen which had served the Liberal government well between 1908 and 1914 had broken down.

Historians disagree over which man was the more to blame for the perpetuation of what soon became a damaging vendetta. Although sorely provoked, Asquith it was who probably did more, in a formal sense, to create the division. For example, by deciding to retire to the backbenches if he could no longer serve as Prime Minister (rather than sit as Lord Chancellor in a Bonar Law ministry), Asquith effectively put Lloyd George into Number 10 Downing Street. Moreover, Asquith's resentment over the way in which he had been treated encouraged the other senior Liberal ministers (among them, Grey, Runciman, McKenna and Montagu) to join their Leader on the backbenches. And this, in turn, meant that, whether he liked it or not, Lloyd George, the

new Premier, was heavily dependent on the Conservatives – a situation
that changed only slightly when in mid-July 1917 the Liberal element
in the government was strengthened by Churchill's appointment as
Minister of Munitions and by the conscience-stricken Montagu's acceptance of the India Office.[14]

What made the future prospects of the Liberal Party so hazardous was
that Asquith remained the official Leader of the Liberal Party, and, as
such, the controller of party funds. Even as early as January 1917 Lloyd
George's friends were talking of the need to get together 'the nucleus
of an organisation' to support the Prime Minister, as a counterbalance to
the Asquithian machine.[15] Yet, until well into 1918 an actual Liberal
schism was still far from inevitable. Many backbenchers sincerely professed their admiration both for the Liberal statesman who led the government and for the Liberal statesman who continued to lead their
party. The division between the two groups was anyhow hazy, since it
owed little or nothing to social or economic background and had no connection with pre-war disagreements.[16]

Lloyd George faced a dilemma, in which he remained trapped for
the rest of his premiership. At an appropriate moment he could rejoin the
Liberals within a reunited party. Or he could continue his working
alliance with the Conservatives. Or he could attempt to restructure the
party system by creating, under his own leadership, a new 'national' party
which would embrace his Liberal followers, sympathetic Conservatives
and possibly a handful of co-operative Labour politicians – the underlying
premise here being that the war had destroyed the old party system and
sensible men might as well come to terms with that salient fact.

We can find Lloyd George, at one time or another, expressing
approval of all three strategies. Interestingly, a number of the Prime
Minister's intimates, like Addison, strongly favoured the 'national'
option, which they were discussing with like-minded Conservatives
throughout the winter of 1917–18. Indeed, the programme of 'Reconstruction', which Addison spearheaded, held out the promise that,
through a synthesis of patriotism and social reform (effectively the old
'national efficiency' programme, rehashed to fit the war emergency), the
forces of Liberalism and Conservatism might reach an historic compromise. As an aspiration, this sounded fine. But would enough senior
Conservatives sign up for so risky a venture, when they still disagreed
over so many important issues – not least the Tariff?[17]

Lloyd George's own mind was largely made up for him in May 1918
by the so-called Maurice Debate, when Asquith's ill-judged challenge to

the government's handling of the issue of troop reinforcements prior to the German Spring Offensive enabled the Prime Minister to stage a showdown with his critics, among them a group of backbench Liberals who had been sniping at his ministry for several months, albeit without Asquith's express authority.[18] In the event, Lloyd George won this crucial parliamentary division, with seventy-one Liberal MPs coming to its support; but ninety-eight Liberal MPs, including tellers, voted with Asquith and another eighty-five abstained or were absent from the House.

The Prime Minister was emboldened by his success to make preparations to fight an election in partnership with the Conservative Party (via his Patronage Secretary, Captain 'Freddie' Guest), although it is important to recall that at this stage it was a wartime election that everyone had in mind. Yet, even now, all hope of Liberal reunion had not been abandoned. In late September an emissary sounded Asquith out about his willingness to rejoin the government as Lord Chancellor, with the power to nominate a certain number of his colleagues.[19] An embittered Asquith rejected the olive branch. Events now developed with bewildering rapidity. The German army suddenly disintegrated; in October its military high command sued for peace; and within a few weeks of the signing of the Armistice the country was plunged into a general election campaign.

The 'Coupon Election' of 1918 (so called because Lloyd George and Bonar Law issued a joint 'coupon' to their favoured candidates) still further split the Liberal Party and intensified the bitterness between its two wings. In general, those Liberals who had supported the government in the Maurice Debate received coupons and were sheltered from the opposition of Conservative candidates, while those who had voted the other way were abandoned to their fate.[20] Not surprisingly, the new House of Commons had an overwhelming Conservative majority, but 133 'National Liberals' (i.e. Liberal supporters of Lloyd George) were returned, while the official Liberals came back, a pathetic rump of 28. Most prominent Asquithians (McKenna, Runciman, Simon, and so on) lost their seats, as did Asquith himself.

The atmosphere of the election campaign mattered almost as much as the result. Initially Asquith and several of his senior colleagues had tried to give the Coalition government their qualified, outside support. But in the heat of the contest Lloyd George alleged that, at a critical point in the war, Asquith had tried to bring down the government for unworthy reasons. To the official Liberals, of course, the real 'traitor' was Lloyd

George himself. The party was now formally divided, and although, as we shall later see, reunion was achieved in November 1923, the scars of the wounds which the Liberals inflicted on themselves in the last two years of the war never properly healed.

With the Liberal Party visibly disintegrating, Labour was given a chance of establishing a claim to being the principal party of reform – the one serious alternative to the Conservatives. From late 1917 onwards it gradually began to disengage from the coalition and, once the Armistice had been signed, it withdrew completely. The imminent enlargement of the electorate may also have influenced Labour's decision to run several hundred candidates in the ensuing general election. In December 1917 Henderson mentioned to a startled Liberal sympathiser that these might number 'as many as 500', though perhaps this presupposed the introduction of the Alternative Vote (see pp. 159–60).[21] Some historians go further and allege that it was in order to take advantage of the Liberals' decline that Labour reorganised itself in 1918 and finally, through Clause 4 of its new constitution, made the commitment to socialism.[22] Therefore, there are grounds for arguing that Labour's rise to power came about because it consciously moved to fill the political vacuum left by the Liberal Party's various acts of self-immolation.

Yet there seems something unsatisfactory about an interpretation which lays such heavy emphasis upon accident and the vagaries of personality. Take, for example, the issue of the Asquith–Lloyd George quarrel. Why should the two men, whose differences of social background and temperament had made them complement one another so effectively between 1908 and 1914, to the great benefit of the Liberal Party, have allowed their relationship to deteriorate seriously once war had broken out? It makes little sense to dwell on Lloyd George's slipperiness and ambition, since these character traits were of long standing. Why should Lloyd George's ambition have driven him to advance his career *through* the Liberal Party before 1914, while it drove him into actions damaging to Liberalism thereafter? Further explanation inevitably leads one to an examination of some of the more fundamental dilemmas which all Liberals were facing in these years.

Quite the most persuasive of such interpretations is the one furnished by Trevor Wilson in *The Downfall of the Liberal Party*. In a metaphor that has achieved fame, Wilson contends that the Liberals on the eve of war resembled a man experiencing symptoms of illness (Ireland, Labour Unrest, the Suffragettes, and so on), who then had the misfortune to be hit by a rampant omnibus (the Great War) which mounted the pavement and inflicted on him injuries from the effects of which he eventually died.[23]

Wilson's thesis is that the Liberals were ideologically ill-equipped for near total war, which required for its prosecution the abandonment or at least the temporary suspension of nearly all the principles and values which they held dear. The dilemma arose most acutely over the issue of conscription, which the military high command insisted was essential to break the deadlock on the Western Front. It was hard for Liberals to deny the generals the extra men that they said they needed, yet at the same time the adoption of conscription seemed a gross betrayal of the cause for which Britain had initially entered the war: the destruction of Junkerdom. What would be gained by an Allied victory if this involved the 'Germanisation' of the British people? Conscription was eventually passed in two stages in 1916, but one prominent Liberal, the Home Secretary, Sir John Simon, resigned, and only Asquith's parliamentary skill prevented others from following suit. The Liberal Party underwent a traumatic experience during the struggle over conscription: patriotic duty and the will to win the war pulled it one way, inherited traditions and beliefs pulled it another. It follows from this analysis that the leadership difficulties, and the Asquith–Lloyd George antagonism itself, should properly be interpreted as *symptoms* of a more fundamental malaise, not as its principal *cause*.

The Liberal Party found itself under similar strain over other issues. The Chancellor of the Exchequer, Reginald McKenna, instituted a departure from strict Free Trade (the 'McKenna Duties' of 1915), and there was talk in government circles of organising a trade war against Germany even after hostilities had ended. Encroachments on customary civil liberties, such as press censorship and the proliferation of Orders-in-Council issued under the Defence of the Realm Act, were further violations of the Liberal conscience.

As a consequence, the party began to split into three separate groups. The more high-principled Radicals simply despaired of Liberalism altogether and began to desert their party for Labour. This was made easier for them because of the existence of a pressure group called the Union of Democratic Control (UDC), which MacDonald and a number of left-wing Liberals had created in the autumn of 1914 to express their hostility to Grey's conduct of foreign affairs. Dissident Radical intellectuals, like E. D. Morel, C. P. Trevelyan and Arthur Ponsonby, got into the habit of co-operating in the UDC with kindred spirits from the socialist movement, like MacDonald. In time many of them gravitated into the Labour Movement.[24]

Second, there were the middle-of-the-road loyalists. These men did their best to conceal their unhappiness, and continued to look to the Leader, Asquith, for guidance and inspiration. Asquith, his personal life in disarray, was not at this time an inspirational figure, but many Liberals (especially rank-and-file activists) went on backing him because they feared for what might happen were he to be overthrown.[25]

This position contrasted totally with that of a third group: a ginger group of 'patriotic' Liberals, some of them, incidentally, advanced Radicals before 1914, whose open exasperation with Asquith's 'wait and see' approach mounted the longer the war progressed.

The crisis of war certainly drove some highly unlikely people into criticising Asquith and calling for ruthless and decisive action. Even James Bryce, Gladstone's old friend, was once heard to observe: 'War is one of those things that if done at all ought to be done with all one's might.'[26] Patriotic zeal persuaded such men that the conscientious scruples of Liberals and maybe the short-term interests of the Liberal Party itself must be subordinated to the greater national good. They wanted the war to be won, and they failed to see how the Germans would ever be defeated by a government half-paralysed by an over-developed moral conscience. Moreover, neither did these Liberals see why the Conservatives should be allowed to claim a monopoly of patriotism and belligerent ardour. Those who took this view of things became very powerful indeed, and no wonder – for these 'patriots' soon found a spokesman in Lloyd George.

Impatient with half-measures that threatened to prolong the war, Lloyd George identified himself in the public mind with a policy of 'Thorough', a dedication to efficiency which overrode all other considerations. In alliance with the Conservatives, it was Lloyd George who made the running over conscription in 1916.[27] It was also Lloyd George, the high-minded opponent of British military operations during the Boer War, who proclaimed fifteen years later that he intended to make life very hard for the conscientious objectors. And it was Lloyd George who in November 1916 called for a 'knock-out blow' against the enemy – so quashing any possibility of a compromise settlement which might have ended the bloodbath.

From an orthodox Liberal viewpoint, this was shocking behaviour indeed. But even Radicals who distrusted Lloyd George personally could see that, while the very existence of the Empire hung in the balance, his approach offered certain advantages. In December 1916 the 'progressive' Barbara Hammond mused: 'the Asquith regime means certain & moderate disaster; the Ll.G. either absolute disaster or success'.[28] By the end of 1916 the country was in such desperate straits that it seemed worth taking a gamble on Lloyd George, and a significant number of Liberal MPs were ready to give him their support, even though they realised that this might mean a temporary breach with Asquith, the party Leader. Looked at in this way, Lloyd George was perhaps not so much 'deserting' Liberalism as providing an alternative version of it suited to the prevailing circumstances. It can also, more plausibly, be argued that, as a charismatic popular leader who appealed to people from all points of the political spectrum, the Welshman was, consciously or otherwise, powerfully propelling forward the 'national party' project.

Let us, however, go back to *The Downfall of the Liberal Party* and examine it more closely. The book is so persuasive that one is tempted to swallow all its claims uncritically. Yet Trevor Wilson's interpretation can be challenged on several fronts. For a start, his is a study of the morale of the Liberal Party which concentrates almost entirely on members of the Parliamentary Party. Opinion amongst Liberal constituency workers was probably different. For example, in a study of Yorkshire Liberalism, George Bernstein has suggested that 'by focussing on the parliamentary party, historians have exaggerated the strains that war-time policies imperilling tenets of liberalism placed upon Liberal loyalties. This tension between policy and principle was a norm of Liberal politics.'[29] In any case, argues Bernstein, Liberal activists and pressmen were prepared to accept compromises from Asquith because they basically trusted him (although conscription and the formation of the coalition ministry created disquiet), and most went on following him even after the split in December 1916. In Bernstein's view, then, the real blow to Liberal unity did not come until the allocation of the coupon in December 1918: the wartime 'crisis of Liberalism' was not the decisive factor.

Moreover, it is also arguable that, in the nature of things, all three British parties suffered from the impact of war and the 'distortions' of political life occasioned by coalition government. For example, the Conservatives, like their Liberal counterparts, were sharply divided between 'Westerners' and 'Easterners' (those who wanted to concentrate the fighting on the Western Front and those who favoured operations in other theatres of war), and could by no means agree over the desirability of conscription and the 'sacrifices' of property rights that needed to be made in the cause of military efficiency.[30] A few prominent Conservatives, like the former Leader in the Upper House, Lord Lansdowne, author of the famous 'Letter' of 1917, even questioned publicly whether the pursuit of total victory justified the enormous loss of men and money which was being sustained. In addition, the cessation of 'normal' political life weakened the authority of *all* party leaders; Bonar Law played a major part in the construction of both Asquith's and Lloyd George's coalition ministries, but in each case he did so partly to shore up his own declining authority.[31] Even the prospective enlargement of the franchise, agreed to in the last period of the war, worried the Conservatives, who feared (needlessly, it later transpired) that 'democracy' would seriously damage their party's electoral fortunes.[32]

The Labour Party found itself in an even more precarious position. Indeed, after the establishment of the first coalition, Labour MPs were actually sitting on both sides of the House. The ILPers, among them MacDonald and Snowden, were so seriously estranged from Henderson and the bulk of the trade union members that the very survival of a united Labour Party sometimes seemed to be in question. The struggle for power between the shop stewards, articulating a primitive syndicalist philosophy, and those party leaders participating in a coalition government whose policies they could only marginally influence, also illustrates the dilemmas facing the party in these years. These dissensions had the effect of hamstringing many of Labour's constituency organisations.[33]

Yet, helped in part by its federal Constitution, Labour managed to surmount its difficulties, and, following its reorganisation, was able to enter the electoral fray in 1918 in good heart. Of course, the extension of collectivist controls during the war removed much of the earlier feeling that socialism was merely 'utopian', a change of attitude that was very much to Labour's benefit. But the contrast between the two 'parties of progress' was not simply that the Labour Movement found it easier than the Liberals to live with the demands of total war. More important, the social changes, which the war accelerated, had created an environment in which Labour felt confident that it could operate with success, and this confidence gave its various factions an interest in minimising their differences and presenting a more or less united face to the wider world. True, Trevor Wilson acknowledges the significance of such developments, in one place ascribing the Liberal decline to 'the impact of the war on the nation's economy' which 'so increased the importance of the trade unions, and so stimulated their political consciousness, that it correspondingly enhanced the position of the Labour party'.[34] But this is an *obiter dictum* which his book in no way demonstrates.

The gist of the Trevor Wilson thesis is his claim that 'the Liberal Party fell . . . because of a revolution in ideas occurring in the minds of men'.[35] But this approach leaves questions of organisation and of class relationships entirely out of account. And it is to these that we must now turn.

Why, in the long run, did the Labour Party emerge from the war with increased strength? We have already seen that participation in the wartime ministries gave the Labour leadership a new self-confidence and ambition, and also that the very fact of coalition government forced the party to free itself from an electoral alliance which, perhaps, had long been something of a trap. But, in addition, Labour's base was enlarged by the war, which created an economic boom, causing the total number of trade unionists to double between 1914 and 1919 – from about four million to nearly eight million. And this enabled the TUC to claim, for the first time, that it represented the majority of working people, skilled and unskilled, women as well as men, over a wide range of industries.

Given the close links between the political and industrial wings of the Labour Movement, such a development, it has been argued, was bound to help the party – not least because trade union expansion automatically enriched it, since all the big trade unions were affiliated to Labour and only a minority of workers chose to contract out of the political levy. By 1918 the Labour Party was flush with funds. The fact that early in the year Henderson was speaking confidently of Labour's ability to run up to 500 candidates at the next election is eloquent testimony of his party's new found opulence.

But the perspectives of the Labour leadership perhaps changed because the working-class community itself was undergoing a profound transformation in these years. Most historians believe that the gap in living standards between the skilled man and the labourer considerably narrowed during the course of the war. This particularly happened in the so-called 'controlled establishments', factories doing contract work for the Ministry of Munitions under official supervision, where piecework and the bonus system squeezed income differentials hard. The semi-skilled machine operators who were recruited in large numbers into munitions production were often earning more money than the skilled craftsmen who were put in charge of them.[36] But that was not all. For the dividing line between the skilled and the unskilled was itself becoming blurred as a result of 'dilution', that is to say, the breaking-down of skilled craft procedures into a series of simpler operations which could be performed by unskilled and semi-skilled machinists, many of them women. This had immediate social consequences. As one well-placed observer later put it, the social barriers of caste between the skilled worker and the lower industrial grades were permanently lowered during the war; from then on 'the artisan felt less superiority, the labourer and semi-skilled man more self-assurance'.[37]

Average real wages increased during the Great War, but the main benefits accrued to the unskilled. Apart from anything else, it was the unskilled, the much-despised 'residuum' of Edwardian Britain, whose circumstances were transformed by the virtual disappearance of unemployment. The unemployment rate fell below one per cent in May 1915 and then stayed at a very low point for the rest of the war. There was now a chronic labour *shortage*. Work was available for all who were not suffering from some physical or mental handicap. The so-called 'unemployables' were soon as busily occupied as anyone else. So, in many cases, were their wives, and the double income made possible a standard of living for the poor which before 1914 would have been inconceivable.

Admittedly, in the short run, such changes gave rise to a certain amount of friction within the working-class community. The newspapers were full of amazing revelations about unskilled workers, drawing good pay in the munitions factories, who were able to purchase luxury items like pianos and gramophones. Many 'labour aristocrats' agreed with middle-class moralists that it was a topsy-turvy world in which ordinary labourers could acquire these prestige consumer goods.

But, despite this sort of jealousy, the changes initiated by the war probably succeeded, in the long run, in uniting working people more than they divided them. It was a more cohesive Labour Movement, as well as a more broadly based one, that was flexing its industrial muscles in the 1920s. For working-class groups that previously had had little in common with one another had been subjected during the war to similar experiences, and this welded them together and made them conscious, perhaps for the first time, of their identity as a class with interests that conflicted with those of other classes. To a large extent this new working-class culture also cut across the local peculiarities which had been so pronounced in the Edwardian period.[38] Such developments could not but help Labour. Buoyed up by a new mood of confidence, the Labour Party rewrote its Constitution in 1918, which now contained the famous

Clause 4 committing its members to socialism. It is unlikely that any of this would have happened so quickly but for the First World War.

Labour also improved its position at the Liberals' expense by quickly seizing the initiative on social reform, agitating vigorously over practical working-class grievances, such as rent levels, food prices and profit-eering. These activities, centrally co-ordinated by the War Emergency Workers' National Committee, on which all sectors of the Labour Move-ment were represented, also served the useful purpose of distracting attention from its own political divisions.[39] The Liberals, by contrast, largely let these social and economic issues go by default. Many of the Radical activists most in sympathy with the problems of the poor had in any case already discredited themselves by opposition to the war, while others, on the point of being deselected, now lived in a kind of political no man's land. As for the bulk of the Liberals in the country, for them the main issue of the day seems to have been, not social reform, but the restoration of liberty.[40] Consequently, whereas many Labour Party members hailed 'war socialism' as proof of socialism's viability,[41] Liberals tended to see it as a 'Prussian innovation' which was both dangerous and inefficient. The recent wartime controls, opined Sir Thomas Whittaker, MP for Spen Valley, 'meant that all the foolish talk we had heard for years about Socialism had been blown to the winds'.[42] This was a dangerously negative stance to take, but one which the Lib-erals' parliamentary leaders did little to counter.

Finally, there is some evidence that, although businessmen did very well out of war contracts, many *professional* middle-class groups living on fixed incomes suffered a severe decline in their standard of living. If we are to accept Masterman's considered judgement that this stratum had provided the pre-war Liberal Party with its bedrock support, its later demoralisation may have had a damaging impact on Liberalism itself.[43]

Yet one should not be carried away by wisdom of hindsight into por-traying an optimistic Labour Party surging irresistibly forward at the end of the war, sweeping aside all the obstacles in its path. A closer exam-ination of developments in the constituencies does not confirm this pic-ture. Many trade unions were still apathetic about electoral politics, party organisation was weak or non-existent in many areas, and the old ideological and sectional divisions had by no means disappeared. Although artificially boosted by the impact of total war, the Labour Party still had an enormous mountain to climb before it could establish itself as a party of government.[44] By the same token, there remained a possibility that the Liberals could recover much of their former influence. It is always a mistake to 'read off' political events as mere indicators of social change. In any case, many of the developments apparently favouring Labour between 1914 and 1918 had been reversed by the mid-1920s, when wage differentials were widening once more, unemployment was rising sharply, and so on.[45] Such changes did not lead to Labour's decline. Neither did economic circumstances by themselves decree the Liberal Party's downfall. All one *can* say is that the social environment created by the war helped the Labour Party, whereas the Liberals would have had difficulty in coping with it, even had they avoided the ideological wrangling that accompanied its conduct.

But, in addition, the growing power of the Labour Movement impinged upon the Liberal Party even more directly. Against the background of the Russian Revolutions of 1917, a new mood of apprehension developed in governing circles about the threat which the working classes seemingly posed to the stability of British society. Continued coalition government could now be defended by reference to the importance of keeping socialism at bay. It may be an exaggeration to claim that ministers after December 1916 were pursuing 'a strategy, albeit half-hearted, of counter-revolution', with the consequence that under Lloyd George 'the Liberal Party was sacrificed to the need to defeat the Labour movement in a general election'.[46] All the same, fear of Labour and anti-socialism were beginning to emerge as powerful political emotions – emotions which were to stir up much strife within the Liberal Party once the war ended.

9

THE 1920S

In many respects the Great War proved disastrous for the Liberal Party. Yet, paradoxically, it also accomplished many of the Liberals' traditional objectives. The 'modernisation' of society, in fact, was speeded up by the war in a way that the Liberal Party had itself never succeeded in doing. The big landowners had been bringing their land on to the market from 1909 onwards, before heavy wartime taxation, high military casualties among the aristocracy and a temporary rise in demand for land provided a fine chance to rid themselves of what, in many cases, had come to be seen as a burdensome liability. Between 1917 and the end of 1921 one-quarter of England probably changed hands. The whole aristocratic 'system', centred on the ownership of big estates, was irrevocably destroyed. By 1927, 36 per cent of land was owned by farmer-proprietors, compared with 12.3 per cent in 1908.[1]

But this belated collapse of 'feudalism' was a mixed blessing for the Liberal Party, since it meant the loss of one of its great defining 'causes'. Although Lloyd George launched a new Land Campaign in 1925, it soon petered out, being largely superseded by the Industrial Inquiry. The trouble with the Land Campaign was that its proffered 'solution', 'cultivating tenure', was not easy to understand and threatened to divide the interests of farmers from those of their labourers. In any case, an alliance between farmers and labourers would be more difficult than ever to construct, now that the economic power of landlordism, which had provided the common enemy before 1914, had been broken. In the 1920s the great landowners were objects of pity, rather than of hatred.[2]

Something similar happened in the sphere of sectarian politics. With the settlement of the Welsh Church issue on a compromise basis in 1919 and with temperance less of a public issue now that heavy drinking had been reduced by higher living conditions and more recreational outlets, as well as by tight restrictions of licensing hours, there was nothing very significant upon which the 'Nonconformist Conscience' could focus. True, Nonconformity still rallied to the party's support. But after 1924 there were more Dissenters, in absolute terms, on the Labour than on the Liberal benches – but as a proportion of the Liberal parliamentary party they increased, as Liberalism was driven back into the 'Celtic Fringe'.[3] Even in Scotland many United Free Church ministers, who could once have been relied upon to support the party through thick and thin, had deserted it by 1924, a development likened by one historian to the Barbary apes leaving Gibraltar![4]

Yet it was these 'dying' issues with which the Liberals still felt most at home. Hence, the importance to the party of the atrocities committed in nationalist Ireland in 1920–1 by the notorious 'Black and Tans', the hastily assembled auxiliary police force, which revived a historic Liberal cause and gave Asquith an opportunity to attack the coalition government with real verve and effectiveness – rather as, when a young man, he had attacked the Unionists' 'coercion' in Ireland. Baldwin's challenge to Free Trade in 1923 had similar consequences.[5] Indeed, the final abandonment of Free Trade in 1931–2 was to deal the party a frightful blow, since it entailed the disappearance of the issue which, more than any other, had given the Liberals their identity.[6]

Unfortunately, the zest with which the Liberals threw themselves into these familiar controversies tended to give them a somewhat dated appearance. It is hardly to be wondered at that one Liberal candidate should have had his election meeting disrupted by his working-class audience bursting out into the hymn, 'Tell me the old, old story'! It may be significant, given this context, that the Liberals seem to have had some difficulty in enlisting young recruits for municipal contests; in Wolverhampton, for example, the average age of new Liberal councillors during the 1920s was forty-nine, ten years older than that of their Labour counterparts.[7]

This did not necessarily mean that there was no place for the Liberal Party in the post-war world. As their defence of Free Trade in 1923 showed, Liberals still performed well when they could launch a principled attack on the Conservative Party from a broadly 'conservative' position. But such opportunities would only arise infrequently. Given the growth of the Labour Party, the Liberals' best bet was therefore to try to carve out a role for themselves as a 'centre' party – mediating between the two extremes of Conservatism and Socialism. But was such a strategy feasible? And, even if feasible, did it offer the Liberals a chance to re-establish themselves as a party of government?

The facts, one might think, spoke for themselves. Up until October 1922 the Liberals remained divided, with Lloyd George continuing to head a coalition government, while the 'Wee Frees', as the Independent Liberals were called, languished in impotent opposition. Even with the fall of the coalition, the two parties led almost entirely separate exist- ences. True, the Conservatives, by clumsily challenging Free Trade, brought about the Liberal Reunion of late 1923, shortly to be followed by a general election in which the Liberals were only narrowly beaten into third place. But that was the best electoral performance that they were to achieve in the entire decade. After 1929 (and perhaps by late 1924) a new two-party system had come into existence, centring upon Conservatives and Labour. In municipal politics, too, the Liberal decline proceeded apace. By 1930 Huddersfield was the only English borough where the Liberals held control, though they were the largest single party in another five.[8]

But, once again, the subject is one over which historians have sharply differed. To illustrate these differences I shall first present the 'pessim- istic' case, then suggest that a more 'optimistic' view of the Liberals' sur- vival chances is possible, before concluding with an interpretation which combines elements of both.

The Pessimistic Case

Some historians believe that the Liberal Party never recovered from its wartime divisions. The perpetuation of the coalition in 1918 was a great disaster; it would have been better if a reunited Liberal Party had suffered a severe electoral defeat rather than undergoing a schism which left some of its prominent leaders reliant for office on the Conser- vative Party, the hereditary enemy.[9] Not surprisingly, the split within the party later deepened as the 'official Liberals' took stock of their situation. At the Leamington meeting of the NLF in May 1920 the party faithful booed and hustled out of the hall those Liberal MPs who were support- ing Lloyd George. The National Liberals (i.e. the Lloyd George Lib- erals) were denounced as 'traitors' to their party and their creed. These bitter divisions spilled over into the country. In Scotland, for example, seventeen constituency parties were disaffiliated in the post-war years

for supporting the Prime Minister, and in the 1922 general election there were sixteen constituencies where Liberals fought one another.[10]

The Asquithian contempt for the coalition Liberals was not entirely justified. Some of the Liberal ministers, notably Montagu at the India Office, H. A. L. Fisher at the Board of Education, and Addison, the first Health Minister, worked with courage and determination in pursuit of genuinely progressive policies. But all of this was eclipsed in the minds of the Independent Liberals by the atrocities committed by the 'Black and Tans' against Sinn Fein sympathisers, as the government sought to crush nationalist resistance to British rule in Ireland; it was all the more humiliating that the Irish Secretary responsible for these activities happened to be a National Liberal, Hamar Greenwood. The 'Liberal' credentials of the Prime Minister were then further undermined when he abandoned, first, Addison in July 1921, and then Montagu in March 1922, in a vain attempt to appease his restless Conservative 'allies'.[11]

All of this, the Irish issue in particular, gave Asquith a splendid opportunity for launching an attack on the immorality and unscrupulous attachment to power of the Prime Minister. Returned to the Commons once more in February 1920 at the Paisley by-election, Asquith took back the chairmanship of the parliamentary party from its stopgap leader, Donald McLean (who had, in fact, done surprisingly well), and for a brief time an Independent Liberal revival seemed possible. But disillusion with Asquith's tired performances soon set in: in 1921 and early 1922 serious moves were afoot to replace him by Grey as leader of a new 'Centre' grouping which would also take in 'liberal' Conservatives, notably Lord Robert Cecil.[12] These intrigues came to nothing, and it was the revamped Labour Party which was the better placed to take advantage of the government's unpopularity. Consequently, when the coalition finally fell in October 1922, Asquith and his friends could do little but watch from the sidelines.

From the Liberal point of view, it was particularly unfortunate that the coalition's demise came about, not as a result of Lloyd George breaking free from his Conservative allies (as he had sometimes threatened to do), but because of a Conservative revolt. This gave the impression that Lloyd George and his friends, who maintained their own 'National Liberal' organisation, had only returned to Liberalism because more promising options had temporarily been closed down. How long would it be, many people wondered, before Lloyd George once again tried to link up with his many Conservative friends (Austen Chamberlain, Balfour and Lord Birkenhead among them)?

Since Asquith's inner circle continued to view Lloyd George with suspicion and contempt, the Liberal schism continued for the next twelve months. Reunification, when it came in November 1923, owed more to Baldwin's incompetence than to any desire for reconciliation, and, although in many constituencies the old camaraderie was quickly restored, at national level the new-found unity of the party (which Asquith formally led) was never anything other than superficial. The Asquithians, particularly close associates of the leader like Herbert Gladstone and Vivian Phillipps (the 'Holy Family'), continued to view Lloyd George with loathing. Meanwhile Lloyd George refused to hand over to the official Liberal coffers the very sizeable fund which he had amassed over the previous few years (not least by the sale of honours during the period of the post-war coalition) until the party machine had been organised to his satisfaction – a transparent device for increasing his own authority within the party.

Lloyd George's behaviour only makes sense if one supposes that he was 'riding for a fall', confident in the knowledge that he would be able to seize control of the party in the wake of another election defeat. If so, the scheme was well contrived. When a snap election was called in October 1924, financial uncertainty meant that the Liberals could only field 340 candidates, 113 fewer than had stood in the successful campaign eleven months earlier.[13] Even before the polling booths had opened (shades of 1900), the Liberals had publicly renounced any ambition of forming their own government.

The 1924 election reduced the Liberals from 158 MPs to 40. Asquith lost his seat, though he took a peerage (becoming Lord Oxford and Asquith) and remained the titular Liberal Leader. Day-to-day running of the parliamentary party devolved on to Lloyd George, the chairman of the Liberal MPs. It was almost an exact re-run of the unhappy period of 1894–5 when Rosebery had tried to lead the Liberals from the Lords, in the face of obstruction from Harcourt, the Leader in the Commons. Haggling over the disposition of the by now notorious 'Fund' continued to poison the atmosphere of Liberal politics: Asquith's friends insisted that the money be 'pooled' (in effect be handed over to them), but Lloyd George had no intention of losing control over a resource which, he believed, guaranteed him an extended political career, however hostile the environment.

The existence of the 'Fund' was damaging to the Liberal Party for three reasons. First, it meant that a party which prided itself on being the embodiment of morality[14] had become associated in the public mind with chicanery and corruption. Second, the Fund made it difficult for the Liberals to put their finances on to a sound footing. Asquith's officials tried, belatedly in 1925, to raise a central fund from a number of small subscriptions (the 'Million Fund'), but sympathisers with Liberalism, affluent or otherwise, felt understandable reluctance to dig deeply into their pockets when a sum of money, rumoured to amount to some £3 million, was in existence to which access was being blocked (according to sources close to Lloyd George) by the petty-mindedness of the Asquithians. The Liberals, it seemed, were damned whether they accepted Lloyd George's 'tainted' money or whether they refused it. But the 'Fund' was also damaging to Lloyd George himself for a rather different reason. Public discussion of the matter kept alive in the electorate's mind memories of the circumstances in which it had been accumulated and drew attention to Lloyd George's coalition past, even when the Welshman sincerely wanted to be seen as a 'man of the Left'.[15]

A resolution of sorts was achieved in the summer of 1926 when differences between Asquith and Lloyd George over how to respond to the General Strike led to the final showdown which resulted in Asquith's retreat into private life. Now that Lloyd George had become the undisputed party leader, his commitment to a Liberal revival dramatically increased, and, although to the end of his life he continued to cling tenaciously to his separate Fund, he began making generous disbursements from it to improve the party organisation and to help the intellectuals of the Liberal Summer School movement formulate a modern programme.[16] But, to the Asquithian faithful, their once great party had been 'bought' by an unprincipled adventurer. In 1927 these men formed the Liberal Council, under the presidency of the aged Grey, to keep 'independent Liberalism' alive – its real driving force was Walter Runciman. As a result, when the Liberals fought a spirited campaign in the 1929 election, with their bold 'We Can Conquer Unemployment' slogan, the effect was marred by the more or less open scepticism expressed by old Asquithians like Runciman and Simon.[17] In any case, by this time Liberal fortunes may have sunk too low for them to be revived by any party campaign, however inspired – indeed, the provincial activists of the West Country (and doubtless elsewhere) still clung to the 'old-time religion' and resisted the allure of Lloyd George's programme.[18] Even at the height of the Liberal 'revival' Lloyd George himself was privately expecting nothing better than to be left holding the balance of seats after the next general election.[19]

Over Liberal politics in the 1920s there hangs, in Michael Bentley's telling phrase, an atmosphere of 'regret and recrimination'.[20] The Asquithians' sense of outrage at what they considered the 'betrayal' of their party and their creed never really abated, and, for the likes of Lord Cowdray, the 'feud' against the Welshman became the main purpose of their existence.[21] The depths of this bitterness can be seen from the fact that when in 1927 the right-wing newspaper, the *Morning Post*, ran a series of articles about the 'Fund', some of its material was being secretly provided by Vivian Phillipps, while other Liberals cheered him on in his attempt to drive their 'Leader' from public life.[22] Moreover, many Liberals succumbed to a mood of self-pity, in which nostalgia for a supposedly glorious past was combined with a stubborn pride in resisting the wiles of the sordid post-war world. 'You have helped the remnant of us to think rightly and to hold out', one Liberal intellectual, Gilbert Murray, wrote to Asquith in 1925.[23] Given this frame of mind, do we need to look further for an explanation of the Liberals' failure to return to power?[24]

Once again, however, Liberal factionalism may have been in part the symptom of a deeper demoralisation. Liberals had good grounds for querying whether after 1918 Lloyd George was truly committed to their party; in 1920 he was saying privately to his 'National Liberal' colleagues: 'Liberal labels ... [lead] nowhere; we must be prepared to burn them.'[25] But *why* did Lloyd George feel this way? Can it not also be argued that the introspective quarrelsomeness displayed by the Liberals for most of the 1920s was as much the consequence, as it was the cause, of the Liberals' failure to win power?

In two respects the Liberals were faced by an entirely new challenge after the First World War, with which, in the opinion of some historians, they were ill-equipped to deal: a mass electorate and the Labour challenge. Let us take these one by one.

In the summer of 1918 Parliament passed the Representation of the People Act, which, for the first time, gave the vote to all adult men and many women, so trebling the electorate at a stroke. In a famous article Matthew, McKibbin and Kay have claimed that the Conservative and Labour Parties were able to appeal to this new mass electorate more effectively than their Liberal rivals, and this for two reasons. First, the newly enfranchised male voters naturally inclined towards Labour, which was able for the first time to exploit its class appeal to the maximum. Second, Liberals, or so it is claimed, were too rational to make emotive appeals to less educated voters, unlike Labour, which could employ class slogans, and the Conservatives, with their shameless appeals to the electorate's 'patriotism'.[26]

Both claims are shaky. For a start, the assumption that the 1918 Act enfranchised a hitherto excluded 'class', the casual poor, has been shown to be false. Tanner calculates that in those constituencies, which before and after 1918 had only a small plural vote, the class impact of franchise change was mostly 'negligible'.[27] In any case, the Labour Party performed almost as well in municipal elections, which operated on a franchise similar to the 'household franchise' of pre-war days.[28] Indeed, if one statistical analysis is to be believed, 'the more new voters, the *less* the constituency tended towards the Labour Party'.[29] If Labour benefited from the new electoral system at all, this, it seems, was largely because of the changes made to constituency boundaries. It has also been suggested that the cohort of radicalised working-class males who had been disfranchised before 1914 'grew up' to become Labour voters after the war – something which would presumably have happened, regardless of the passing of the Representation of the People Act.[30]

As for the relationship between the Liberal Party and the new parliamentary electors, Asquith privately viewed them with a mixture of detached amusement and mistrust: the recently enfranchised women were 'hopelessly ignorant of politics, credulous to the last degree, and flickering with gusts of sentiment like a candle in the wind', the Irish working class were at the mercy of their 'bosses', and so on.[31] But Lloyd George, author of the slogan of '9d for 4d' (when promoting Health Insurance after 1911), had never in the past been averse to a spot of vulgar demagoguery, nor did he become austerely scrupulous after 1918. Indeed, the opposite criticism of him was often made. Asquith's daughter wrinkled up her nose during the 1923 Election at Lloyd George 'cartwheeling round the country with his apparatus of loudspeakers, journalists, jokes, etc.', and Herbert Gladstone worried lest Lloyd George's 'American' campaigning methods would alienate the 'highbrows'.[32] The relevance of all this to the survival chances of the Liberal Party is unclear.

The rise of Labour, on the other hand, really did present the Liberals with a major problem. For the Liberals could not easily decide whether Labour should be treated as allies, rivals or enemies. This uncertainty was, of course, bound up with uncertainty over where they themselves stood.[33]

Given the problems faced by their party in the 1920s, it was natural that many Radicals should look back nostalgically to the old 'progressive alliance' with Labour and try to re-create it. This was a favourite idea of C. P. Scott, the influential editor of the *Manchester Guardian*, who pressed it on moderate Labour politicians like Henderson. L. T. Hobhouse, who could never quite bring himself to join Labour, as other 'New Liberals' had done, would also have welcomed such a development. He even speculated privately about what he regarded as a logical party realignment, in which the 'bad Liberals' would join up with 'ordinary Tories', while 'good [i.e. progressive] Liberals' would fuse with 'ordinary Labour', leaving both Diehards and theoretical socialists on the political fringes.[34] It seemed absurd to Hobhouse that the forces of progress should, through their divisions, play into the hands of the Conservative enemy. A number of historians, including Trevor Wilson, have agreed.

But these were mere paper schemes. The last thing that Labour wanted was a reversion to the pattern of pre-war politics. Moreover, as it steadily built up its popular vote, Labour had no need of Liberal support. So much became apparent when MacDonald formed his minority ministry in 1924 after Asquith had made his fateful decision to 'put Labour in'. Far from being grateful for Asquith's assistance, the new Cabinet went its own way and refused even to consult with the Liberal MPs on whose votes it depended. Backbench Labour MPs were equally unaccommodating. Accordingly, when a Liberal brought forward a Bill to establish proportional representation, twenty-eight Labour MPs voted in its favour, but ninety-one went through the 'No' lobby (there was a free vote). Most galling of all, Liberal MPs found that, while they had been staying up late into the night sustaining MacDonald in office, the Labour Party was preparing to run candidates against them at the forthcoming election – even when this meant intervening in a constituency for the first time and thereby almost certainly handing it over to a Conservative (this actually happened in the Oxford by-election in June).[35]

Too late, Asquith and Lloyd George recognised that they had walked into a trap. If the Labour ministry displayed moderation and acted in ways of which Liberals approved, as happened with Philip Snowden's Budget or with MacDonald's attempts to act as a conciliator between the French and German governments, the Liberals found that a rival party had stolen their clothes. But when the Labour ministry seemed to be pandering to its 'extreme' socialist backbenchers, for example, through its attempts to reach a commercial and financial settlement with the Bolshevik regime in Russia, the Liberals could do little about it, yet were open to the taunt that it was *they* who bore responsibility by having put these dangerous revolutionaries into power in the first place. Indeed, Labour showed by its behaviour during the 'Campbell Case'[36] that it was even prepared to countenance its own ejection from office if this would damage the Liberals. Relations between the two parties were little better between 1929 and 1931, when the Liberals, holding the balance of seats, once again installed Labour in government.

But there was more to Labour hostility than mere scepticism over whether a bargain with the Liberals was worth pursuing. In the mind of Henderson, the key Labour figure in the 1920s, the memory of the 'doormat incident' still rankled. Moreover, Lloyd George's cynical attacks on 'Bolshevism' during the coalition years had alienated nearly all Labour activists.[37] Finally, with the adoption of Clause 4, an ideological chasm now separated the two parties in an entirely new way.

Yet this was not really the main obstacle. 'Socialism', important at a rhetorical level, did not mean much in practice, and at Westminster there was still a great deal that the Liberals and the Socialists had in common. As we have seen, it was this very closeness of view which made for so much rivalry between the two parties. Conversely, Labour dreaded a Liberal revival more than it did the Conservative challenge, precisely because it realised that Liberals and Labour were, to some extent, 'fishing in the same pond' – in policy terms, at least.

The Liberals also caused offence, mainly unwittingly, by their patronising attitude towards the Labour Party, which they pitied for being so raw and inexperienced. Asquith's private reference to Labour's Commons performance in 1920 – the Labour people 'know as much about Parliamentary politics . . . as a hen does of Astrology'[38] – expressed a deep contempt which he scarcely bothered to conceal in public. Masterman's ostentatious 'coaching' of Labour ministers in 1924 also lacked tact (as did Keynes, who wanted some kind of 'alliance' with Labour, yet showered its spokesmen with ridicule for their stupidity and philistinism).[39] Most Labour politicians were very touchy on these matters, and MacDonald was speaking for many of his colleagues when, during the 1923 election, he compared the dishonourable behaviour of the Liberals with the Conservatives, who had at least fought like gentlemen.

Rational calculation and emotion alike suggested that Labour's policy should be one of treating individual Liberals considerately in the hope of persuading them to join its ranks, while treating the Liberal *Party* with bitter hostility. Since the Labour leaders believed the Liberal Party to be historically doomed, they were in any case tempted to behave in such a way as to make these predictions come true.

But even if Labour had proved more co-operative, it is not clear that this would have been acceptable to the bulk of the Liberal Party. The loss of several thousand disillusioned left-wing Radicals to Labour between 1917 and 1919 (one historian thinks that 2000 joined the ILP alone) had undoubtedly shifted the political centre of gravity within the Liberal Party.[40]

This quickly manifested itself at the level of political thought. Michael Freeden, author of a study of the Edwardian New Liberals, has noted how much less adventurous were what he calls the 'Centre Liberals' of the 1920s. The latter tended to treat economics as something lying outside the control of governments and of society. This more conservative intellectual approach was in part a reaction against wartime controls, but it was reinforced by the slump, which destroyed the earlier Liberal belief that the problem of production had been largely solved and all that now mattered was how to redistribute wealth. 'The grievances of today are mainly economic', said the authors of the *Liberal Industrial Inquiry*, popularly known as the 'Yellow Book'. In practice, this meant that Liberals sought to restore capitalism's lost dynamic (rediscovering 'economic man' in the process), while neglecting social reform: for they were reluctant to divert money from productive investment into welfare. The improvement of industrial relations, on the other hand, greatly interested Liberals – perhaps because it cost nothing! No one expressed this new emphasis better than the Liberal Party's most distinguished intellectual, John Maynard Keynes. It is particularly significant, thinks Freeden, that Keynes and his Summer School friends seem to have been totally unaware of many of the important pre-war writings of Hobson and Hobhouse. A challenging, even subversive, element in Liberal thought had, at least for the time being, disappeared.[41]

Indeed, far from wanting any kind of co-operation with Labour, a not inconsiderable number of Liberals after 1918 hoped to make resistance to socialism the cornerstone of their politics. Shocked by the astonishing success of the Labour Party in the 1919 municipal elections, the Liberals joined the Conservatives in many parts of the country, either forming 'anti-Socialist' parties, like the 'Hull Municipal Alliance', or operating an informal pact, as in the Bristol region, Merseyside, western Scotland, and parts of West Yorkshire.[42]

As pre-war events had shown, anti-socialist pacts did not necessarily mean that the Liberal Party's ability to contest parliamentary elections would be inhibited, still less that it would always side with the Conservatives in national politics.[43] However, in the twelve two-member 'territorial' constituencies which had survived the 1918 Redistribution, there was a strong tendency for the Liberal vote to be shared with the Conservatives rather than with Labour. This even happened in a city like Norwich, which, as we have seen, had been one of the boroughs in which the 'progressive alliance' had worked very effectively before 1914.[44] As a result, only nine of the Liberals who survived the debacle of 1924 had had to fight a genuine triangular contest; of the rest, all but two had been spared the ordeal of fighting a Conservative opponent.[45] In the long run, this boded ill for the future of the party.

Can we be more specific about where the Liberal Party's electoral support was located? This is difficult, since Liberalism meant different things in different parts of the country. Indeed, in one historian's opinion, the sporadic electoral successes which the Liberals enjoyed during the 1920s 'appear to have been partly fortuitous or the result of local initiative', not something which had much connection with the actions of the national leaders.[46] For example, the old Lib-Lab parliamentary pact largely survived in Preston throughout the 1920s,[47] in sharp contrast to what was happening in most other double-member constituencies. But an analysis of the general elections between 1918 and 1929 shows clearly that the regions in which the Liberals enjoyed the highest success rate were Rural Wales and the Scottish Highlands, followed by the South-West Peninsula (Cornwall and parts of Devon). It seems, in fact, as if constituencies with a very high percentage of the population working in agriculture were especially prone to elect Liberals. In 1923 the Liberals won nearly one-third of the country's most rural constituencies; in 1929, over 40 per cent of them.[48] By contrast, the party was generally weak in urban Britain, though it retained a powerful presence in some industrial towns, for example, Huddersfield, Middlesborough and Preston, as well as in Bethnal Green. Indeed, areas where the Liberal Party had hitherto been dominant, like Clydeside and South Wales, quickly became Liberal 'deserts', following Labour's breakthrough in the 1922 General Election.

The omens, then, were not very promising for the electoral chances of the Liberals, for the kind of constituencies where they performed best were few in number – their three strongest areas only returned thirty-two MPs in total. Labour and the Conservatives had a much stronger platform from which to launch their assault on power. This is what clearly lies behind the interesting statistic that, whereas the Liberals in the 1920s were quite successful in *winning* seats (they won 281, compared with Labour's 304 and the Conservatives' 445), their problem was rather one of *holding on to their gains*: in only 41 seats did they win in 4 or more contests, compared with 112 for Labour and 259 for the Conservatives.[49] Even in 1929, when the Liberals achieved a net gain of 19 seats, they still managed to lose 19 of the 40 seats which they had won in the disastrous election of 1924. In other words, the Liberals had nothing equivalent to Labour's mining seats or the Conservatives' strength in the wealthy suburban districts of Outer London. This put the Liberals at a permanent disadvantage in the sort of class-based politics which characterised Britain in the 1920s.

The Liberals liked to believe that they were able to transcend these class divisions with an appeal that reached out to all members of the community. This was true, up to a point; in 1923 the defence of Free Trade enabled them to pick up seats in both counties and towns in all regions of mainland Britain. At the same time, the Liberals could not, after 1922, boast many secure working-class seats. Where they were successful in working-class constituencies, this usually owed much to the personal popularity of a particular MP – for example, Percy Harris, who had built up a strong rapport with the poverty-stricken people of South-West Bethnal Green. As for municipal contests, Chris Cook has shown that in Manchester the Liberals actually enjoyed less success in poor working-class wards than the *Conservatives*, let alone Labour, and that they fared only slightly better in such wards in Leicester.[50] Indeed, there were times in the 1920s when the Liberals looked like becoming 'a bourgeois special interest party' – which was why they posed such a serious potential threat to the Conservatives.[51]

At the parliamentary level, too, Liberalism in the 1920s gives the appearance of being a party of the right rather than a party of the left. Only a handful of Liberal MPs throughout the decade came from the working class; Barnet Kenyon, a Primitive Methodist who was President of the Derbyshire Miners and MP for Chesterfield, was a highly untypical Liberal member. In sharp contrast to the PLP, the Liberal parliamentary party, like the women's organisation, clearly gave the impression of being an overwhelmingly middle-class body.[52]

The right-wing tendencies within Liberalism were exposed by the events of 1924. True, the leadership decided to allow MacDonald to create a minority ministry, but the decision was not popular in all quarters of the parliamentary party; ominously, ten Liberal MPs voted against the Liberal motion which destroyed Baldwin's government (another seven were absent unpaired).[53] Among the activists in the country, too, there was much dismay. Asquith had received a letter from five leading local businessmen in his Paisley constituency (both Liberals and Conservatives) appealing to him to keep Labour out of office, and when he ignored this advice the leading Liberal newspaper in the Glasgow area, the *Daily Record*, threw in its lot with the Unionists.[54]

Opinion among the Liberal MPs soon polarised. Time and again Liberal MPs found themselves going through different division lobbies. Lloyd George himself protested that Labour was behaving with shocking moderation, but a larger number were clearly unhappy about Labour being in office at all. These disaffected right-wing Liberals were already embarking on a political journey that would eventually take them out of the party altogether. When Parliament dissolved in October, many of these men were allowed by their Conservative friends to stage a straight fight against Labour. Of course, such behaviour disgusted most of the party's remaining working-class supporters in the country, who seem to have regarded it as a betrayal.

There were three further stages on this journey to the right. First, there was Lloyd George's Land Campaign of 1925–6, which alienated not only the old-fashioned stalwarts of Devon and Cornwall but also some of the party's wealthier members like Hilton Young and Alfred Mond, the great chemicals magnate, who responded by defecting to Conservatism.[55] Second, there was the 1926 General Strike when, despite the backing given to Baldwin's government by most senior Liberals, especially Asquith and Simon, some Liberals reached the conclusion that the enemies of Labour could not safely stay divided. In the immediate aftermath of the Strike the Conservatives managed to persuade several prominent members of the Leeds City Council (including the leader of the Liberal Group) to defect.[56] And finally there was the creation of the National Government in August 1931, when the 'Liberal Nationals', led by Simon, effectively abandoned the historic Liberal Party and joined forces with the Conservatives.

The General Strike was particularly disruptive to Liberalism because it forced the party to do what it had always tried to avoid: take sides in a stark confrontation between capital and labour. As we have seen, when this happened, Asquith took the former side, Lloyd George the latter. But the split was not confined to the leadership. For while many Liberals felt that the crisis obliged them to throw in their lot with the Conservatives, some genuine Radicals, including the Liberal MP for Central Hull, Commander Kenworthy, formally joined the Labour Party. It was (to use one of their own favourite metaphors) a classic example of the Liberals being crushed between the 'upper and nether millstones'.[57]

The Optimistic Case

But pessimism can be carried too far. In 1923 the Liberal vote fell only fractionally below Labour's: 4 311 147 as compared with 4 438 508. If one makes allowance for uncontested seats (eleven Liberal, as against three Labour), the two parties were virtually running neck and neck. In Scotland, the Liberals regained their old ascendancy over the Tories, winning twenty-two seats to their rivals' fourteen. True, the Free Trade issue may have artificially revived Liberal electoral fortunes in 1923, but the same had been said about the 1906 victory. There is something unsatisfactory about simply *assuming* that the Liberals were losers and then dismissing all their successes as 'aberrations'. True, the 1924 election was a disaster, but some good by-election performances, following the publication of the 'Yellow Book' in early 1928 (see below),[58] suggested that the electoral corner might have been turned. Indeed, in 1929 the Liberals polled more votes than ever before in their history, over five and a quarter million (admittedly on a wider franchise). The bias of the electoral system (of which more in a moment) cruelly disguised the underlying Liberal strength. Whatever socialist theory might predict, the Liberals took a long time to die – no wonder that they were viewed by their opponents (until late 1924 anyway) with such deep fear.

It is still less convincing to present Liberalism as a 'Victorian' creed, of no relevance to post-war needs. For example, the popularity of the League of Nations, acknowledged by both Labour and Conservative front benches, testified to the continuing vitality of an essentially liberal approach to the problems of international life – an approach which harmonised well with the aspirations of many of the new female voters.[59] Admittedly, in matters of economic management the Liberals were less favourably situated. Under Asquith's leadership the party gave the impression of living on past memories. But, as Masterman ruefully conceded, 'When Lloyd George came back to the party, ideas came back to the party.'[60] The first of the annual Summer Schools took place in 1921, when the movement was associated with Liberal intellectuals generally sympathetic to Asquith, but by the middle of the decade it was Lloyd George who was treating the Summer Schools as a kind of 'think-tank'.

Two groups can be identified in the Summer School movement. On the one hand, there was a group of radical Manchester businessmen, led by E. D. Simon, whose main interest lay in the restructuring of industry with a view to creating a more co-operative relationship between capital and labour. On the other, there were the Cambridge economists, led by

Hubert Henderson (who had replaced Massingham as editor of the revamped *Nation*) and John Maynard Keynes. To the latter group the primary task was the formulation of a reflationary financial and fiscal strategy, the implementation of which could lift the country out of Depression.[61] Both groups made their contribution to the so-called 'Yellow Book', *Britain's Industrial Future*, which, published in 1928, provided the Liberals with the economic proposals on which they fought the 1929 election. According to one historian, it was the most intellectually distinguished manifesto ever put before the British voters.[62]

More recently, economists who have fed the Liberal programme into a computer model of the economy have expressed scepticism over the Liberals' pledge to 'conquer' unemployment (Lloyd George spoke on the eve of the election of reducing it within the space of two years to 'normal dimensions'). Apart from anything else, in the absence of tariffs (and the Liberals remained a Free Trade party), a reflationary programme would probably have run quite quickly into severe balance of payments problems.[63] A question mark also hangs over the commitment of the party as a whole towards the implementation of the radical economic ideas that Lloyd George and his Summer School friends had imposed upon it.[64]

All the same, the Liberals had the energy and the boldness to confront what was an unprecedented economic situation, and they did at least try to do something about the slump, unlike their opponents, most of whom were sunk in apathetic fatalism. Lloyd George and his friends certainly went out of their way to make the electorate draw such a contrast. It was Socialists and Conservatives, mocked the Liberals, who were living in the past: 'We refuse ... to spend time or energy over the controversy between Individualism and Socialism. . . . If it ever were a real issue, it is certainly now obsolete.'[65] The fight between laissez-faire capitalism and socialism, claimed Lloyd George's circle, was anyhow a bogus fight: businesses had been 'socialising themselves', as more and more were converted into joint-stock companies, with the result that the capitalism which socialists were attacking had already been largely superseded – something which only a devotion to dogma prevented them from seeing.[66]

Underlying such gibes, of course, was the traditional Liberal belief that class divisions were either mischievous or unimportant. The 'Yellow Book' pitched its appeal to the intelligent and public-spirited from all social backgrounds – to people who were tired of class animosities and party political cries. But this studied 'classlessness' (an index of the party's own lack of a clear class base) should not be seen as an unmitigated weakness. As the Liberals themselves realised, there was a growing class of white-collar workers and professional people unable to identify with either the Labour Movement or with big business. The 'Yellow Book' tried to tap precisely this social grouping with its references to 'the "third party" in industry' (the managerial and technical staffs) who were being left out of the process of collective bargaining between organised bodies of employers and workpeople.[67] Finally, the very depth of bitterness aroused by such episodes as the General Strike created a widespread yearning for social and political reconciliation which the Liberals were better placed than the other parties to exploit.

In the view of the 'optimists', then, there is nothing 'inevitable' about Liberal decline, which came about, rather, as a result of a series of mistakes. Even as late as 1923–4, they claim, the Liberals still had a good chance to re-establish their credentials as a party of government. Certainly, at the start of 1924 Asquith seemed to have the ball at his feet. Indeed, it was widely predicted that since the Liberals held the balance of seats in the Commons and no new dissolution could take place for many months, it was quite possible that, perhaps following a short-lived Labour administration, the King would turn to Asquith to form a caretaker ministry, for, of the three party leaders (Baldwin and MacDonald being the other two), Asquith was quite the most experienced and able. That the Liberals would have been pushed back by the end of the year to the margins of the political system, with a mere forty MPs, was not an outcome which seemed 'inevitable' or even probable at the time, and only the wisdom of hindsight makes it seem so today.[68]

In the view of several historians, the real rot only set in after Asquith had made the fatal mistake of putting Labour into office. True, the Liberals, having just fought an election on the issue of Free Trade versus Protection, had little option but to throw their weight, for the time being, on the side of Labour, another Free Trade party, rather than prop up the Conservative administration. But neither Asquith (nor, indeed, Lloyd George) took sufficient account of the dangers they were running. At the least, they should have pressed Labour for an 'understanding' that could have formed a basis for their support of the new government. If, as seems probable, Labour had then refused to strike a deal, the public would at least have been left in no doubt as to who was responsible for the resulting deadlock.[69]

But if a failure of strategy did indeed take place, then this owed something to the bad relationship between the two Liberal factions, which found expression in internal wrangling and introspection, and militated against a cool appraisal of the wider political situation. Nor can this internal squabbling easily be accepted as a manifestation of deep-seated ideological fissures within Liberalism. True, the final split between Asquith and Lloyd George took place on an issue, the General Strike, involving two quite different conceptions of what Liberalism meant. But this was atypical. In any case, although on this occasion Lloyd George seemed to be articulating a 'radical', 'left-wing' point of view, *most* of the Liberals closely associated with the Welshman, like Freddie Guest and Sir William Edge, were on the right wing of the party and eventually landed up in the Conservative (or Liberal National) Party. Inasmuch as the Asquith–Lloyd George dispute was largely a personal vendetta, the Liberal Party can be said to have been the author of many of its own misfortunes.

But there is yet another way of looking at the subject. The question of whether or not the Liberal Party could have 'survived' depends very much on what one means by 'survival'. Given the 'first-past-the-post' system, there was little room for a Liberal Party which had sunk to the level of 'perpetual thirds'. But electoral reform would have transformed the Liberals' prospects. This is no mere debating point. For the Speakers Conference, whose Report laid the basis for the 1918 Representation of the People Act, *unanimously* recommended the adoption of Proportional Representation (PR) on the Single Transferable Vote (STV) system in all boroughs currently returning three or more MPs, while a majority also recommended the Alternative Vote (AV) in the remaining constituencies.

Unfortunately for the Liberals, Lloyd George, then Prime Minister, neither made these recommendations part of government policy nor even, when the matter came before the House, declared his own personal commitment to a fundamental change in the voting system in the way that he lent his authority to the enfranchisement of women. This probably accounted for the loss of the various PR amendments – one of which was defeated by only eight votes. An extremely confused parliamentary situation then developed, with much cross-party voting. To simplify slightly, the House of Lords resolved in favour of PR, the Commons insisted on replacing this with the AV, and eventually a compromise was reached, whereby PR was adopted for the seven university constituencies, while the status quo was otherwise maintained until further investigations had been made. By the time the matter was next reviewed, the majority of MPs had lost interest in change.[70]

In retrospect, it seems ironical that the Liberal leaders did not more quickly grasp the importance of electoral reform. Perhaps in 1918 Asquith could not have been expected to foresee the imminent Liberal decline which soon made this innovation so necessary. As for Lloyd George, he was understandably preoccupied in 1918 with the running of the war and had little leisure to study electoral reform; perhaps also he instinctively distrusted any change which would have meant the handing over of seats in rural North Wales, 'his' fiefdom, to the old Conservative enemy.[71] Whatever the explanation, the fact is that the Liberals, as a party, only became keen about electoral reform (they preferred PR but would have welcomed AV as a second best) during the course of 1924 when they started to worry in earnest about their long-term survival. But this very situation meant that Labour's former support for electoral reform quickly evaporated. Why should Labour have made its own quest for power more difficult by throwing out a life-line in the direction of the Liberals? True, the second Labour ministry did agree in 1930, under strong Liberal pressure, to agree to a scheme of AV, but the Bill embodying this was held up by the House of Lords and was lost when the government collapsed the following year. Consequently, against all expectations, the traditional electoral system managed to survive. No one could seriously claim that this outcome was in any way 'inevitable'.

Yet the consequences for the Liberals were serious. AV would have helped them considerably, since most Labour and Conservative voters would probably have chosen the Liberal candidate as their 'second choice'. It has been calculated that its likely effect would have been to raise the number of Liberal MPs from 159 to 217 in 1923, from 40 to 74 in 1924, and from 59 to 137 in 1929. PR would have been even more advantageous. The best informed guess is that it would have left the Liberals holding the balance of seats, not just in 1923 and 1929, but in 1922 and 1924 as well. Moreover, all such calculations probably underestimate likely Liberal gains, since a change in the electoral system would have altered political behaviour: the Liberals would have been encouraged to put up more candidates and, with the disappearance of the 'wasted vote' argument, electors would have been more likely to vote for them.[72] In these circumstances, Britain might well have had something resembling the political system of post-Second World War Germany, in which the 'Free Democrats' allied themselves sometimes with the Left and sometimes with the Right but stayed almost continuously in office. Would such a development have constituted a Liberal 'survival'?

However, there is yet another way in which the Liberal Party might have survived, albeit in a different guise. In the immediate post-war years, the Conservative Party did not look well equipped to cope with the Labour challenge. This was one reason why the life of the Lloyd George coalition had been extended in the first place. In Scotland, for example, the Unionists felt little confidence in their ability to go it alone in this traditionally Liberal terrain and so tended to support the coalition to the very end.[73] Moreover, the old issues which had formerly divided Conservatism from Liberalism seemed to many observers to have fallen into permanent abeyance. If this were so, how absurd for the two 'capitalist' parties to maintain their vendetta, thereby playing into the hands of a radicalised (some called it 'Bolshevik') Labour Movement. The obvious answer seemed to be a 'fusion' of 'Coalition Liberalism' and 'moderate' Conservatism within a new broad-based Centre Party: in other words, the 'national party' project re-emerged once more.

Lloyd George personally had a strong interest in encouraging such a political development. Having been partly responsible for splitting his own party, his personal survival depended upon splitting the Conservatives, too. Moreover, had the much-vaunted Centre Party come into existence, Lloyd George, its natural leader, would presumably have been Prime Minister for as long as his health held good.

Strangely enough, the Prime Minister was able in early 1920 to talk prominent Conservatives, even a somewhat reluctant Bonar Law, into endorsing such an initiative. But, more strangely still, when 'fusion' finally collapsed in March, it did so because of the hostility of most coalition *Liberal* MPs and ministers, the two groups which, one would have thought, had most to gain from the arrangement. The opportunity to restructure the party system never arose again – at least not until the 1980s. The Conservatives thereafter drifted more or less steadily away from the coalition towards independence, leaving Lloyd George in a very exposed position. The events at the Carlton Club in October 1922, when the Conservative MPs defied their leader, Austen Chamberlain, and voted to break with Lloyd George, finally put paid to the Coalition experiment itself.[74]

What, in retrospect, is so fascinating about the 'fusion' talks, however, is the element of accident which shaped the outcome. In his two meetings with his supporters, Lloyd George, normally so adroit and sensitive to the 'atmosphere' of his audience, seems to have presented his case ineptly, gratuitously alarming Liberals nervous of severing their links with the Liberal past. Some also disliked what they saw as an attempt 'to divide the nation into two camps, the "haves" and the "have nots"', a division which they thought 'would inevitably lead to a bitter class war'.[75]

In consequence, a chain of events was set off which eventually led to the establishment of a reunited but impotent Liberal Party. Liberalism itself, of course, did not disappear. Its Radical elements became incorporated into the moderate democratic socialism espoused by MacDonald's Labour Party, while its 'anti-socialist' strands formed an essential part of Baldwinian Conservatism. And this might be seen as testimony to the continuing resilience and vitality of the Liberal creed. But it was Liberalism without the Liberal Party. A long chapter of British history had come to an end.

10
CONCLUSION

In politics all success is ephemeral. Parties may achieve electoral triumphs and fulfil some of their goals, but they satisfy transient needs and in time, having lost their *raison d'être*, they are replaced. Sometimes this is disguised by the accident of institutional survival. There is a party which calls itself a Conservative Party today, just as there was in the 1840s; but little connects the two organisations except the name and a few hazy historical memories. Nor would Keir Hardie and other Labour pioneers easily recognise any affinities with the political party which bore the 'Labour' title in the 1980s, still less its 'New Labour' descendant. The once-mighty Liberal Party of Gladstone, Campbell-Bannerman, Asquith and Lloyd George served its turn before fading into insignificance. Does that make it any different from other political parties?

The Liberal Party's achievements during the Victorian and Edwardian periods were certainly substantial. For a start, in its heyday, it was highly successful at winning elections, being in power with only a few brief interruptions from 1846 to 1886, and then, despite a twenty-year period in the doldrums following the Home Rule split, re-emerged to win another three general elections in a row. Compare this record with that of the twentieth-century Labour Party which, before the triumph of Tony Blair's 'New Labour' in 1997, had won only two decisive victories at national level in nearly 100 years of existence. As an institution capable of winning power and keeping the Conservatives at bay, the Liberal Party has never (to date) had an adequate successor. Lloyd George therefore had a valid point when he warned in 1906: 'You are not going to make socialists in a hurry out of farmers and traders and professional men in this country, but you may scare them into reaction.'[1]

Moreover, the Liberal Party put its electoral success to effective use. It presided over the development of industrialisation, creating the conditions for spectacular economic growth. It helped 'modernise' society by removing or reforming older social practices and institutions that were weakening competitiveness. It helped establish a concept of citizenship and of individual rights and gave them a central position in political life. In the early twentieth century it also laid the foundations of what later became known as the 'Welfare State' (to use an anachronistic expression) by making public provision for certain categories of disadvantaged people: for example, the sick, the aged and the unemployed.

Paradoxically, the Liberals may eventually have weakened themselves by dint of their own successes – a common fate of reforming parties. For the more completely they removed 'abuses', the less intelligible their mission became. This particularly affected the always intimate relationship between Liberalism and Nonconformity. 'It is perhaps harder to be a Nonconformist today than it has ever been in the history of England', one of their divines said in 1897. 'The very decay of the disabilities from which our fathers suffered has made it harder for us than it was for them to dissent.'[2] The same was perhaps also true of the Liberals themselves. As we have seen, the end of the war brought about the long-awaited 'fall of feudalism' (though this owed more to agricultural depression and the impact of war than to the Liberals' own policies). Thereafter, the Liberal Party ceased to be a party of radical change; the sense of intellectual adventure was still there, as the work of the Summer Schools testified, but Liberals no longer sought fundamental institutional changes (except to the voting system) and their posture accordingly became a defensive rather than an aggressive one. But did this change of circumstances condemn the party to near-extinction?

Prophets of doom certainly existed from the 1880s onwards. Marxists predicted the inevitable triumph of the proletariat. Meanwhile many Conservatives, surveying what was happening on the Continent, concluded that Liberalism could not be reconciled with democracy and popular nationalism. Long before the Radical project had been completed (with Lloyd George's Budget and Land Campaign still to be launched), Radical Tories were mocking Liberalism as a 'Victorian' creed. In the aftermath of his party's defeat in 1906, George Wyndham, could write to his mother, lambasting 'the blatant, lower-middle-class, fraud, called Liberalism or "Free Trade"':

Two things – that are real – emerge: –
Labour and Imperialism.... I believe in my method. They believe in their
method.... But whether we are Socialists or Imperialists, we are living
men. The others are old women and senile professors.[3]

Such prognostications had two practical consequences. First, in times
of adversity like the early 1920s even Liberals sometimes wondered
whether Liberalism had outlived its usefulness; perhaps, they mused,
it was too noble a creed to prosper in the modern decadent world.
Second, such a view of politics encouraged members of the other
two parties to act in such a way as to make their predictions of Liberal
decline come true. For example, Maurice Cowling has argued that in
the late summer of 1924 the minority Labour Government 'colluded'
with the Conservative Opposition in engineering its own defeat, know-
ing that in the resulting general election the Liberals would be the
real losers.[4] Irritated at the 'survival' of a party they believed to be historically doomed, Labour showed in 1924 that it was prepared to put up
with a (hopefully temporary) loss of office and reduction of representation if this extinguished the recent Liberal revival. The Conservatives
showed similar animosity. L. S. Amery warned Baldwin in December
1923 not in any circumstances to offer any support to the Liberals:
'the real healthy and *natural* [my emphasis] division of parties in this
country is between constructive Conservatism on the one side and
on the other Labour-Socialism'.[5] Contrary to the popular view that the
Liberals committed suicide, there is a strong case for saying that they
were murdered.

Yet the spectacle of Liberal decline in other countries also had
the effect of stimulating the Liberals into working hard to save their
own skins. Some drew a 'conservative' moral: 'The fate of the Liberal
Party, unless experience teaches it wisdom, will doubtless be that of
the German National Liberal Party which coquetted with Socialism
till Socialism, grown strong, destroyed it as a political force.'[6] But
the possibility that, in Rosebery's words, Liberalism would disappear
'leaving the two forces of socialism and Reaction face to face',[7] spurred
many Liberals, Lloyd George included, into trying to modernise the
party's programme.

Before that enterprise is dismissed as an impossibility, it is worth
remembering that the Conservatives were not necessarily better placed
than the Liberals to cope with social and economic change. Indeed,
still over-dependent on the landed classes, Edwardian Conservatives
had good reasons for fearing the advent of 'democracy'; yet they

successfully refurbished their image and broadened their appeal. Why, despite all their efforts, could the Liberals not do likewise?

To the generation of historians growing up in the aftermath of the Liberals' humiliations in the early 1930s, the answer presented few difficulties. Liberal failure seemed to have been preordained – not just for the reasons given by Marxists – but because by this time Liberalism itself had taken on a dated appearance. The great Liberal statesmen of the Victorian and Edwardian eras now looked, to those whose memories of the period were non-existent or vague, both quaint and absurd – custodians of an old-fashioned creed with an aura surrounding it redolent of top hats and mutton-chop whiskers. Mocking the values and idols of one's parents' generation is, of course, a favourite pastime of the young. It is precisely such an attitude which inform George Dangerfield's famous book, *The Strange Death of Liberal England*, first published in 1935, which combines a modishly psychological interpretation of the subject (England on the eve of the Great War was experiencing a 'nervous breakdown') with a sub-Lytton Strachey vein of 'debunking'.[8] Of course, the wheel has now turned full circle, and in many ways Dangerfield's book seems much more of a period piece than the objects of his mockery.

However, in the 1960s and 1970s a belief in the obsolescence of Liberal values gained new adherents, not just among those caught up in the renewed interest in Marxist theory. Historians of various political persuasions tried to demonstrate that, in the Edwardian years in particular, Britain had shared in the same 'crisis' which had afflicted many continental states, particularly Germany, and, like them, had seen a determined assault on older liberal practices and values. Accordingly, historians made their readers' flesh creep with their lurid accounts of 'anti-Liberal' ideologies, chronicling not only the rise of revolutionary socialism but also bringing out the contemporary importance of 'Radical Right' causes such as National Efficiency, Imperialism, militarism and eugenics.

This was a healthy reaction against an earlier view of the past which had rather smugly emphasised Britain's virtuous attachment to parliamentary institutions and its good fortune in being insulated from the murderously 'illiberal' ideologies which were wreaking havoc on the Continent. But this historiographic reaction may have gone too far. After all, the Edwardian 'crisis of Liberalism' was a relatively minor affair: the impotent rage of opponents unable to dislodge a popular Liberal Party from office. Liberalism, to use a Gramscian phrase, was still the hegemonic creed – a position which, in a way, it never subsequently lost. True, the later abandonment of Free Trade in 1931–2 represented a repudiation of a cardinal liberal belief. But most other elements of the creed survived. In fact, to this very day, few British politicians of any substance have chosen to assault liberal values head-on, and those who have done so (Oswald Mosley comes particularly to mind) have not fared well.

Indeed, far from Liberalism having become discredited, it is easier to argue the opposite: namely, that because most liberal beliefs and values came to be so widely accepted there seemed no need for a separate party to campaign on their behalf. By the 1920s it could almost be claimed that 'We are all Liberals now.' After all, both Labour and Conservatives drew heavily upon the Liberal tradition. Writing about the late 1920s, Michael Bentley has drawn attention to this paradox: 'Everyone believed in liberalism but no one would actually vote for it.'[9] Ten years later even a Communist and Marxist like Stephen Spender, who wanted to go 'forward from Liberalism', did not propose to abandon it – appropriately enough, since his father and uncle had both been prominent Liberal journalists, on close terms with the party leadership. Writing in 1937, Spender could dismiss Liberal politicians with contempt as 'capitalist hirelings',[10] but the classless society he advocated was to be an extension of the Liberal state, not a complete repudiation of it. Peter Clarke goes further. The post-Second World War Labour Party, in his view, was an uneasy coalition of socialists, trade unionists and 'social democrats', in which the latter, the inheritors of the Liberal tradition, had simply attached themselves to Labour because the decline of the Liberal Party had, for the time being, left them with no alternative.[11]

There are, in any case, two ways of approaching Liberalism. It can be seen as an economic theory expressing the interests of a particular social class. Alternately, its main mission may have been the creation of social conditions in which individuals had the greatest possible chance of self-realisation, in which case, as Michael Balfour has argued, Liberalism 'is a permanent rather than a transient creed, which changes its detailed aims from period to period in accordance with changes in the general environment'.[12] And if this be true, then there seems no *necessary* reason why the party with which it was identified could not have survived.

Yet by 1935 the Liberal Party *had* self-evidently all but disappeared as a significant force in British politics. Why did this happen and at what point did the process of Liberal decline become irreversible?

Basically, the explanations furnished by historians fall under three heads. Some see the party's collapse as the consequence of a deep moral or ideological crisis, a loss of belief in Liberalism as a creed; they accordingly emphasise the emergence of a 'revisionist' school in the 1890s (i.e. Liberal Imperialism), the later cult of efficiency, the 1910 Secret Coalition talks, and, of course, the damage wrought by the 'rampant omnibus'. Other historians draw attention to class divisions, though they disagree over the timing of the Labour Party's crucial breakthrough: was it the formation of the LRC in 1900, the return of twenty-nine Labour MPs in 1906, the Great Labour Unrest of 1911–14, or the industrial conflicts which culminated in the 1926 General Strike? By contrast, a third historical school (the 'accidentalists') emphasises matters of contingency, individual decision and chance. Would the Liberal Party, they ask, have floundered so badly in the 1890s but for Gladstone's Home Rule bombshell? Or might Liberalism have bounced back in the 1920s but for the fateful 'mistake' of putting Labour into office in early 1924? Moreover, the Liberals, note the 'accidentalists', seriously injured their own party by the quarrels which rent the leadership in the 1890s involving those three prima donnas, Harcourt, Rosebery and Morley, followed a quarter of a century later by the implacable vendetta waged between the followers of Asquith and Lloyd George.

These are complex issues about which historians are unlikely ever to agree. It is particularly difficult to guess what might have happened but for the outbreak of the Great War. The following observations, then, are only personal ones.

Winston Churchill rightly observed in 1906: 'War is fatal to Liberalism.'[13] The Great War did, indeed, inflict great damage on the party, but not so much as to prevent a subsequent recovery. In the 1918 general election the two halves of the divided Liberal Party polled over 350 000 more votes than Labour, which was perhaps significant, given the edgy relationship between many 'Lloyd George Liberals' and the Conservative Party and the widespread belief (especially in Scotland) that the coalition was only a temporary arrangement.[14]

It is therefore tempting to assume that the Liberal Party's collapse was due to some more profound cause, perhaps an inability to adapt to changes in the structure of capitalism. An examination of the backgrounds of Liberal businessmen lends some support to this contention. Right through its history, the party made an appeal to 'petit-bourgeois' groups, like small shopkeepers, who belonged to a dwindling sector of the economy. Moreover, though the Liberals continued to do well in the manufacturing districts of northern England, from an early stage they lost the confidence of people engaged in the financial services sector: no Liberal was ever returned for the City of London constituency after 1880.

Yet this does not mean that by the start of the new century the Liberals lacked support in the world of corporate capitalism. For example, the great industrialist Alfred Mond, the creator of ICI, did not desert the Liberal Party for Conservatism until 1925. Indeed, Mond's case is also a reminder of Liberalism's formidable powers of adaptation. Traditionally, Liberals had been proponents of a market ideology, which extolled competition and sought to maximise its scope. This continued to be the case. But some Liberals, like Mond himself, had come out by the 1920s in favour of a 'managed capitalism' and were advocates of 'rationalisation' – which they saw, in quintessentially liberal terms, as a way of tempering the excesses of competition by the application of reason and science.[15] A similar emphasis marked the Liberals' Industrial Inquiry in the late 1920s. In this way early twentieth-century Liberalism bequeathed to posterity a legacy of laissez-faire (to be revived by 'neo-Liberals' like Hayek in later decades), while also providing a rationale for economic planning and pioneering the welfare capitalism which dominated the political agenda of Britain (and many other industrialised countries) in the period following the Second World War.

Unfortunately for the Liberals, they seem to have been slower to grasp the *political* implications of the emergence of the corporate economy. For example, whereas J. C. C. Davidson, the Chairman of the Conservative Party, made great efforts to tap the big industrial and financial companies in the run-up to the 1929 general election, the Liberals continued, despite the 'Million Fund', to look to sympathetic entrepreneurs to replenish their central war chest.[16] This was unsatisfactory, not least because many of these wealthy subscribers were looking for 'recognition'. The Liberals were unwise to have risked incurring another 'Honours Scandal' like the one which had so damaged Lloyd George's reputation in 1922. Unwilling or unable to modernise their fund-raising methods, the Liberals therefore became stuck in what one historian has called the 'Plutocratic Era', without properly making the transition to the class-based system adopted by Labour (reliant on trade union subventions) and by the Conservatives (closely connected to big business).

But this, in turn, takes us on to what was perhaps the Achilles' Heel of Liberalism: its particular attitude towards class. 'The Liberal Party is not to-day, it never has been, and so long as I have any connection with it, it never will be, the party of any class, rich or poor, great or small, numerous or sparse in its composition. We are a party of no class', Asquith was still defiantly telling the faithful in 1921.[17] Lloyd George did not dissent. To quote from a historian who has made a specialised study of Preston: 'The Liberals remained essentially populist, being unable to make any specific appeals to members of the working class as such, and this allowed leading Liberals to present themselves as leaders of a popular coalition which did not in fact exist.'[18]

Now, admittedly, it was a convention of British political life, observed by all Conservatives and many Socialists, that parties should disclaim any exclusive association with a single social class. Even Ramsay MacDonald, the socialist, took this line.[19] Yet no one could doubt where the sympathy of the Labour and socialist movement lay. The Conservative Party provided a mirror image of this. Leaders like Baldwin denounced 'class politics' as essentially 'un-English', a foreign commodity imported from Russia. But while managing to attract a considerable working-class following, the Conservatives owed most of their electoral success to the skill with which they played upon middle-class anxieties. This meant that they were able both to have their cake and eat it.

But the Liberals had little chance of pulling off a similar trick. Theoretically, they could have consolidated their position as the party which traditionally most manual workers supported by establishing formal links with the trade union movement, while at the same time protesting their devotion to the interests of the 'nation' as a whole. But though they were willing to reformulate their programme in order to accommodate the new welfare issues, the Liberals could not bring themselves to make any very great effort to place significant numbers of working-class candidates in winnable seats.

Moreover, whereas the Conservative Party enjoyed close ties with big business (though it was usually deemed prudent not to draw public attention to this fact), the Liberals continued, right until the end, to have very ambivalent feelings about trade unionism. In most of the big industrial disputes of the period, the Liberals were at best neutral and more often hostile to the cause of the strikers. This allowed the Labour Party to establish itself in the affections of many working-class communities. And as Labour extended its organisation in the 1920s, the old working-class Liberal vote atrophied. True, the rise of Labour also created hostility to socialism which the Liberal Party might have exploited; indeed, many of their municipal and parliamentary candidates did precisely this. Yet, when all is said and done, by the 1920s the

Conservatives were better placed than the Liberals to function as a 'party of resistance'; for, in Ross McKibbin's words, 'it was *known* that the Conservative Party was the party of bourgeois propriety and dignity'.[20]

Even so, electoral reform could still have saved the Liberals. But luck was not on their side. The traditional 'first-past-the-post' system militates against a third party acquiring a representation commensurate with its national vote. The narrow failure to carry either the Alternative Vote or Proportional Representation at the end of the Great War therefore left the Liberals in a very weak position, while the bungled attempt at 'fusion' in the spring of 1920 shut off the possibility of a rather different kind of comeback.

Finally, the Asquith–Lloyd George feud further weakened the party at a crucial historical turning point, for the collapse of the coalition ushered in a confused phase of three-party politics between 1922 and 1924, the outcome of which could not easily be foreseen. Yet the Liberals, given a great opportunity in early 1924, had blown their chances before the end of the year. By the time the party had reorganised itself around a new leader and a new programme, it was too late to break up the Conservative–Labour duopoly presided over by MacDonald and Baldwin. Despite the creation of the 'Alliance' in the 1980s and the subsequent formation of the Liberal Democrats, this is still, in essence, the political system within which we are living.

NOTES

1 Introduction

1. Wilson, T., *The Downfall of the Liberal Party, 1914–1935* (London, 1966), pp. 15–16.
2. Clarke, P. F., 'The electoral position of the Liberal and Labour parties, 1910–1914', *English Historical Review*, 90 (1975), 828–36.
3. Though Roy Douglas has written a mischievous article, 'Labour in Decline, 1910–14', in Brown, K. D. (ed.), *Essays in Anti-Labour History* (London, 1974), pp. 105–25.
4. Cooke, A. B. and Vincent, J., *The Governing Passion: Cabinet Government and Party Politics 1885–86* (Brighton, 1974), p. 164.
5. See the first three essays in Langan, M. and Schwarz, B. (eds), *Crises in the British State 1880–1930* (London, 1985), which provide a more sophisticated 'modern' Marxist reading of the turn-of-the-century British Liberal Party.
6. The most important book in this 'school' is that of Clarke, P. F., *Lancashire and the New Liberalism* (Cambridge, 1971). This interpretation is examined later in the book, esp. in Chapter 6.
7. For example, Roy Douglas was a prominent Liberal activist in the 1960s, standing on five occasions as a Liberal parliamentary candidate, an experience which in places colours *The History of the Liberal Party, 1895–1970* (London, 1971).
8. See Chapter 8.
9. See Chapter 9.
10. A useful survey of the literature, which focuses on the Edwardian period, is Thompson, J. A., 'The Historians and the Decline of the Liberal Party', *Albion*, 22 (1990), 65–83.
11. The best starting point for an exploration of the methodological assumptions underlying such an approach would be Patrick Joyce's important (but difficult) *Visions of the People: Industrial England and the question of class, 1848–1914* (Cambridge, 1991), esp. Ch. 2. Eugenio Biagini's work falls broadly within the same tradition – see the next chapter.

2 The Rise of the Liberal Party

1. Inglis, K. S., 'Patterns of Religious Worship in 1851', *Journal of Ecclesiastical History*, 11 (1960), esp. 82–6; see also Pickering, W. S. F., 'The 1851 religious census – A useless experiment', *British Journal of Sociology*, 18 (1967), 403–5.

2. Scotland's situation differed in that those who upheld and those who opposed the established Presbyterian Kirk otherwise professed the same faith.

3. In any case, the removal of Nonconformist disabilities did not immediately obliterate them as political issues. Alfred Illingworth, the Bradford mill owner, a Congregationalist who later became a Liberal MP, singled out the requisitioning of his father's goods in 1866 (for non-payment of church rates) as the most important factor in determining his own political career (Jowitt, T., 'Patterns of Religion in Victorian Bradford', in Wright, D. G. and Jowitt, J. A. [eds], *Victorian Bradford* [London, 1981], p. 42).

4. Barker, M., *Gladstone and Radicalism: The Reconstruction of Liberal Policy in Britain 1885–1894* (Hassocks, 1975), p. 39.

5. Taylor, A. J. P., *The Trouble Makers: Dissent over Foreign Policy 1792–1939* (London, 1957). For a more nuanced account of the mid-Victorian years, see Taylor, M., *The Decline of British Radicalism, 1847–1860* (Oxford, 1995).

6. Cobden to F. Cobden, 11 Sept. 1838, in Morley, J., *The Life of Richard Cobden* (London, 1881; 1896 ed.), Vol. I, p. 130.

7. There were important respects, however, in which Chamberlain differed markedly from Cobden. See below and Ch. 4.

8. For example, Edward Baines of Leeds, the leader of the 'voluntaryists', which comprised those Dissenters who wanted education to be entirely separate from the state.

9. Hurst, M., 'Liberal Versus Liberal: The General Election of 1874 in Bradford and Sheffield', *Historical Journal*, 15 (1972), 669. Among the early defectors from within the northern business community were H. W. Ripley of Bradford and Edward Akroyd of Halifax. The latter had always been an Anglican; the former left the Congregational Chapel in which he had been brought up for the Church of England.

10. Howe, A., *The Cotton Masters 1830–1860* (Oxford, 1984), esp. Ch. 7.

11. On Whiggery's capacity to survive and adapt, see Jenkins, T. A., *Gladstone, Whiggery and the Liberal Party 1874–1886* (Oxford, 1988); Parry, J., *The Rise and Fall of Liberal Government in Victorian Britain* (New Haven and London, 1993). An older, but still very valuable, study of the subject is Southgate, D., *The Passing of the Whigs 1832–1886* (London, 1962).

12. John Vincent, *Pollbooks: How Victorians Voted* (Cambridge, 1967), *passim*.

13. Lubenow, W. C., *Parliamentary Politics and the Home Rule Crisis: The British House of Commons in 1886* (Oxford, 1988), pp. 178–82.

14. Jenkins, *Gladstone, Whiggery*, p. 3, fn. 10.

15. It has been argued that this coolness of temper was more a characteristic of 'true' Liberalism than Gladstonian 'enthusiasm'. See Parry, *Liberal Government*.

16. A Cornish squire, Sir John Trelawny, was the parliamentary leader of the agitation against church rates, but he baulked at Disestablishment. See

Jenkins, T. A. (ed.), *The Parliamentary Diaries of Sir John Trelawny 1858–1865* (London, 1990).

17. Bagehot, W., *The English Constitution* (London, 1867; Fontana edn, 1963), p. 175.
18. Perkin, H., *The Origins of Modern English Society 1780–1880* (London, 1969; 1972 edn), p. 380. Gladstone's life has been dextrously covered in the one-volume biography by Roy Jenkins, *Gladstone* (London and Basingstoke, 1995). For more detailed treatment of his later career, see two excellent, but very different, accounts: Matthew, H. C. G., *Gladstone 1875–1898* (Oxford, 1995) and Shannon, R., *Gladstone: Heroic Minister 1865–1898* (Harmondsworth, 1999).
19. Biagini, E. F., *Liberty, Retrenchment and Reform: Popular Liberalism in the Age of Gladstone, 1860–1880* (Cambridge, 1992).
20. Biagini, E. F., 'Popular Liberals, Gladstonian finance, and the debate on taxation, 1860–1874', in Biagini, E. F. and Reid, A. J. (eds), *Currents of Radicalism: popular radicalism, organised labour and party politics in Britain, 1850–1914* (Cambridge, 1991), pp. 137–8.
21. Joyce, P., *Visions of the People: Industrial England and the question of class, 1848–1914* (Cambridge, 1991), p. 49.
22. Barker, *Gladstone and Radicalism*, pp. 250–1. Steele, E. D., 'Gladstone and Ireland', *Irish Historical Studies*, 17 (1970–1), 58–88.
23. Southgate, *Whigs*, p. 372.
24. Ibid., p. 374. But note Jenkins's point: that 'if the Irish question was going to provoke a split in the Liberal party simply along "class" lines, it would have happened in 1881' (Jenkins, *Gladstone, Whiggery*, p. 172).
25. Hunter, J., 'The Politics of Highland Land Reform, 1873–1895', *Scottish Historical Review*, 53 (1974), 45–68.
26. Dissenters particularly resented Clause 25 of the Education Act, which provided that children from the workhouses should be sent, at the ratepayers' expense, to a local school, which in practice was often an Anglican school. A Conservative government later repealed this clause in 1876.
27. For the view that Chamberlain was willing to make an accommodation with Hartington and was not primarily concerned with driving him out of the party, see Jenkins, *Gladstone, Whiggery*, p. 195. But that is not to say that Chamberlain, in his eagerness to impose his will on the Liberal Party, might not have been quite willing to run the risk of a Whig secession.
28. Hamer, D. A. (ed.), *The Radical Programme*, with a Preface by J. Chamberlain, 1885 (Hassocks, 1971).
29. See Jones, G. S., *Outcast London* (Oxford, 1971).
30. Armytage, W. H. G., *A. J. Mundella 1825–1897: The Liberal Background to the Labour Movement* (London, 1951). A controversial account of what the author claims to be an early version of 'New Liberalism' is provided in Finn, Margot C., *After Chartism: Class and nation in English radical politics, 1848–1874* (Cambridge, 1993), Ch. 7.
31. Spinner, T. J., *George Joachim Goschen: The Transformation of a Victorian Liberal* (Cambridge, 1973). There were many other 'conservative' businessmen who by the 1880s were beginning to lose confidence in Gladstone and the Liberal Party, like Nathan de Rothschild, Liberal MP for Aylesbury. On the political perspectives of the 'railway interest', see Ch. 4.

32. Roach, J., 'Liberalism and the Victorian Intelligentsia', *Cambridge Historical Journal*, 13 (1957), 58–81; Harvie, C., *The Lights of Liberalism: University Liberals and the Challenge of Democracy, 1860–86* (London, 1976); Dunne, T., 'La trahison des clercs: British intellectuals and the first home-rule crisis', *Irish Historical Studies*, 23 (1982–3), 134–73.

33. Perkin, H. J., 'Land Reform and Class Conflict in Victorian Britain', in Butt, J. and Clarke, I. F. (eds), *The Victorians and Social Protest* (Newton Abbot, 1973), pp. 177–217.

34. Southgate, *Whigs*, p. 389.

35. See Roach, 'Liberalism and the Victorian Intelligentsia'; Harvie, *Lights of Liberalism* and Dunne, 'La trahison des clercs'. Among the defectors were A. V. and Edward Dicey, W. E. H. Lecky, James Fitzjames Stephen and Henry Sidgwick. But others, notably James Bryce, stayed loyal to official Liberalism.

36. There are numerous accounts of the Irish Crisis and the party realignment. A good starting point might be Hamer, D. A., *Liberal Politics in the Age of Gladstone and Rosebery* (Oxford, 1972), Chs. 5–6. Aspects of the subject are examined at greater length in the following two chapters.

3 The Assault on Feudalism, 1886–1905

1. In Scotland the Liberal Unionists comprised both the most cautious of Whigs and the most fiery of Radicals. The 'crofters', for example, can be found on both sides of the divide. See Savage, D. C., 'Scottish Politics, 1885–6', *Scottish Historical Review*, 40 (1961), 118–35, and Hutchison, I. G. C., *A Political History of Scotland 1832–1924* (Edinburgh, 1986), pp. 162–8, 171.

2. Labouchere to Chamberlain, 15 April 1886, in Thorold, A. L., *The Life of Henry Labouchere* (London, 1913), p. 291.

3. Joseph Chamberlain to Arthur Chamberlain (his brother), 8 March 1886, in Garvin, J. L., *The Life of Joseph Chamberlain, Vol. 2* (London, 1933), p. 185.

4. Barker, M., *Gladstone and Radicalism: The Reconstruction of Liberal Policy in Britain 1885–94* (Hassocks, 1975), pp. 173–4.

5. During the 1885 general election Parnell issued his 'Vote Tory' manifesto, urging the Irish on mainland Britain to vote for Conservative rather than for Liberal candidates – a course of action which many Irishmen were anyhow predisposed to take because of their educational beliefs. It is difficult to estimate how many seats may have changed hands as a result of this appeal, but Liberals thought it responsible for many of their losses. The resulting bitterness did not make it any easier for Gladstone to 'sell' Home Rule to his party a few months later.

6. Admittedly, Professor Lubenow, in examining the 1885–6 Parliament, concludes that there was already considerable agreement on policy between the Radical–Liberals and the Irish Nationalists, prior to Gladstone's commitment to Home Rule (W. C. Lubenow, *Parliamentary Politics and the Home Rule Crisis: The British House of Commons in 1886* [Oxford, 1988], pp. 157–8).

7. Bebbington, D. W., *The Nonconformist Conscience: Chapel and Politics 1870–1914* (London, 1982), p. 90.

8. Hutchison, *Scotland*, pp. 162–3.
9. Bebbington, *Nonconformist Conscience*, p. 99.
10. Ibid., p. 103; Matthew, H. C. G., *The Liberal Imperialists: The ideas and politics of a Post-Gladstonian élite* (Oxford, 1973), p. 270; Machin, G. I. T., *Politics and the Churches in Great Britain 1869–1921* (Oxford, 1987), pp. 226–7.
11. Hamer, D. A., *Liberal Politics in the Age of Gladstone and Rosebery* (Oxford, 1972), Ch. 6; Hamer, D. A., 'The Irish Question and Liberal Politics, 1886–1894', *Historical Journal*, 12 (1969), 511–32.
12. Barker, *Gladstone and Radicalism*, p. 235; Stansky, P., *Ambitions and Strategies: The Struggle for the Leadership of the Liberal Party in the 1890s* (Oxford, 1964), pp. 1–2.
13. Howarth, J., 'The Liberal Revival in Northamptonshire, 1880–1895: A Case Study in Late Nineteenth Century Elections', *Historical Journal*, 12 (1969), 101.
14. Biagini, E. F., *Liberty, Retrenchment and Reform: Popular Liberalism in the Age of Gladstone, 1860–1880* (Cambridge, 1992), p. 424.
15. Bebbington, *Nonconformist Conscience*, p. 92. See also Pelling, H., *Social Geography of British Elections 1885–1910* (London, 1967), pp. 220, 163.
16. Matthew, *Liberal Imperialists*, p. 271.
17. The Liberal Imperialists were divided amongst themselves over whether it was best to postpone Home Rule or to abandon it altogether (Matthew, *Liberal Imperialists*, Ch. 8). Their stand did persuade a few former Liberals, like the Duke of Sutherland, to return to the fold (ibid., p. 98). See Gutzke, D. W., 'Rosebery and Ireland, 1898–1903: A Reappraisal', *Bulletin of the Institute of Historical Research*, 53 (1980), 88–98.
18. On Radical protests at Rosebery's assumption of the premiership, see Stansky, *Ambitions*, p. 80. Similarly in Scotland, where the great landowners remaining loyal to official Liberalism included Rosebery, Elgin and Aberdeen (Hutchison, *Scotland*, p. 163).
19. Loughlin, J., *Gladstone, Home Rule and the Ulster Question 1882–93* (Dublin, 1986), esp. pp. 184–91.
20. Professor Lubenow is keen to deny any connection between social class and voting on the Home Rule Bill. But his own statistics suggest that 37 per cent of Liberal landowning MPs opposed Gladstone in 1886, as compared with 29 per cent of all Liberal MPs (*Home Rule Crisis*, p. 200). See also the table on p. 205, showing that peers and Whigs were disproportionately likely to oppose Home Rule.
21. Howarth, 'Liberal Revival', 105; Goodman, G. L., 'Liberal Unionism: The Revolt of the Whigs', *Victorian Studies*, 3 (1959–60), 173–89.
22. Barker, *Gladstone and Radicalism*, p. 113. But Gladstone also referred to 'a small minority of wealthy men'.
23. Many examples of such co-operation can be found in Hollis, P., *Ladies Elect: Women in English Local Government, 1865–1914* (Oxford, 1987). For the reluctance of former Liberals, hostile to Home Rule, to abandon their Liberal affiliations, see Lubenow, W. C., 'The Liberals and the National Question: Irish Home Rule, Nationalism, and its Relationship to Nineteenth-Century Liberalism', *Parliamentary History*, 13 (1994), 136–40.
24. In fact, before the 'Newcastle Programme', the Liberal Unionists in the Lords voted with the Liberals more often than with the Conservatives:

only slowly did the Unionist Alliance cohere, partly as result of changes in Conservative policy (Phillips, G. D., 'The Whig Lords and Liberalism, 1886–93', *Historical Journal*, 28 [1981], 168–72).

25. Lee, J. M., 'Parliament and the Appointment of Magistrates: the Origins of Advisory Committees', *Parliamentary Affairs*, 13 (1959–60), 85–94; Phillips, G. D., *The Diehards: Aristocratic Society and Politics in Edwardian England* (Cambridge, Mass., 1979), pp. 60–8.

26. Barker, *Gladstone and Radicalism*, pp. 89–92. But Barker also shows how conservative Gladstone was on the land question, attacking Harcourt's Budget, though he accepted graduated taxation on income derived from ground rents (ibid., pp. 250–1).

27. Douglas, R., *Land, People and Politics: A History of the Land Question in the United Kingdom, 1878–1952* (London, 1976), pp. 106–7.

28. Russell, A. K., *Liberal Landslide; the General Election of 1906* (Newton Abbot, 1973), p. 65.

29. Phillips, 'Whig Lords', 168–72.

30. Ramsden, J., *The Age of Balfour and Baldwin, 1902–1940* (London, 1978), p. 98.

31. Bebbington, D. W., 'Nonconformity and Electoral Sociology, 1867–1918', *Historical Journal*, 27 (1984), 643–6.

32. Machin, *Politics and the Churches*, p. 206; Bernstein, G. L., *Liberalism and Liberal Politics in Edwardian England* (London, 1986), p. 18: over 40 per cent, according to Bernstein.

33. Koss, S., *Nonconformity in Modern British Politics* (London, 1975), p. 230.

34. Taking the 1892 election and the two elections of 1910, in which the Liberal Party did well but not spectacularly so, the English regions where the Liberals achieved the highest percentage of possible wins were: the North-East (78 per cent), the West Riding (72 per cent), the East Midlands (63 per cent), Eastern Lancastria (59 per cent), the South-West Peninsula (57 per cent) and East Anglia (55.5 per cent). All these regions bar Eastern Lancastria contained populous Nonconformist communities.

35. Koss, *Nonconformity*, pp. 28–30; Bebbington, *Nonconformist Conscience*, Ch. 4.

36. Chamberlain to Devonshire, 22 Sept. 1902, Amery, J., *Life of Joseph Chamberlain*, Vol. 4 (London, 1951), p. 496.

37. On Lloyd George's early life, see Grigg, J., *The Young Lloyd George* (London, 1973); George, W. R. P., *Lloyd George Backbencher* (Gomer, 1983). See also Machin, G. T. I., 'Lloyd George and Nonconformity', in Loades, J. (ed.), *The Life and Times of David Lloyd George* (Bangor, 1991), pp. 33–47.

38. Morgan, K. O., *Wales in British Politics 1868–1922* (Cardiff, 1970), pp. 217–18; Machin, *Politics and the Churches*, p. 269.

39. Morgan, *Wales*, pp. 189–91.

40. Bebbington, *Nonconformist Conscience*, p. 144.

41. The Unionist Ministry had bowed to the insistence of Lord Milner, High Commissioner in South Africa, that indentured Chinese labourers should be brought in to work in the goldmines of the Witwatersrand, to replace the 'Kaffirs' who had disappeared during the course of the recent war. The decision was attacked by the Opposition parties (Labour as well as the Liberals) on both economic and humanitarian grounds; the Chinese

178 Notes

workers, they complained, were to all intents and purposes, living in a condition of 'slavery'.

42. Bebbington, *Nonconformist Conscience*, p. 8.
43. Russell, *Liberal Landslide*, pp. 184–5.
44. Bebbington, *Nonconformist Conscience*, p. 77; Koss, *Nonconformity*, p. 59.
45. Matthew, *Liberal Imperialists*, esp. Ch. 7.
46. Hutchison, *Scotland*, pp. 235–6.
47. 'French vices do not find favour with the women of England', the WLF declared. See Walker, L., 'Party Political Women: A Comparative Study of Liberal Women and the Primrose League, 1890–1914', in Rendall, J. (ed.), *Equal or Different: Women's Politics 1800–1914* (Oxford, 1987), pp. 176–7. The WLF is discussed at greater length in Ch. 7.
48. Glaser, J. F. 'English Nonconformity and the Decline of Liberalism', *American Historical Review*, 63 (1957–8), 359.
49. Lawrence, J., *Speaking for the People: Party, Language and Popular Politics in England, 1867–1914* (Cambridge, 1998).
50. In fairness, the Irish Nationalists themselves helped create this situation. Shannon also notes that Gladstone felt personally betrayed by Parnell's behaviour and that, in any case, 'he was used to treating the Liberal party with equal lack of consideration' (Shannon, R., *Gladstone: Heroic Minister 1865–1898* [Harmondsworth, 1999], pp. 497–500).
51. Waley, S. D., *Edwin Montagu* (London, 1964), p. 30 (where, however, the lady is wrongly called 'Allen').
52. Bebbington, *Nonconformist Conscience*, p. 158; Machin, *Politics and the Churches*, p. 12. On the situation in Wales, see Morgan, *Wales*, pp. 172–3, 262.
53. This means that Paul Thompson's account of Liberal weaknesses in London cannot be used as an indicator of what was happening to the party elsewhere. See Thompson, P., *Socialists, Liberals and Labour. The Struggle for London 1885–1914* (London, 1967).
54. Doyle, B. M., 'Urban Liberalism and the "Lost Generation": Politics and Middle Class Culture in Norwich, 1900–1935', *Historical Journal*, 38 (1995), 617–34.
55. Bebbington, 'Nonconformity and Electoral Sociology', 654–5.
56. Koss, *Nonconformity*, p. 115; Bebbington, *Nonconformist Conscience*, p. 80.
57. That is not to say that all Dissenters were middle-class: Primitive Methodism had a strong following amongst farm labourers and miners, and the Baptist Chapels attracted many skilled workers. But sects like the Congregationalists were overwhelmingly middle-class.
58. This is a point particularly emphasised in Tanner, D., *Political Change and the Labour Party 1900–1918* (Cambridge, 1990).
59. Bernstein, *Liberalism, passim*.
60. Douglas, *Land, People and Politics, passim*. Though it deals with a later period, there is a useful discussion of the different 'schools' amongst land reformers in Emy, H. V., 'The Land Campaign: Lloyd George as a Social Reformer, 1909–14', in Taylor, A. J. P. (ed.), *Lloyd George: Twelve Essays* (London, 1971), pp. 35–68.
61. Howarth, 'Liberal Revival', 106.

62. Adonis, A., 'Aristocracy, Agriculture and Liberalism: The Politics, Finances and Estates of the Third Lord Carrington', *Historical Journal*, 31 (1988), 890–5.

63. Gladstone offended many working men when, attempting to sound a class note, he said that drinking was 'excusable [and] not unnatural' for workers (Barker, *Gladstone and Radicalism*, pp. 210–11).

64. In the two 1910 general elections 41 per cent of Labour candidates were Nonconformists, compared with 35 per cent of Liberal candidates (Blewett, N., *The Peers, the Parties and the People; the British General Elections of 1910* [London, 1972], p. 232).

65. This is one of the main themes in Lawrence, *Speaking for the People*.

66. 'Faddists' were also keen on abolishing compulsory vaccination and many campaigned for a repeal of the Contagious Diseases Acts (Howarth, 'Liberal Revival', 102).

67. Stansky, *Ambitions*, p. 143.

68. For a good survey of wartime divisions, see Sykes, A., *The Rise and Fall of British Liberalism 1776–1988* (Harlow, 1997), pp. 136–40. On the two 'extreme' factions, Matthew, *Liberal Imperialists, passim*, and Koss, S. (ed.), *The Pro-Boers: the anatomy of an antiwar movement* (Chicago, 1973).

69. Brown, S. J., '"Echoes of Midlothian": Scottish Liberalism and the South African War, 1899–1902', *Scottish Historical Review*, 71 (1992), 156–83.

4   The 'Problem of Labour', 1886–1905

1. William Woodall's pro-suffrage amendment was defeated by 137 votes to 273. See Ch. 7.

2. Chadwick, M. E. J., 'The Role of Redistribution in the Making of the Third Reform Act', *Historical Journal*, 19 (1976), 665–83. On the way in which the division of Leeds into five separate parliamentary constituencies damaged the Liberal Party in Leeds, see Roberts, A. W., 'Leeds Liberalism and Late Victorian Politics', *Northern History*, 5 (1970), 154–6.

3. Blewett, N., 'The Franchise in the United Kingdom, 1885–1918', *Past and Present*, 32 (1965), 27–56; Matthew, H. C. G., McKibbin, R. I. and Kay, J. A., 'The Franchise Factor in the Rise of the Labour Party', *English Historical Review*, 91 (1976), 723–52.

4. As a result of various legal decisions, it was relatively easy for some urban working men to achieve the vote: see Davis, J., 'Slums and the vote, 1867–90', *Bulletin of the Institute of Historical Research*, 64 (1991), 375–88.

5. Liberals were keen to abolish Plural Voting, which they clearly believed to work to the disadvantage of their own party. In 1906 they introduced a Bill on the subject, which was thrown out by the Lords, and made further attempts to end the 'abuse' with the equally abortive Franchise and Registration Bill of 1912. The government was again promoting a Plural Voting Bill when war broke out in 1914.

6. Tanner, D., 'The Parliamentary Electoral System, the "Fourth" Reform Act and the Rise of Labour in England and Wales', *Bulletin of the Institute of Historical Research*, 56 (1983), 205–19. Michael Childs broadly agrees, but, unlike Tanner, thinks that the bias against the younger age groups mainly affected manual workers ('Labour Grows Up. The Electoral System, Political Generations and British Politics, 1890–1929', *Twentieth-Century British History*, 6 [1995], 123–44).

7. Hamer, D. A., *Liberal Politics in the Age of Gladstone and Rosebery* (Oxford, 1972), pp. 9–18. Though he admits that to treat 'Labour' as a section and not as a class was already becoming difficult.

8. Pelling, H., *Social Geography of British Elections 1885–1910* (London, 1967), pp. 418–20.

9. Jay, R., *Joseph Chamberlain: A Political Study* (Oxford, 1981), especially pp. 175–80.

10. Barker, M., *Gladstone and Radicalism: The Reconstruction of Liberal Policy in Britain 1885–94* (Hassocks, 1975), pp. 175–93; Matthew, H. C. G., *The Liberal Imperialists: The ideas and politics of a post-Gladstonian élite* (Oxford, 1973), pp. 3–14.

11. Mundella was forced to resign: see Armytage, W. H. G., *A. J. Mundella, 1825–1897: the Liberal Background to the Labour Movement* (London, 1951), pp. 300–5. On the reforms of the 1892–5 Liberal Ministry, see Powell, D., 'The New Liberalism and the Rise of Labour, 1886–1906', *Historical Journal*, 29 (1986), 369–93, and D. Powell, 'The Liberal Ministries and Labour, 1892–1895', *History*, 68 (1983), 408–26.

12. Stansky, P., *Ambitions and Strategies: The struggle for the leadership of the Liberal Party in the 1890s* (Oxford, 1964), pp. 130–5.

13. On the wider issues raised by the Budget, see Emy, H. V., *Liberals, Radicals and Social Politics 1892–1914* (Cambridge, 1973), pp. 191–2. But it is not clear whether Harcourt saw the Budget, in traditional Radical terms, as an attack on the privileges of the landowners, or whether he saw it as a device for appealing to the working-class masses.

14. Matthew, *Liberal Imperialists*, Ch. 7.

15. Lubenow, W. C., *Parliamentary Politics and the Home Rule Crisis: The British House of Commons in 1886* (Oxford, 1988), p. 166.

16. Ibid., p. 338.

17. Ibid., pp. 320, 144. See also Lubenow, W. C., 'Irish Home Rule and the Social Basis of the Great Separation in the Liberal Party in 1886', *Historical Journal*, 28 (1985), 125–42.

18. Alderman, G., *The Railway Interest* (Leicester, 1973), Ch. 4, esp. p. 80. The railway interest had been offended by the Liberals' Employers Liability Act of 1880. Nevertheless, in 1881, 53.6 per cent of railway directors in Parliament were Liberals. Yet a decade later the proportions had dropped to just over 30 per cent and by 1911 it was as low as 15.6 per cent (ibid., pp. 234–50). The defection of Sir Edward Watkin, the great railway magnate, to Liberal Unionism in 1886 is symptomatic of this trend. However, the railways were not typical of the business world. Many manufacturers and merchants saw them as quasi-monopolies, whose privileges needed to be curbed by state action, in the interest of the wider business community. Many of the attacks on the railways, in fact, came from other Liberal businessmen.

19. Blewett, N., *The Peers, the Parties and the People: the General Elections of 1910* (London, 1972), pp. 14–15. The distribution of MPs by region and the social description of the various English constituencies is based upon Blewett's *Peers*. In the 1885 general election the Liberals picked up ten of the forty-eight urban seats which Blewett categorises as 'urban: predominantly middle class', but in the following four elections they won only one, one, none and two, respectively.

20. Rubinstein, W. D., 'Wealth, Elites and the Class Structure of Modern Britain', *Past and Present*, 76 (1977), 99–126.

21. Blewett, *Peers, Parties and People*, pp. 380–1. This division was one of long standing. In the 1892 election, for example, the Liberals won 68 seats in the south of England, but 125 in the north.

22. See Ch. 6.

23. Bernstein, G. L., *Liberalism and Liberal Politics in Edwardian England* (London, 1986), p. 24.

24. See Laybourn, K. and Reynolds, J., *Liberalism and the Rise of Labour 1890–1918* (London, 1984), *passim*.

25. Lloyd, T. O., 'The Whip as paymaster: Herbert Gladstone and party organisation', *English Historical Review*, 89 (1974), 785–813.

26. Barker, *Gladstone and Radicalism*, pp. 149–50.

27. See Illingworth's letter to Harcourt of 12 July 1894, declaring his unwillingness to be associated with a party which interfered with the hours of adult labour by legislation, as the government was currently doing with its Miners' Eight-Hours' Bill (*The Holden-Illingworth Letters* [Bradford, 1927], 597–9). On Illingworth and Bradford Liberalism, see Laybourn and Reynolds, *Liberalism*, esp. pp. 79, 112–13.

28. Powell, 'The New Liberalism', 378.

29. Laybourn and Reynolds, *Liberalism*, pp. 51, 80.

30. The concept is used in Clarke, P., 'The End of Laissez Faire and the Politics of Cotton', *Historical Journal*, 15 (1972), 493–512.

31. Hutchison, I. G. C., *A Political History of Scotland 1832–1924* (Edinburgh, 1986), pp. 218–19. In Paisley one of the Vice-Presidents of the Paisley Unionist Association defected to the Liberal camp (ibid., p. 220).

32. Harris, J., *Unemployment and Politics: A Study in English Social Policy 1886–1914* (Oxford, 1972), pp. 222–6.

33. Gilbert, B. B., *The Evolution of National Insurance in Great Britain: the Origins of the Welfare State* (London, 1966), p. 247.

34. Masterman, L., *C. F. G. Masterman* (London, 1939); David, E., 'The New Liberalism of C. F. G. Masterman, 1873–1927', in Brown, K. (ed.), *Essays in Anti-Labour History* (London, 1974), pp. 17–41.

35. Hamer says his creed drew on Benthamism and on America; 'Government of the people by the people' (Escott, T. H. S., *The Radical Programme* {1885} [ed. with introduction by Hamer, D. A., Brighton, 1971], p. xiv). The same was even more obviously the case with some of Chamberlain's collaborators, like T. H. S. Escott and Francis Adams.

36. Matthew, *Liberal Imperialists*, pp. 140–7; Searle, G. R., *The Quest for National Efficiency, 1899–1914* (Oxford, 1971; new edn, London, 1990).

37. Barker, *Gladstone and Radicalism*, p. 174.

38. Bebbington, D. W., *The Nonconformist Conscience: Chapel and Politics 1870–1914* (London, 1982), Ch. 3.
39. Clarke, P. F, 'The Progressive Movement in England', *Transactions of the Royal Historical Society*, 24 (1974), 159–81; Freeden, M., *The New Liberalism: An Ideology of Social Reform* (Oxford, 1978); Clarke, P., *Liberals and Social Democrats* (Cambridge, 1978); Collini, S., *Liberalism and Sociology: L. T. Hobhouse and Political Argument in England, 1880–1914* (Cambridge, 1979); Weiler, P., 'The New Liberalism of L. T. Hobhouse', *Victorian Studies*, 16 (1972), 141–61; Blaazer, D., *The Popular Front and the Progressive Tradition: Socialists, Liberals, and the Quest for Unity, 1884–1939* (Cambridge, 1992), Chs. 1–2.
40. H. V. Emy, *Liberals, Radicals and Social Politics*, p. 101. Some of the Liberal MPs returned in 1906 were members of the Fabian Society.
41. Ibid., p. 105; Freeden, M. (ed.), *Minutes of the Rainbow Circle, 1894–1924* (London, 1989).
42. Clarke, P., 'Liberals and Social Democrats in Historical Perspective', in Bogdanor, V. (ed.), *Liberal Party Politics* (Oxford, 1983), pp. 27–34.
43. Hobhouse, L. T., *Liberalism* (London, 1909; New York edn, 1964), p. 48.
44. Emy, H. V., 'The Impact of Financial Policy on English Party Politics Before 1914', *Historical Journal*, 15 (1972), *passim*.
45. Powell, 'The New Liberalism', 393.
46. Emy, *Liberals, Radicals and Social Politics*, p. 142.
47. This theme is powerfully argued in Sykes, A., *The Rise and Fall of British Liberalism 1776–1988* (Harlow, 1997), esp. pp. 170–6, though the discussion tends to conflate 'New Liberalism' with the more authoritarian creed of 'National Efficiency'. Incidentally, by no means all 'advanced' Radical intellectuals subscribed to the 'New Liberalism'. Bertrand Russell, for example, who later accepted the case for Socialism and joined the Labour Party, continued up until 1914 to adhere to a traditionally Radical view of the world (Rempel, R. A., 'Conflicts and Change in Liberal Theory and Practice, 1890–1918: the case of Bertrand Russell', in Waller, P. J. [ed.], *Politics and Social Change in Modern Britain* [Brighton, 1987], pp. 117–39).
48. Clegg, H. A., Fox, A. and Thompson, A. F. (eds), *A History of British Trade Unions Since 1889, Vol. I* (Oxford, 1964), p. 279.
49. Shepherd, J., 'Labour and parliament: the Lib.-Labs. as the first working-class MPs, 1885–1906', in Biagini, E. F. and Reid, A. J. (eds), *Currents of Radicalism: popular radicalism, organised labour and party politics in Britain, 1850–1914* (Cambridge, 1991), pp. 187–213; Gregory, Roy, *The Miners and British Politics 1906–1914* (Oxford, 1968).
50. Wrigley, C., 'Liberals and the Desire for Working-Class Representatives in Battersea, 1886–1922', in Brown, K. D. (ed.), *Essays in Anti-Labour History* (London, 1974), pp. 126–58.
51. MacDonald's rejection at Southampton is described in Marquand, D., *Ramsay MacDonald* (London, 1977), pp. 34–6.
52. In fairness, one must add that perhaps two-thirds of the delegates who rejected Henderson were manual workers (Wrigley, C., *Arthur Henderson* [Cardiff, 1990], p. 17; Purdue, A. W., 'Arthur Henderson and Liberal, Liberal-Labour and Labour politics in the North-east of England 1892–1903', *Northern History*, 11 [1976], 200).

53. Brown, J., 'Attercliffe, 1894: How One Local Liberal Party Failed to Meet the Challenge of Labour', *Journal of British Studies*, 14 (1975), 48–77. Even a middle-class Liberal setting out to 'represent' the working-class community, like W. P. Byles in Shipley in 1892, had great difficulty in securing the backing of the local Liberal caucus (Laybourn and Reynolds, *Liberalism*, pp. 81–2).

54. Clarke, P. F., *Lancashire and the New Liberalism* (Cambridge, 1971), pp. 198–9, and also pp. 220–1, for the constant stream of financial demands on candidates of both parties from local clubs and associations. Multiply the sums by about forty-six to establish their rough equivalent in today's money.

55. On the attempts of the Liberals in the North-West to escape dependence on 'Old Liberal' manufacturing interests, see Tanner, D., *Political Change and the Labour Party 1900–1918* (Cambridge, 1990), pp. 135–6. On the earlier problems associated with the running of working-class candidates, see Barker, *Gladstone and Liberalism*, pp. 130–8.

56. This theme is explored, mainly in relation to the Edwardian decade, in Searle, G. R., *Corruption in British Politics, 1895–1930* (Oxford, 1987), Ch. 7. See also Coetzee, F., 'Pressure Groups, Tory Businessmen, and the Aura of Political Corruption Before the First World War', *Historical Journal*, 29 (1986), 833–52.

57. Wrigley, C. J., *David Lloyd George and the British Labour Movement* (Hassocks, 1976), p. 25. Even a tried friend of Labour like Channing can be found bursting out about 'the baser motives ... grudges and disappointments ... noxious weeds to choke pure democratic instincts', when unrest in the shoe-making industry produced independent labour candidates in the 1894 local government elections in Northamptonshire (Howarth, J., 'The Liberal Revival in Northamptonshire, 1880–1895: A Case Study in Late Nineteenth Century Elections', *Historical Journal*, 12 [1969], 113).

58. Bealey, F., 'Negotiations between the Liberal Party and the Labour Representation Committee before the General Election of 1906', *Bulletin of the Institute of Historical Research*, 29 (1956), 261–74; Bealey, F. and Pelling, H., *Labour and Politics, 1900–1906* (London, 1958), Chs. 6, 10.

59. Douglas, R., *History of the Liberal Party, 1895–1970* (London, 1971), p. 73. The remark was made by Samuel Storey, Chairman of the Northern Liberal Federation, in July 1903, while the 'Pact' was still being negotiated.

60. Tanner, *Political Change*, p. 23. The Pact did not apply in Scotland, because Labour was weakened by ethnic divisions and by the popularity of Liberalism. The Liberal Party accordingly had no incentive to give ground (Hutchison, *Scotland*, pp. 259–60).

61. Bealey and Pelling, *Labour and Politics*, p. 50.

62. Important differences on the Tariff issue separated socialist theoreticians like Snowden from the 'consumerism' that characterised mainstream Liberalism (Trentmann, F., 'The strange death of free trade: the erosion of "liberal consensus" in Great Britain, *c.*1903–1932', in Biagini, E. F., *Citizenship and community: Liberals, radicals and collective identities in the British Isles 1854–1931* [Cambridge, 1996], pp. 231–4), but both could at least agree in rejecting Chamberlain's proposals. For an interpretation stressing the way in which Free Trade *unified* the Left, see Howe, A., 'Towards the "hungry

forties": free trade in Britain, c.1880–1906' (ibid., pp. 193–218) and Howe, A., *Free Trade and Liberal England, 1846–1946* (Oxford, 1997), Ch. 7.
63. Bealey and Pelling, *Labour and Politics*, pp. 144–6.
64. Powell, 'New Liberalism', 383. But Campbell-Bannerman added that 'if the time ever came when they [i.e. the Liberal and Labour Parties] parted they would deal with that when it arrived'.
65. J. Herbert to H. Gladstone, 6 Mar. 1903, in Bealey, 'Negotiations', 266.
66. Herbert believed that the Pact would give the Liberals an extra ten seats. In the event there were thirty-three constituencies where the Liberals stood down for Labour in the 1906 Election (either by refusing to put up a candidate at all or by putting up only one candidate in a double-member constituency). But in only two of these cases did the Liberals 'give up' a seat which they had won in 1900: Clitheroe and Barnard Castle, both of which the LRC had captured in recent by-elections. It is also significant that, of the twenty-nine newly elected Labour MPs, as many as thirteen had been returned for the North-West, where the Liberal Party had been weak since 1886, as against only three from Yorkshire, where Liberalism was very much stronger.
67. Powell, 'New Liberalism', 391. Hamer sees the Pact as a way of restoring a class balance which the Liberals themselves had earlier upset (Hamer, *Gladstone and Rosebery*, p. 309).
68. Lawrence, J., *Speaking for the People: Party, Language and Popular Politics in England, 1867–1914* (Cambridge, 1998), p. 131.
69. Biagini, E. F., *Liberty, Retrenchment and Reform: Popular Liberalism in the Age of Gladstone, 1860–1880* (Cambridge, 1992), p. 425.

5   The Radicals in Office, 1905–14

1. Stephens, H. W., 'Party Realignment in Britain, 1900–1925', *Social Science History*, 6 (1982), 42, and Table 1.
2. See Boyle, T., 'The Formation of Campbell-Bannerman's Government in December 1905: A Memorandum by J. A. Spender', *Bulletin of the Institute of Historical Research*, 45 (1972), 283–302.
3. Russell, A. K., *Liberal Landslide; the General Election of 1906* (Newton Abbot, 1973). The Liberals won as many as eighteen of the forty-eight heavily middle-class constituencies in England identified by Professor Blewett – which had been barren territory for the Liberals since the 1886 schism.
4. H. V. Emy, *Liberals, Radicals and Social Politics, 1892–1914* (Cambridge, 1973), p. 187; Tanner, D., *Political Change and the Labour Party 1900–1918* (Cambridge, 1990), p. 45.
5. Bealey, F. and Pelling, H., *Labour and Politics, 1900–1906* (London, 1958), p. 265.
6. Koss, S., *Nonconformity in Modern British Politics* (London, 1975), p. 74.
7. Richards, N. J., 'The Education Bill of 1906 and the Decline of Political Nonconformity', *Journal of Ecclesiastical History*, 23 (1972), 49–63; Machin, G. T. I., *Politics and the Churches in Great Britain 1869–1921* (Oxford, 1987), pp. 284–9. A major licensing Bill shortly followed.

8. Koss, *Nonconformity*, pp. 85–9, Ch. 5; Bebbington, D. W., *The Nonconformist Conscience: Chapel and Politics 1870–1914* (London, 1982), pp. 147–52; on the more general process of disillusionment, see ibid., pp. 79–83.

9. Hepburn, A. C., 'The Irish Council Bill and the Fall of Sir Antony Mac-Donnell', *Irish Historical Studies*, 17 (1970–1), 470–98.

10. Pelling, H., 'Two By-Elections: Jarrow and Colne Valley, 1907', in *Popular Politics and Society in Late Victorian Britain* (London, 1968), pp. 130–46.

11. Blewett, N., *The Peers, the Parties and the People; the British General Elections of 1910* (London, 1972), Ch. 3; Blewett, N., 'Free Fooders, Balfourites, Whole Hoggers. Factionalism Within the Unionist Party, 1906–10', *Historical Journal*, 11 (1968), 95–124; Sykes, A., *Tariff Reform in British Politics 1903–1913* (Oxford, 1979), Chs. 6–11.

12. The most useful short account is Pugh, M., *Lloyd George* (London, 1988). More detailed studies covering this period are Gilbert, B. B., *David Lloyd George: The Architect of Change 1863–1912* (London, 1987), Gilbert, B. B., *David Lloyd George, The Organizer of Victory 1912–16* (London, 1992) and Grigg, J., *Lloyd George: The People's Champion: 1902–1911* (London, 1978). For a useful collection of essays, see Loades, J. (ed.), *The Life and Times of David Lloyd George* (Bangor, 1991).

13. Koss, *Nonconformity*, p. 106; Machin, G. T. I., 'Lloyd George and Nonconformity', in Loades (ed.), *Lloyd George*, pp. 33–47.

14. Koss, *Nonconformity*, p. 102.

15. Murray, B., 'The Politics of the "People's Budget"', *Historical Journal*, 16 (1973), 555–70. The theme is explored in greater detail in Murray, B. K., *The People's Budget 1909–10* (Oxford, 1980).

16. Harris, J., *Unemployment and Politics: A Study in English Social Policy 1886–1914* (Oxford, 1972), pp. 340–6.

17. On land campaign, see Douglas, R., *Land, People and Politics: A History of the Land Question in the United Kingdom, 1878–1952* (London, 1976), pp. 160–6; Emy, H. V., 'The Land Campaign: Lloyd George as a Social Reformer, 1909–14', in Taylor, A. J. P. (ed.), *Lloyd George: Twelve Essays* (London, 1971), pp. 35–68; Douglas, R. '"God gave the land to the people"', in Morris, A. J. A. (ed.), *Edwardian Radicalism 1900–1914* (London, 1974), pp. 148–61; Offer, A., *Property and Politics, 1870–1914* (Cambridge, 1981), Ch. 22; Fforde, M., *Conservatism and Collectivism, 1886–1914* (Edinburgh, 1990), Ch. 5; Packer, I., 'Lloyd George and the Land Campaign, 1912–1914', in Loades (ed.), *Lloyd George*, pp. 143–52. On the 1914 Budget, see Gilbert, B. B., 'David Lloyd George: The Reform of British Landholding and the Budget of 1914', *Historical Journal*, 22 (1978), 117–41; Emy, H. V., 'The Impact of Financial Policy on English Party Politics before 1914', *Historical Journal*, 15 (1972), 129–30.

18. Emy, 'Land Campaign', p. 42.

19. The best introduction to this complex subject is still Jenkins, R., *Mr Balfour's Poodle* (London, 1954).

20. In Scotland there was a vigorous campaign for Scottish Home Rule (Hutchison, I. G. C., *A Political History of Scotland 1832–1924* [Edinburgh, 1986], pp. 241–2). The view that Free Trade, land reform and the old sectarian issues made the Liberal Party popular with the Scottish working class right

up until the Great War is argued in W. Hamish Fraser, 'The Labour Party in Scotland', in Brown, K. D. (ed.), *The First Labour Party 1906–1914* (London, 1985).

21. Packer, 'Land Campaign', pp. 147–8.
22. Fforde, *Conservatism and Collectivism*, p. 130.
23. Masterman, L., *C. F. G. Masterman* (London, 1939), p. 259.
24. Packer, 'Land Campaign', pp. 150–2, and Packer, I., 'The Land Issue and the Future of Scottish Liberalism in 1914', *Scottish Historical Review*, 78 (1996), 52–71. In Scotland, Packer concludes, the Liberal leadership had handled the complexities of the land question skilfully and the omens were looking good (ibid., 70). See also Hutchison, *Scotland*, pp. 243–5; Fforde, *Conservatism and Collectivism*, p. 157.
25. Cannadine, D., *The Decline and Fall of the British Aristocracy* (New Haven, 1990), p. 110; Thompson, F. M. L., *English Landed Society in the Nineteenth Century* (London, 1963), pp. 321–6.
26. Weston, C. C., 'The Liberal Leadership and the Lords' Veto, 1907–1910', *Historical Journal*, 11 (1968), 508–37; Fair, J. D., *British Interparty Conferences* (Oxford, 1980), Ch. 4.
27. On 'federalism', see Kendle, J., *Federal Britain: A History* (London, 1997) and Kendle, J., *Ireland and the Federal Solution, 1870–1921* (Kingston, Ont., 1989).
28. Searle, G. R., *The Quest for National Efficiency, 1899–1914* (Oxford, 1971; new edn, London, 1990), Ch. 6; Scally, R. J., *The Origins of the Lloyd George Coalition: The Politics of Social Imperialism, 1900–1918* (Princeton, 1975), Ch. 7.
29. Jalland, P., 'A Liberal Chief Secretary and the Irish Question: Augustine Birrell, 1907–1914', *Historical Journal*, 19 (1976), 421–51; Jalland, P., *The Liberals and Ireland: the Ulster Question in British Politics to 1914* (Brighton, 1980); Jenkins, R., *Asquith* (London, 1964), Chs. 18–19. Perhaps because his heart had gone out of the Home Rule cause after the Irish betrayal over the 1902 Education Act, Lloyd George gave the impression of wishing to extricate Liberalism from the Gladstonian commitment.
30. This is the theme of a now classic book, Dangerfield, G., *The Strange Death of Liberal England* (London, 1935). On the problems associated with women's suffrage, see Ch. 7.
31. The view that landed society adapted surprisingly well to the problems it faced is vigorously argued in Phillips, G. D., *The Diehards: Aristocratic Society and Politics in Edwardian England* (Cambridge, Mass., 1979). The opposing view is put by Cannadine, *Decline and Fall, passim*.
32. Fforde, *Conservatism and Collectivism*, p. 152.
33. Clarke, I. F., *Voices Prophesying War 1763–1984* (Oxford, 1966); Hynes, S., *The Edwardian Turn of Mind* (Princeton, 1968), pp. 35–53.
34. Phillips, *Diehards, passim*.
35. Morris, A. J. A., *Radicalism Against War 1906–1914* (London, 1972); Morris, A. J. A. (ed.), *Edwardian Radicalism 1900–1914* (London, 1974); Weinroth, H. S., 'The British Radicals and the Balance of Power, 1902–1914', *Historical Journal*, 13 (1970), 653–82; Weinroth, H. S., 'Left-Wing Opposition to Naval Armaments in Britain before 1914', *Journal of Contemporary History*, 6 (1971), 93–120.

36. Williamson, S. R., *The Politics of Grand Strategy: Britain and France Prepare for War, 1904–1914* (Cambridge, Mass., 1969); for a harsh view of Grey's diplomacy, Wilson, K. M., *The Policy of the Entente: essays on the determination of British foreign policy, 1904–1914* (Cambridge, 1985).
37. These xenophobic outbursts are graphically described in Koss, S. E., *Lord Haldane: Scapegoat for Liberalism* (N. York, 1969), Ch. 5.
38. Searle, G. R., 'Critics of Edwardian Society: the Case of the Radical Right', in O'Day, A. (ed.), *The Edwardian Age: Conflict and Stability 1900–1914* (London, 1979), pp. 79–96; Searle, G., 'The "Revolt from the Right" in Edwardian Britain', in Kennedy, P. and Nicholls, A. (eds), *Nationalist and Racialist Movements in Britain and Germany Before 1914* (London, 1981), pp. 21–39; Phillips, G. D., 'Lord Willoughby de Broke and the Politics of Radical Toryism, 1909–14', *Journal of British Studies*, 20 (1980), 205–24. A different perspective is offered in Coetzee, F., *For Party or Country: Nationalism and the Dilemmas of Popular Conservatism in Edwardian England* (N. York, 1990) and in Sykes, A., 'The Radical Right and the Crisis of Conservatism Before the First World War', *Historical Journal*, 26 (1983), 661–76.
39. Cannadine, *Decline and Fall*, pp. 516–30.
40. Searle, 'Critics of Edwardian Society', p. 85.

6 Liberalism, Labour and Social Reform, 1905–14

1. However, one-half of the Land Enquiry was devoted to issues centring around *urban* land, even if it was the rural campaign which attracted far more attention.
2. For the most convenient general introduction, see Hay, J. R., *The Origins of the Liberal Welfare Reforms 1906–1914* (London, 1975). The best single study of the subject remains Gilbert, Bentley B., *The Evolution of National Insurance in Great Britain: The Origins of the Welfare State* (London, 1966).
3. Emy, H. V., 'The Impact of Financial Policy on English Party Politics Before 1914', *English Historical Review*, 15 (1972), esp. 130.
4. Tanner, D., *Political Change and the Labour Party 1900–1918* (Cambridge, 1990), pp. 123, 448–50. The Liberal Government tried to establish 'one man one vote' with its 1906 Plural Voting Bill, but the House of Lords rejected it. The more wide-ranging Franchise and Registration Bill of 1912 became entangled with the divisive issue of women's suffrage and was withdrawn. Incidentally, between 1886 and 1918 the Liberal Party failed to win a single seat in any of the university constituencies, whose electorate consisted of graduates. The 1912 Franchise Bill would have abolished these constituencies.
5. Blewett, N., 'Free Fooders, Balfourites, Whole Hoggers. Factionalism within the Unionist Party, 1906–10', *Historical Journal*, 11 (1968), 95–124.
6. Emy, H. V., *Liberals, Radicals and Social Politics, 1892–1914* (Cambridge, 1973), p. 226. For the circumstances in which this Budget was produced, see Murray, B. K., 'Lloyd George, the Navy Estimates, and the Inclusion of Rating Relief in the 1914 Budget', *Welsh Historical Review*, 15 (1990), 58–78.

7. Emy, 'Financial Policy', 112–16. Indeed, as Emy argues, it was the Liberals' reneguing over Retrenchment after 1906 which caused so much anger among Conservatives.
8. Blewett, N., *The Peers, the Parties and the People: The British General Elections of 1910* (London, 1972), Ch. 12.
9. Clarke, P. F., *Lancashire and the New Liberalism* (Cambridge, 1971).
10. Cited in Tanner, *Political Change*, p. 60 fn 46.
11. Emy, *Liberals, Radicals and Social Politics*, pp. 171–3.
12. Paradoxically, old-style plebeian Radicals (some of whom had by now made the transition to socialism) may have responded far more favourably to this kind of Liberal rhetoric than to promises of social reform, as Patrick Joyce intimates (*Visions of the People: Industrial England and the question of class, 1848–1914* [Cambridge, 1991], p. 80).
13. Blewett, *Peers*, pp. 346–8; Koss, S., *Nonconformity in Modern British Politics* (London, 1975), pp. 117–18, 105.
14. Blewett, *Peers*, pp. 348–9; Koss, *Nonconformity*, Ch. 5.
15. Beveridge, Lord, *Power and Influence* (London, 1953), p. 92.
16. Clarke, P., *Liberals and Social Democrats* (Cambridge, 1978).
17. Lloyd George and Masterman later quarrelled. See Masterman, L., *C. F. G. Masterman* (London, 1939); David, E., 'The New Liberalism of C. F. G. Masterman', in Brown, K. D. (ed.), *Essays in Anti-Labour History* (London, 1974), pp. 17–41. Another interesting figure is the former President of the teachers' union, the NUT, T. J. Macnamara: see Betts, R., *Dr Macnamara 1861–1931* (Liverpool, 1999).
18. Perkin, H., *The Rise of Professional Society* (London, 1989), pp. 155–70.
19. Hay, R., 'Employers and social policy in Britain: the evolution of welfare legislation, 1905–14', *Social History*, 2 (1977), 435–55.
20. Tanner, *Political Change*, pp. 88–9.
21. Turner, J., 'The Politics of "Organised Business" in the First World War', in Turner, J. (ed.), *Businessmen and Politics* (London, 1984), pp. 34–5.
22. Older accounts of the 1914 Budget and its critics need to be revised in the light of Ian Packer's important article, 'The Liberal Cave and the 1914 Budget', *English Historical Review*, 111 (1996), 620–35.
23. Emy, *Liberals, Radicals and Social Politics*, esp. p. 285.
24. Clarke, P., 'The End of Laissez Faire and the Politics of Cotton', *Historical Journal*, 15 (1972), 493–512.
25. Blewett, *Peers*, p. 215.
26. Searle, G. R., 'The Edwardian Liberal Party and Business', *English Historical Review*, 98 (1983), 28–60.
27. Bernstein, G. L., *Liberalism and Liberal Politics in Edwardian England* (London, 1986), pp. 22–4; Bernstein, G. L., 'Liberalism and the Progressive Alliance in the Constituencies 1900–1914', *Historical Journal*, 26 (1983), 617–40. On the West Riding 'millocrats', see Laybourn, K. and Reynolds, J., *Liberalism and the Rise of Labour 1890–1918* (London, 1984), esp. pp. 6, 80, 123, 167. For evidence that such old business oligarchies were coming under challenge from within the Liberal organisation during the Edwardian years, see Tanner, *Political Change*, pp. 255–8, 269–73.
28. Searle, 'Edwardian Liberal Party', 44–6.

29. Searle, G. R., *Corruption in British Politics, 1895–1930* (Oxford, 1987), Ch. 6.
30. Ibid., Ch. 8; Gilbert, B. B., 'David Lloyd George and the Great Marconi Scandal', *Historical Research*, 62 (1989), 295–317.
31. Searle, *Corruption*, Ch. 7.
32. Significantly, Lloyd George's Land Inquiry was a largely personal venture, funded by his friends.
33. Bentley, M., *The Climax of Liberal Politics: British Liberalism in Theory and Practice 1868–1918* (London, 1987), citing Ellins, pp. 144–5.
34. Blewett, *Peers*, pp. 317, 326.
35. For example, Pringle in North-West Lanark in January 1910 and MacCallum Scott in Bridgeton in December 1910 (Hutchison, I. G. C., *A Political History of Scotland 1832–1924* [Edinburgh, 1986], p. 239).
36. Tanner, *Political Change*, p. 344.
37. Bernstein, *Liberalism*, p. 123.
38. Morgan, K. O., 'The New Liberalism and the Challenge of Labour: The Welsh Experience, 1885–1929', in Brown (ed.), *Essays in Anti-Labour History*, p. 170.
39. Hutchison, *Scotland*, p. 237; Dawson, M., 'Liberalism in Devon and Cornwall, 1910–1931: "The Old-Time Religion"', *Historical Journal*, 38 (1995), 427–8. In 1913 the Scottish Temperance Act was passed, allowing local authorities to ban alcohol sales if this had been agreed to by referendum.
40. The movement among working men and women to establish a school meal service had been strongly resisted by leading Liberals in the West Riding (Laybourn and Reynolds, *Liberalism*, especially pp. 168–9).
41. Bernstein, 'Liberalism and the Progressive Alliance'.
42. Ibid., pp. 635, 639–40.
43. Tanner, *Political Change*, pp. 127–8.
44. John Howe, 'Liberals, Lib-Labs and Independent Labour in North Gloucestershire, 1890–1914', *Midland History*, 11 (1986), 135.
45. Cook, C., 'Labour and the Downfall of the Liberal Party, 1906–14', in Sked, A. and Cook, C. (eds), *Crisis and Controversy* (London, 1976).
46. Sheppard, M. G. and Halstead, J., 'Labour's Municipal Election Performance in Provincial England and Wales, 1901–13', *Bulletin of the Society for the Study of Labour History*, 39 (1979), 42. For the working of the anti-Labour pact in Bradford, see Laybourn and Reynolds, *Liberalism*, pp. 150–1.
47. See Appendix, pp. 210–11. Only by treating Labour MPs as surrogate Liberals is it possible to conclude that the Liberals had strengthened their hold over working-class constituencies in England between 1892 and 1910, and even then the improvement is hardly dramatic. The Liberals won 100 seats in English urban working-class and mining constituencies in 1892, and 89 in January 1910 (when Labour won 31 seats in this type of constituency). Of course, the Liberals did better in 1910 than they had done in 1895 and 1900, when the party as a whole was in the doldrums, but that was to be expected.
48. However, Asquith thought that the class of small employers was the most hostile (Rowland, P., *The Last Liberal Governments: Unfinished Business, 1911–1914* [London, 1971], pp. 80–1.
49. Clegg, H. A., Fox, A. and Thompson, A. F., *A History of British Trade Unions Since 1889: Vol. I 1889–1910* (Oxford, 1964), pp. 402–3. See also Thane, P.,

'The Working Class and State "Welfare" in Britain, 1880–1914', *Historical Journal*, 27 (1984), 898–9.

50. Lloyd George to brother, 6 May 1908, in George, W., *My Brother and I* (London, 1958), p. 220. Churchill to Asquith, 29 December 1908, Churchill, R. S., *Winston Churchill, Vol. 2 Young Statesman 1901–1914* (London, 1967), pp. 307–8.

51. Thane, 'Working Class and "Welfare"', 877–900. The article is a response to an earlier claim that the 'Welfare State' initially encountered heavy working-class and Labour resistance (Pelling, H., 'The Working Class and the Origins of the Welfare State', in *Popular Politics and Society in Late Victorian Britain* [London, 1968], pp. 1–18).

52. On the Great Labour Unrest, see Clegg, H. A., *A History of British Trade Unions Since 1889: Vol. II 1911–1933* (Oxford, 1985), Ch. 2; Tanner, *Political Change*, pp. 62–3. On the Liberal dilemma, see Fletcher, I. C., '"Prosecutions...Are Always Risky Business": Labor, Liberals, and the 1912 "Don't Shoot" Prosecutions', *Albion*, 28 (1996), 251–78.

53. Gregory, R., *The Miners and British Politics 1906–1914* (Oxford, 1968), *passim*.

54. Cited in Richter, M., *The Politics of Conscience: T. H. Green and His Age* (London, 1964), pp. 374–5.

55. See Phelps Brown(ed.), E. H., *The Growth of British Industrial Relations: A study from the standpoint of 1906–14* (London, 1959), Ch. 6. But the government was sometimes accused of not being sufficiently willing to employ the police to maintain order during industrial disturbances; see Morgan, J., *Conflict and Order: The Police and Labour Disputes in England and Wales 1900–1939* (Oxford, 1987), pp. 43–4. On the tangled story of what really happened at Tonypandy, see O'Brien, A. M., 'Churchill and the Tonypandy Riots', *Welsh Historical Review*, 17 (1994), 67–99.

56. In May 1910, with industrial tension mounting in the valleys, the Welsh journal, *Llais Llafur*, pointed out that the Liberal MPs representing South Wales included seven major industrialists, as well as five ministers and many lawyers (Peter Stead, 'Establishing a Heartland – The Labour Party in Wales', in Brown, K. D. [ed.], *The First Labour Party 1906–1914* [London, 1985], p. 67).

57. McKibbin, R., *The Evolution of the Labour Party 1910–1924* (Oxford, 1974), Chs. 3–4. For a very different view, see Douglas, R., 'Labour in Decline, 1910–14', in Brown (ed.), *Essays in Anti-Labour History*, pp. 105–25.

58. McKibbin, *Evolution*, p. 76.

59. Tanner, *Political Change*, pp. 319–20.

60. Ibid., pp. 336–7.

61. Ibid., *passim*.

62. By 1914 Labour was holding 171 seats on municipal councils in England (outside London). True, there were cities where the Labour Party significantly increased its representation on the eve of the War, such as Bradford and Leeds (Laybourn and Reynolds, *Liberalism*, p. 152). In Birmingham, Sheffield, and the East End of London, on the other hand, Labour was very slow to make any impact at all (Michael Cahill, 'Labour in the Municipalities', in Brown [ed.], *First Labour Party*, p. 99; Adams, T., 'Labour and the

First World War: Economy, Politics and the Erosion of Local Peculiarity?',
Journal of Regional and Local Studies, 10 [1990], 24–5), while in Scotland,
which remained overwhelmingly pro-Liberal before 1914, Labour could
only claim sixty-nine town councillors and thirteen county councillors even
as late as 1915 (W. Hamish Fraser, 'The Labour Party in Scotland', in
Brown [ed.], *First Labour Party*, p. 57). On Scottish politics, see Fry, M.,
Patronage and Principle: A Political History of Modern Scotland (Aberdeen, 1987).

63. McKibbin, R. I., 'James Ramsay MacDonald and the Problem of the Inde-
    pendence of the Labour Party, 1910–1914', *Journal of Modern History*, 42
    (1970), 216–35. The Osborne Judgement, a legal ruling upheld by the
    House of Lords in 1909, restricted the use of trade union funds for political
    purposes and thus struck a serious blow against the Labour Party.

64. Marquand, D., *Ramsay MacDonald* (London, 1977), pp. 150–1, 159–62.

65. See Ch. 7.

66. Clarke, P. F., 'The electoral position of the Liberal and Labour parties,
    1910–14', *English Historical Review*, 90 (1975), 828–36.

67. Tanner, *Political Change*, pp. 22, 317, 422.

68. For a statistical analysis of elections in five English boroughs which suggests
    that class realignment was not taking place on a significant scale, see Wald,
    K. D., 'Class and the Vote Before the First World War', *British Journal of
    Political Science*, 8 (1978), 441–57.

69. McKibbin, *Evolution*, p. 54; Petter, M., 'The Progressive Alliance', *History*, 58
    (1973), 58.

70. Childs, M., 'Labour Grows Up. The Electoral System, Political Generations
    and British Politics, 1890–1929', *Twentieth-Century British History*, 6 (1995),
    132–5. Childs believes that before 1914 the Labour Party's growing hold on
    a younger generation of working-class males was being 'masked by the
    inequalities of the franchise' (134).

7 The Liberals, Women's Suffrage and the Women's Vote

1. Cited in Dangerfield, G. *The Strange Death of Liberal England* (London, 1935:
   New York edn, 1961), p. 179.

2. F. Pethick-Lawrence, cited in Harrison, B., 'Women's Suffrage at Westminster, 1866–1928', in Bentley, M. and Stevenson, J. (eds), *High and Low Politics in Modern Britain* (Oxford, 1983), p. 82.

3. Pugh, M., 'The limits of liberalism: Liberals and women's suffrage, 1867–
   1914', in Biagini, E. F. (ed.), *Citizenship and community: Liberals, radicals and
   collective identities in the British Isles, 1865–1931* (Cambridge, 1996), pp. 45–8.

4. Walker, L., 'Party Political Women: A Comparative Study of Liberal
   Women and the Primrose League, 1890–1914', in Rendall, J. (ed.), *Equal or
   Different: Women's Politics, 1800–1914* (Oxford, 1987), p. 187.

5. Howe, A., *Free Trade and Liberal England 1846–1946* (Oxford, 1997), p. 272;
   Russell, A. K., *Liberal Landslide: The General Election of 1906* (Newton Abbot,
   1973), p. 177.

6. Indispensable reading is Hollis, P., *Ladies Elect: Women in English Local Government, 1865–1914* (Oxford, 1987). However, not until 1907 could women *sit* as councillors or aldermen on borough councils or county councils (as distinct from *vote*), though they had from the start played both roles on School Boards and were later to do so on Boards of Guardians.

7. Harrison, B., *Separate Spheres: The Opposition to Women's Suffrage in Britain* (London, 1978), pp. 133–6; Kent, S. S., *Sex and Suffrage in Britain* (Princeton, 1987).

8. Hume, L. P., *The National Union of Women's Suffrage Societies 1897–1914* (New York, 1982), p. 37.

9. Pugh, M., *The Tories and the People 1880–1935* (Oxford, 1985), Ch. 3; Walker, 'Party Political Women', pp. 170–4.

10. Walker, 'Party Political Women', p. 169.

11. Ibid., pp. 176–8. The morally censorious tone of the WLF did not always help the party (see above, Ch. 3).

12. From Mrs W. Phillips's *An Appeal to Women* (c.1890), cited in Walker, 'Party Political Women', p. 174.

13. Hirschfield, C., 'A Fractured Faith: Liberal Party Women and the Suffrage Issue in Britain, 1892–1914', *Gender and History*, 2 (1990), 177.

14. See Ch. 4.

15. In 1907 ten of the twenty members of the Executive of the NUWSS were Liberals, as against two Labour supporters and one Conservative (Hume, *National Union*, p. 36).

16. See Liddington, J., and Norris, J., *One Hand Tied Behind Us: The Rise of the Women's Suffrage Movement* (London, 1978), Ch. IX.

17. Rosen, A., *Rise Up Women! The Militant Campaign of the Women's Social and Political Union 1903–1914* (London, 1974), pp. 30–2; Liddington and Norris, *One Hand*, Ch. X.

18. Pugh, 'Limits of liberalism', pp. 59–60.

19. Mrs Fawcett was a member of the Women's Liberal Unionist Association, although she held the NUWSS itself to political neutrality (Walker, 'Party Political Women', p. 190).

20. Harrison, *Separate Spheres*, p. 40.

21. Letter of 1892, cited in Lewis, J. (ed.), *Before the Vote was Won: Arguments For and Against Women's Suffrage* (London, 1987), p. 446.

22. Harrison believes that this was an influence mediated by Frederic Harrison from French sources (*Separate Spheres*, p. 40). 'As late as 1911 a Liberal agent in East Scotland could tell his leaders privately that in so far as religious issues were prominent, Liberals would suffer from the women's vote at election because "religious bigotry will find a ready response among the women of the Country"' (ibid., p. 42).

23. Harrison, 'Women's Suffrage at Westminster', pp. 108–9; Blewett, N., *The Peers, the Parties and the People; the British General Elections of 1910* (London, 1972), pp. 317, 326.

24. This scuppered the chances of the first two Bills launched by the Conciliation Committee, an all-party grouping which had come together in 1910 to frame a compromise Suffrage Bill. Its 1910 Bill lapsed when Parliament dissolved later in the year, and the following year its Bill proceeded no further because the government would not give it facilities.

25. The first Conciliation Bill (1910) was also a measure of this kind, though the Bill of the following year was drafted in such a way as to permit the franchise to be extended. Quite how many women these measures would have enfranchised remains a subject of dispute.

26. Harrison, 'Women's Suffrage at Westminster', p. 100.

27. Morgan, D., *Suffragists and Liberals: The Politics of Woman Suffrage in Britain* (Oxford, 1975), p. 82.

28. Least of all, Harrison adds, when 'confronted by the militancy of an auto-cratically-led suffragette movement which sought to coerce the majority through tactical violence' (Harrison, 'Women's Suffrage at Westminster', p. 104).

29. Jenkins, R., *Asquith* (1964), p. 250.

30. See Pugh, M., *Electoral Reform in War and Peace 1906–18* (London, 1978), pp. 41–3. The NUWSS itself took this line.

31. When Dickinson introduced his private members' Bill in 1913, a bill for which the government had promised facilities, it, too, failed to secure a majority, this time by 48 votes – with the Irish voting against by 13 votes to 51.

32. Hume, *National Union*, p. 179.

33. Cited in Rowland, P., *The Last Liberal Governments: Unfinished Business 1911–1914* (London, 1971), p. 295.

34. Pugh, M., 'Labour and Women's Suffrage', in Brown, K. D. (ed.), *The First Labour Party 1906–1914* (London, 1985), pp. 233–53.

35. A full Suffrage Bill had actually passed its second reading in 1909, though by a smaller margin than earlier women suffrage motions and in a thin House.

36. Dickinson's 1913 Bill tackled this problem by raising the age of qualification for women to 25 – a similar strategy to that eventually adopted in the 1918 Representation of the People Act.

37. Fletcher, I. C., '"A Star Chamber of the Twentieth Century": Suffragettes, Liberals and the 1908 "Rush the Commons Case"', *Journal of British Studies*, 35 (1996), 519–21.

38. Walker, 'Party Political Women', pp. 175–6.

39. In 1908 an earlier splinter group, several hundred members strong, had been formed – the Forward Suffrage Union.

40. Hirschfield, 'Fractured Faith', 184.

41. This led to a breach between Mrs Pankhurst and Christabel, on the one hand, and, on the other, the younger daughter, Sylvia, who set up her own organisation in the East End of London.

42. Rosen, *Rise Up Women!*, pp. 209–12.

43. However, it is a sign of WLF frustration that even a loyalist like Mrs Acland wanted Asquith's resignation (Hirschfield, 'Fractured Faith', 188).

44. The Liberal women also came to appreciate the values of 'union and combination' (Walker, 'Party Political Women', 178).

45. On the EEF, see Hume, *National Union*, Ch. 5; Holton, S. S., *Feminism and Democracy: Women's Suffrage and Reform Politics in Britain 1900–1918* (Cambridge, 1986), Chs. 4–5; Pugh, *Electoral Reform*, pp. 22–8.

46. Pugh, 'Labour and Women's Suffrage', p. 250.

47. Holton, *Feminism and Democracy*, p. 119.
48. Harrison, 'Women's Suffrage at Westminster', p. 103.
49. Holton, *Feminism and Democracy*, pp. 113–15.
50. Churchill to Elibank, 18 Dec. 1911, cited in Morgan, *Suffragists and Liberals*, p. 87.
51. See Harrison, *Separate Spheres*, on the women 'antis'; Hirschfield, 'Fractured Faith', 181–2.
52. Hume, *National Union*, p. 100; Bentley, 'Women's Suffrage at Westminster', p. 109.
53. In January 1913 Hugh Cecil expressed doubt, as Balfour had also done, on whether votes could change society that much one way or the other (Harrison, B., *Prudent Revolutionaries: Portraits of British Feminists Between the Wars* [Oxford, 1987], p. 305).
54. Cited in Robbins, K., *Sir Edward Grey: A Biography of Lord Grey of Fallodon* (London, 1971), p. 248.
55. Clarke, P. F., *Lancashire and the New Liberalism* (Cambridge, 1971), p. 399; Pugh, *Electoral Reform*, p. 44.
56. The Representation of the People Act set an age threshold for women of 30, thereby excluding most of the very females whose lives had been most at risk during the War (e.g. the munitions workers).
57. Pugh, M., *Women and the Women's Movement in Britain 1914–1959* (Basingstoke, 1992), pp. 142–3.
58. Ibid., p. 143.
59. The WSPU was far less forgiving, but after 1918 its leadership largely withdrew from active politics into nostalgic myth-making.
60. Harrison, B., 'Women in a Man's House: The Women MPs, 1919–45', *Historical Journal*, 29 (1986), 634.
61. Harrison, *Prudent Revolutionaries*, Ch. 7.
62. Though considerably below the combined membership of the WLF and the old WNLF.
63. Thane, P., 'Women, liberalism and citizenship, 1918–1930', in Biagini (ed.), *Citizenship and community*, p. 77.
64. Pugh, *Women and the Women's Movement*, pp. 140–1. In fact, the evidence assembled by Pugh is ambivalent. In the 1922 and 1923 general elections Liberal candidates were more likely to mention women's issues than Conservatives, though less likely than Labour. In 1924 and 1929 they ignored them, compared to the other two parties (ibid., 120). For further information, see Appendix, F.
65. In the general elections of 1918, 1922, 1923, 1924 and 1929 the Liberals fielded 64 female candidates (2.85 per cent of the total), the Conservatives only 35 (1.35 per cent).
66. There is some evidence that, in double-member constituencies, women sometimes allocated their votes in order to maximise the chances of a woman candidate or candidates, as in Sunderland. On the other hand, women candidates could damage the party that adopted them if they provoked a male backlash, for example, by having a strident 'feminist' reputation, as in Norwich. But none of this can have had more than a marginal impact.

67. Harrison, *Prudent Revolutionaries*, pp. 308–9. Women had benefited considerably before 1902 from the cumulative vote system used in School Board elections.
68. Thane, 'Women, liberalism and citizenship', *passim*.
69. Ibid., p. 79.

8 Liberalism and the Great War

1. This is the conclusion of Cook, C., 'Labour and the Downfall of the Liberal Party, 1906–14', in Sked, A. and Cook, C. (eds), *Crisis and Controversy* (London, 1976).
2. Many examples are given in Tanner, D., *Political Change and the Labour Party 1900–1918* (Cambridge, 1990). See also Hutchison, I. G. C., *A Political History of Scotland 1832–1924* (Edinburgh, 1986), pp. 231–2.
3. Ball, S. R., 'Asquith's Decline and the General Election of 1918', *Scottish Historical Review*, 61 (1982), 44–61.
4. A balanced appraisal is to be found in Cassar, G. H., *Asquith As War Leader* (London and Rio Grande, 1994).
5. But Cassar shows that Asquith, initially an admirer, quite quickly became disillusioned with Kitchener, though he felt unable to sack him (ibid., pp. 41, 102).
6. Some historians argue that because there were three times as many Unionist MPs as Liberal MPs serving at the front, the Liberal Ministry might still have held on to power: see Pugh, M. D., 'Asquith, Bonar Law and the First Coalition', *Historical Journal*, 17 (1974), 815–16, 819–20; Cassar thinks that such a course of action would have also been in the national interest (*Asquith As War Leader*, pp. 100–2).
7. Wilson, T., *The Downfall of the Liberal Party, 1914–35* (London, 1966), p. 40.
8. Wilson, T., *The Myriad Faces of War: Britain and the Great War, 1914–1918* (Cambridge, 1988 ed.), pp. 414–15, 422. In the Nigerian Debate of 8 November 1916, Carson, a backbencher once more, divided the House against the government's methods of disposing of captured enemy property in Nigeria. This rebellion triggered off a chain of events which culminated in Asquith's fall from power a month later.
9. Howard, C., 'Expectations born to death: local Labour party expansion in the 1920s', in Winter, J. (ed.), *The Working Class in Modern British History* (Cambridge, 1983), p. 68.
10. Henderson was kept waiting on the doormat outside the Cabinet Room while his colleagues discussed his 'delinquency' in publicly backing Labour participation in an international conference of socialists at Stockholm, where the British delegates would have met their German and Austrian counterparts. This was the incident which prompted Henderson's resignation.
11. Asquith had initially planned to replace Kitchener as War Secretary by Lloyd George, leaving the Treasury to be filled by Bonar Law, but pulled

back when he realised that Kitchener was unsackable. Later, in September 1915, he let Lloyd George veto Bonar Law's request to be made Deputy Leader of the House – another blunder (Cassar, *Asquith As War Leader*, pp. 102–3, 130).

12. McEwen, J. M., 'Lloyd George's Liberal Supporters in December 1916: A Note', *Bulletin of the Institute of Historical Research*, 53 (1980), 265–72.

13. The literature on the Crisis of December 1916 is voluminous. Here are a few short accounts which provide a good introduction to the subject.

   Lowe, P., 'The Rise to the Premiership', in Taylor, A. J. P. (ed.), *Lloyd George: Twelve Essays* (London, 1971), pp. 95–133; Fry, M., 'Political Change in Britain, August 1914 to December 1916: Lloyd George Replaces Asquith: The Issues Underlying the Drama', *Historical Journal*, 31 (1988), 609–27; McEwen, J. M., 'The Struggle for Mastery in Britain: Lloyd George versus Asquith, December 1916', *Journal of British Studies*, 18 (1978), 131–56; Fair, J., *British Interparty Conferences* (Oxford, 1980), Ch. 7; Turner, J., *British Politics and the Great War: Coalition and Conflict 1915–1918* (New Haven and London, 1992), Ch. 3.

14. On the problems which this presented to Asquith, see Scott's diary, 9–11 Aug. 1917, Wilson, T. (ed.), *The Political Diaries of C. P. Scott 1911–1928* (London, 1970), p. 298.

15. Christopher Addison's diary, 11 Jan. 1917, Addison, C., *Four And A Half Years* (London, 1934), Vol. 2, p. 315.

16. David, E., 'The Liberal Party Divided, 1916–1918', *Historical Journal*, 13 (1970), 509–32; Hosking, G. and King, A., 'Radicals and Whigs in the British Liberal Party, 1906–1914', in Aydelotte, W. O. (ed.), *The History of Parliamentary Behaviour* (Princeton, 1977), pp. 154–5.

17. Searle, G. R., *Country Before Party: Coalition and the idea of 'National Government' in Modern Britain, 1885–1987* (Harlow, 1995), pp. 106–8, 111–13.

18. David, 'Liberal Party Divided', 513–18; Turner, *British Politics and the Great War*, pp. 257–8.

19. Gooch, J., 'The Maurice Debate 1918', *Journal of Contemporary History*, 3 (1968), 211–28.

20. Wilson attempts to show that the Maurice Debate was less influential in determining who received a coupon than is commonly supposed, but he exaggerates his case: Wilson, T., 'The Coupon and the British General Election of 1918', *Journal of Modern History*, 36 (1964), 28–42. See also Douglas, R., 'The Background to the "Coupon" Election Agreements', *English Historical Review*, 86 (1971), 318–36; McGill, B., 'Lloyd George's Timing of the 1918 Election', *Journal of British Studies*, 14 (1974), 109–24.

21. Scott's diary, 11–12 Dec. 1917, Wilson (ed.), *C. P. Scott*, pp. 316–17.

22. McKibbin, R., *The Evolution of the Labour Party 1910–1924* (Oxford, 1974), Ch. 5; Winter, J. M., *Socialism and the Challenge of War: ideas and politics in Britain 1912–18* (London, 1974), Ch. 8.

23. Wilson, *Downfall*, pp 18–19. But the book contains two other theses: the 'diabolism' of Lloyd George and the tragic absence of a continued alliance between the two progressive parties. A similar account of the Liberal dilemma, concentrating on the progressive intelligentsia, is provided in Clarke, P., *Liberals and Social Democrats* (Cambridge, 1978), Ch. 6.

24. The best single study of the UDC is Swartz, M., *The Union of Democratic Control in British Politics During the First World War* (Oxford, 1971). There is also a useful discussion in Hanak, H., 'The Union of Democratic Control During the First World War', *Bulletin of the Institute of Historical Research*, 36 (1963), 168–80, and Robbins, K., *The Abolition of War: The 'Peace Movement' in Britain 1914–1919* (Cardiff, 1976). See also Rempel, R. A., 'Conflicts and Change in Liberal Theory and Practice, 1890–1918: the case of Bertrand Russell', in Waller, P. J. (ed.), *Politics and Social Change in Modern Britain* (Brighton, 1987), esp. pp. 127–37.

25. McGill, B., 'Asquith's Predicament 1914–1918', *Journal of Modern History*, 39 (1967), 283–303. The respect which most activists in the country continued to have for Asquith is emphasised in Bernstein, G. L., 'Yorkshire Liberalism during the First World War', *Historical Journal*, 32 (1989), 107–29.

26. Robbins, K. G., 'Lord Bryce and the First World War', *Historical Journal*, 10 (1967), 268.

27. Asquith himself, however, was not in principle opposed to adopting Conscription at an appropriate moment: see Little, J. G., 'H. H. Asquith and Britain's Manpower Problem, 1914–1915', *Historical Journal*, 82 (1997), 397–409.

28. Clarke, *Liberals and Social Democrats*, p. 185.

29. Bernstein, 'Yorkshire Liberalism', 126.

30. Stubbs, J., 'The Impact of the Great War on the Conservative Party', in Peele, G. and Cook, C. (eds), *The Politics of Reappraisal 1918–1939* (London, 1975), pp. 14–38.

31. Pugh, 'Asquith, Bonar Law and the First Coalition', 813–36. On Bonar Law's problems in December 1916, see Blake, R., *The Unknown Prime Minister: Life and Times of Andrew Bonar Law 1858–1923* (London, 1955), Ch. 19; Adams, R. J. Q., *Bonar Law* (London, 1999), Ch. 11.

32. Ramsden, J., *The Age of Balfour and Baldwin 1902–1940* (London, 1978), pp. 119–21.

33. Tanner, *Political Change*, Ch. 12.

34. Wilson, *Downfall*, p. 29.

35. Ibid., p. 390.

36. Waites, B., *A Class Society at War: England 1914–1918* (Leamington Spa, 1987), esp. Ch. 4. But for a contrary view, see Reid, A., 'The impact of the First World War on British workers', in Wall, R. and Winter, J. (eds), *The Upheaval of War: Family, Work and Welfare in Europe, 1914–1918* (Cambridge, 1988), pp. 224–5.

37. Roberts, R., *The Classic Slum: Salford Life in the First Quarter of the Century* (Manchester, 1971; Pelican edn, 1973), Ch. 9, esp. p. 200.

38. Adams, T., 'Labour and the First World War: Economy, Politics and the Erosion of Local Peculiarity?', *Journal of Regional and Local Studies*, 10 (1990), esp. 27–32.

39. Harrison, R., 'The War Emergency Workers' National Committee, 1914–1920', in Briggs, A. and Saville, J. (eds), *Essays in Labour History 1886–1923* (London, 1971), pp. 211–59.

40. Tanner, *Political Change*, pp. 375–6.

41. However, for a contrary view, see Adams, T., 'Labour and the First World War: Economy, Politics and the Erosion of Local Peculiarity?', *Journal of Regional and Local Studies*, 10 (1990), 29–30.
42. Bernstein, 'Yorkshire Liberalism', 124.
43. Waites, *Class Society*, pp. 48–9.
44. Tanner, *Political Change*, Ch. 12.
45. Ibid., pp. 369–70.
46. This is the case brilliantly argued in Turner, *British Politics and the Great War*, esp. pp. 108, 54.

9   The 1920s

1. Thompson, F. M. L., *English Landed Society in the Nineteenth Century* (London, 1963), Ch. 12; Cannadine, D., *The Decline and Fall of the British Aristocracy* (New Haven, 1990), pp. 110–12; Hutchison, I. G. C., *A Political History of Scotland 1832–1924* (Edinburgh, 1986), p. 320.
2. Douglas, R., *Land, People and Politics: A History of the Land Question in the United Kingdom, 1878–1952* (London, 1976), pp. 189–94; Campbell, J., *Lloyd George: the Goat in the Wilderness 1922–1931* (London, 1977), pp. 119–28; Dawson, M., 'The Liberal Land Policy, 1924–29: Electoral Strategy and Internal Division', *Twentieth-Century British History*, 3 (1991), 272–90.
3. Koss, S., *Nonconformity in Modern British Politics* (London, 1975), Chs. 6–7. Machin, G. I. T., *Politics and the Churches in Great Britain 1869–1921* (Oxford, 1987), pp. 310–26. But during the war temperance briefly acquired a new importance as a factor in increasing national efficiency (Koss, *Nonconformity*, pp. 135–8).
4. Hutchison, *Scotland*, p. 327.
5. Protectionism also proved unpopular with women voters. In the 1923 election Lady Terrington, the second woman to be elected as a Liberal, unseated the former Conservative MP, campaigning hard on Free Trade, on a swing of nearly 10 per cent from Conservative to Liberal.
6. Even during the war some Liberal intellectuals had come to the realisation that international cartels, corporate capitalism and economic nationalism were destroying their traditional free-trade theories (Trentmann, F., 'The strange death of free trade: the erosion of "liberal consensus" in Great Britain, *c*.1903–1932', in Biagini, E. F. [ed.], *Citizenship and community: Liberals, radicals and collective identities in the British Isles, 1865–1931* [Cambridge, 1996], pp. 235–41).
7. Cook, C., *The Age of Alignment: Electoral Politics in Britain 1922–1929* (London, 1975), pp. 80–1. But the same situation existed during the Edwardian decade.
8. Cook, C., 'Liberals, Labour and Local Elections', in Peele, G. and Cook, C., (eds), *The Politics of Reappraisal 1918–1939* (London, 1975), p. 170. But in Huddersfield the Liberals' strength on the Council owed a great deal to the existence of a Liberal–Conservative Pact in municipal elections (Reynolds, J. and Laybourn, K., *Labour Heartland: The History of the Labour Party in West Yorkshire during the inter-war years 1918–1939* [Bradford, 1987]), pp. 48–9).

9. For a very full analysis of the 1918 General Election, Turner, J., *British Politics and the Great War: Coalition and Conflict 1915–1918* (New Haven and London, 1992), Ch. 11.

10. Hutchison, *Scotland*, p. 310.

11. On the Coalition, see Morgan, K. O., *Consensus and Disunity: the Lloyd George Coalition Government 1918–1922* (Oxford, 1979); Morgan, K. O., 'Lloyd George's Stage Army: the Coalition Liberals, 1918–1922', in Taylor, A. J. P. (ed.), *Lloyd George: Twelve Essays* (London, 1971), pp. 225–54; Morgan, K. O. and Morgan, J., *Portrait of a Progressive: The Political Career of Christopher, Viscount Addison* (Oxford, 1980); Kinnear, M., *The Fall of Lloyd George: The Political Crisis of 1922* (London, 1973).

12. Bentley, M., 'Liberal Politics and the Grey Conspiracy of 1921', *Historical Journal*, 20 (1977), 461–78; Morgan, *Consensus and Disunity*, Ch. 8.

13. Campbell, *Goat in the Wilderness*, Ch. 3; Cook, *Age of Alignment*, esp. Chs. 13, 15, 17; Wilson, T., *The Downfall of the Liberal Party, 1914–35* (London, 1966), Ch. 15.

14. The association with Nonconformity strengthened rather than weakened in these years, Dissenters comprising over one-half of all Liberal MPs after 1924.

15. Cregier, D. M., 'Lloyd George's Lucre: The National Liberal Fund', in *Chiefs Without Indians* (Washington, DC, 1982); Searle, G. R., *Corruption in British Politics, 1895–1930* (Oxford, 1987), pp. 379–86; Campbell, *Goat in the Wilderness*, pp. 172–7; McGill, B., 'Glittering Prizes and Party Funds in Perspective, 1882–1931', *Bulletin of the Institute of Historical Research*, 55 (1982), 88–93; Pinto-Duschinsky, M., *British Political Finance 1830–1980* (Washington, DC, 1981), pp. 116–19.

16. The conciliatory Herbert Samuel, brought in as head of the Liberal Party Organisation in February 1927, found his financial dependence on Lloyd George an embarrassment (Wasserstein, H., *Herbert Samuel: A Political Life* [Oxford, 1992], pp. 300–2).

17. Campbell, *Goat in the Wilderness*, pp. 158–61. The Liberal Council enjoyed considerable support amongst the Liberal MPs from Devon and Cornwall: see Wrigley, C., 'Lloyd George and the Labour Movement after 1922', in Loades, J. (ed.), *The Life and Times of David Lloyd George* (Bangor, 1991), p. 63. On the bitter rivalry between Lloyd George and Simon, who had once seen himself as Asquith's natural successor: see Dutton, D., 'Lloyd George, John Simon and the politics of the Liberal Party, 1919–1931', in ibid., pp. 71–86.

18. Dawson, M., 'Liberalism in Devon and Cornwall, 1910–1931: "The Old-Time Religion"', *Historical Journal*, 38 (1995), 430–7; Dawson, 'Liberal Land Policy', 283–90. In Norwich, on the other hand, Lloyd George's new programmes were popular with the Liberals' middle-class leaders: Doyle, B., 'A Conflict of Interests? The Local and National Dimensions of Middle-Class Liberalism, 1900–1935', *Parliamentary History*, 17 (1998), 135.

19. Williamson, P., *National Crisis and National Government: British Politics, the Economy and Empire, 1926–1932* (Cambridge, 1992), pp. 24–7.

20. Bentley, M., *The Liberal Mind 1914–1929* (Cambridge, 1977), p. 213.

21. Koss, S., *The Rise and Fall of the Political Press in Britain, Vol. 2: The Twentieth Century Test* (London, 1984), esp. pp. 448–9.

22. Searle, *Corruption*, pp. 401–6.

23. Bentley, *Liberal Mind*, p. 176.

24. Ibid., *passim*. But was this 'frame of mind' a cause or a consequence of the declining fortunes of the party?

25. Wilson, *Downfall*, p. 197.

26. Matthew, H. C. G., McKibbin, R. I. and Kay, J. A., 'The Franchise Factor in the Rise of the Labour Party', *English Historical Review*, 91 (1976), 723–52.

27. Tanner, D., *Political Change and the Labour Party 1900–1918* (Cambridge, 1990), p. 388, also Ch. 4 and pp. 385–92; Tanner, D., 'The Parliamentary Electoral System, the "Fourth" Reform Act and the Rise of Labour in England and Wales', *Bulletin of the Institute of Historical Research*, 56 (1983), 205–19. See also Hart, M., 'The Liberals, the War and the Franchise', *English Historical Review*, 97 (1982), 820–32.

28. One historian argues that Labour's advance was more rapid at municipal than at parliamentary level (Hart, M., 'The Liberals, the War and the Franchise', 824). In parts of West Yorkshire, on the other hand, Labour was winning seats in parliamentary contests but performing weakly at local government level. This disparity, however, seems to be explicable by reference to the existence of a Liberal–Conservative Alliance in local politics (Reynolds and Laybourn, *Labour Heartland*, pp. 46–50).

29. Turner, J., 'The Labour Vote and the Franchise after 1918: an Investigation of the English Evidence', in Denley, P. and Hopkin, D. (eds), *History and Computing* (Manchester, 1987), pp. 139–40. However, as McKibbin notes, Turner seems to be admitting that most of the new voters in 1918 were working-class, which suggests that the critics of his article are divided amongst themselves (McKibbin, R., *The Ideologies of Class* [Oxford, 1990], pp. 66–7, fn).

30. Childs, M., 'Labour Grows Up. The Electoral System, Political Generations and British Politics, 1890–1929', *Twentieth-Century British History*, 6 (1995), 132–5. Or is it Childs's contention that young working-class males were *inherently* more likely to support Labour? If the latter, then the 1918 Act, by ceding adult manhood suffrage, would have helped raise Labour's share of the vote. On the impact of female voters, see Ch. 7.

31. Asquith to 'Friend' (Mrs Harrison), 30 Jan. 1920, in MacCarthy, D. (ed.), *H. H. A.: Letters of the Earl of Oxford and Asquith to a Friend: First Series 1915–22* (London, 1934), pp. 124–5. Colin Matthew returns to a discussion of the importance of the 'political cultural explanation' of the Liberal decline in 'Rhetoric and Politics in Britain, 1860–1950', in Waller, P. J. (ed.), *Politics and Social Change in Modern Britain* (Brighton, 1987), pp. 53–6.

32. Bentley, M., 'The Liberal Response to Socialism, 1918–29', in Brown, K. D. (ed.), *Essays in Anti-Labour History* (London, 1974), p. 54; Campbell, *Goat in the Wilderness*, p. 74. However, Gladstone on this occasion felt that, on balance, Lloyd George's style of campaigning probably won votes. On the other hand, politics in the 1920s was almost definitely less of a rough house and more 'rational' than it had been before the war: Lawrence, J., *Speaking for the People: Party, Language and Popular Politics in England, 1867–1914* (Cambridge, 1998), pp. 183–8; Dawson, 'Liberalism in Devon and Cornwall', 437.

33. The dilemma is brilliantly explored in Bentley, 'Liberal Response', pp. 42–73.
34. Hobhouse to Scott, 7 Nov. 1924, in Wilson, T. (ed.), *The Political Diaries of C. P. Scott 1911–1928* (London, 1970), p. 468.
35. Wilson, *Downfall*, Ch. 14. Hart thinks that Labour's mistaken decision to put Labour in was made 'under a "progressive" delusion' (Hart, 'The Liberals, the War and the Franchise', 821). Labour also damaged the Liberals through its interventions in the 1924 General Election: of the 104 Conservative gains from the Liberal Party, fifty-one involved Labour interventions (plus one Communist intervention).
36. J. R. Campbell, a prominent Communist, had made a 'Don't Shoot' appeal to soldiers in the *Daily Worker*, as a result of which he found himself charged with incitement to mutiny. But the Labour Attorney-General dropped the prosecution after representations had been made on Campbell's behalf by Labour left-wing backbenchers. It was the Opposition attack on the way in which this case had been handled which led to the fall of MacDonald's government and to the dissolution of Parliament in October 1924.
37. Wrigley, C., *Lloyd George and the Challenge of Labour: The Post War Coalition 1918–1922* (Hemel Hempstead, 1990).
38. Asquith to 'Friend', 20 Oct. 1920, in MacCarthy (ed.), *H. H. A., 1915–22*, p. 159. Given the weak leadership of Willie Adamson and, to a lesser extent, of Clynes, this contemptuous attitude towards the PLP was understandable.
39. Masterman, L., *C. F. G. Masterman* (London, 1939), pp. 336–44. Keynes, for example, even while calling for co-operation between Labour and Liberals, could at the same time say that the 'progressive Liberal' could 'work out his policies without having to do lip-service to Trade-Unionist tyrannies, to the beauties of the class war, or to doctrinaire State Socialism – in none of which he believes' (Keynes, 'Liberalism and Labour' [1926], in *Essays in Persuasion* [London, 1933] p. 342). Characteristically, he dismissed Marxism with the words: 'How can I adopt a creed which, preferring the mud to the fish, exalts the boorish proletariat above the bourgeois and the intelligentsia who, with whatever faults, are the quality in life and surely carry the seeds of all human advancement?' ('A Short View of Russia' [1925], in ibid., p. 300). In fairness, Keynes was also consistently rude about the Conservatives.
40. Dowse, R. E., 'The Entry of the Liberals into the Labour Party, 1910–1920', *Yorkshire Bulletin of Economic and Social Research*, 13 (1961), 78–87; Cline, C. A., *Recruits to Labour: The British Labour Party, 1914 to 1931* (Syracuse, 1963).
41. Freeden, M., *Liberalism Divided: A Study in British Political Thought 1914–1939* (Oxford, 1986). Also important was the discrediting of Hegelianism and the new distrust of state intervention caused by the war. One Liberal newspaper wrote in 1918 that 'those who hate and detest the cramping, blundering activities of the State will look to Liberalism alone for escape' (Bernstein, G. L., 'Yorkshire Liberalism During the First World War', *Historical Journal*, 32 [1989], 123–4). But compare Peter Clarke, who stresses the continuity between the Edwardian 'New Liberals' and Keynes ('Liberals and Social Democrats in Historical Perspective', in Bogdanor, V. [ed.], *Liberal Party Politics* [Oxford, 1983], pp. 34–5).

42. On Labour's breakthrough in the 1919 municipal elections and the reaction to this among Liberals, see Wrigley, *Lloyd George and the Challenge of Labour*, pp. 245–6. In Bethnal Green Labour had no councillors at all on the eve of the war; in 1919 it won eighteen out of the twenty-four seats (Bush, J., *Behind the Lines: East London Labour 1914–1919* [London, 1984], pp. 222–3, 239). Examples of many of these anti-Labour arrangements are to be found in Cook, *Age of Alignment*, pp. 56–63. In Norwich the pre-war municipal pact was extended to all wards in the city, though this arrangement began to collapse after 1925 (Doyle, 'Conflict of Interests?', 137–8).

43. Doyle, 'Conflict of Interests?', 131–40.

44. In Blackburn, for example, 82 per cent of the Liberal vote in 1923 was shared with the Conservative candidate, as against only 12.5 per cent shared with one of the two Labour candidates (5.5 per cent were 'plumpers'). In 1924 the proportion of votes shared with the Conservatives had gone up to 90.5 per cent. A similar situation prevailed in Oldham and Norwich. A retrospective poll, carried out in the 1960s, also suggested that former Liberal voters had switched to the Conservatives in somewhat larger proportions than to the Labour Party (Butler, D. and Stokes, D., *Political Change in Britain* [London, 1969; 1971 ed.], pp. 306–11).

45. The figure is wrongly given in Cook, *Age of Alignment*, p. 316.

46. Savage, M., *The Dynamics of Working-Class Politics: the Labour Movement in Preston, 1880–1940* (Cambridge, 1987), pp. 175–6.

47. McKibbin, *Ideologies of Class*, p. 278.

48. Based on the classification of constituencies in Turner, *British Politics and the Great War*, pp. 472–9.

49. Kinnear, M., *The British Voter: An Atlas and Survey Since 1885* (London, 1968), p. 84.

50. Cook, *Age of Alignment*, pp. 85–6.

51. McKibbin, *Ideologies of Class*, p. 276.

52. Many members of the executive of the WNLF were actually titled: see Chapter 7.

53. Cook, *Age of Alignment*, pp. 195–6. However, ten Liberal MPs who had won in straight fights against Labour actually voted for the Labour amendment!

54. Hutchison, *Scotland*, p. 326.

55. Although once the treasurer of the Free Trade Union, Mond had been forced by the experience of the Great War to modify his belief in the orthodox theory of Free Trade. He thereafter defended Safeguarding of Industry legislation and argued for a programme of imperial self-sufficiency in raw materials (Trentmann, 'The strange death of free trade', pp. 245–8).

56. Reynolds and Laybourn, *Labour Heartland*, p. 48.

57. In October 1924 Asquith himself called the Liberal Party 'a dying party set between the upper and nether millstones' (MacCarthy [ed.], *H. H. A.: Letters of the Earl of Oxford and Asquith to a Friend: Second Series 1922–1927* [London, 1934], p. 107). The phrase was also one much liked by Masterman. He wrote to his wife in August 1920, during the coal strike, 'Liberalism is dumb and crushed between truculent Labour and equally truculent

wealth' (Masterman, *Masterman*, p. 317). Increasingly, Masterman defined the 'middle class' as an unfortunate group trapped between the profiteers, on one side, and the proletariat on the other. See Waites, B., *A Class Society at War: England 1914–1918* (Leamington Spa, 1987), pp. 48–50, and Searle, *Corruption*, pp. 292–5.

58. In fact, the Liberals enjoyed mixed fortunes in these early 1928 by-elections (Campbell, *Goat in the Wilderness*, pp. 206–16).

59. See Ch. 7.

60. Masterman, *Masterman*, p. 346.

61. Freeden, *Liberalism Divided*, Ch. 4. Campbell, *Goat in the Wilderness*, pp. 187–201.

62. Skidelsky, R., *Politicians and the Slump* (London, 1967), pp. 51–6, esp. p. 51.

63. E.g. Thomas, T., 'Aggregate demand in the United Kingdom, 1918–45', in Floud, R. and McCloskey, D. (eds), *The Economic History of Britain Since 1700, vol 2* (Cambridge, 1981), pp. 337–8.

64. In the 1929 election campaign, Lloyd George's critics tried, not very successfully, to explain away their earlier dismissals of the 'Yellow Book' programme (Campbell, *Goat in the Wilderness*, pp. 229–30).

65. *Britain's Industrial Future* (1928), p. xx and *passim*.

66. See also Keynes, M., 'The End of Laissez-Faire' (1926), in *Essays in Persuasion*, pp. 312–22.

67. *Britain's Industrial Future*, pp. 464–5.

68. Cowling, M., *The Impact of Labour 1920–1924* (Cambridge, 1971), pp. 350–1. But, as Cowling says, Asquith seemed largely unaware of the great dangers he was running.

69. Bentley calls this decision 'the greatest political mistake Asquith ever made' (Bentley, 'Liberal Response', p. 55). See also Cowling, *Impact of Labour*, Ch. 18. But other historians argue that he really had no choice in the matter (Wilson, *Downfall*, pp. 265–6).

70. For a good introduction to the subject, see Butler, D. E., *The Electoral System in Britain Since 1918* (Oxford, 1963), pp. 10–11, 38–48; Hart, J., *Proportional Representation: Critics of the British Electoral System 1820–1945* (Oxford, 1992). A more detailed account of the political manoeuvres is provided by Pugh, M., *Electoral Reform in War and Peace 1906–18* (London, 1978).

71. Grigg, J., 'Lloyd George and Electoral Reform', in Bean, J. M. W. (ed.), *The Political Culture of Modern Britain* (London, 1987), pp. 165–77.

72. Butler, *Electoral System*, pp. 189–94.

73. At the Carlton Club meeting, of the Scottish MPs seventeen voted with Chamberlain, only six (including Bonar Law and the party chairman, George Younger) against. In the ensuing election a pact operated in nearly two-thirds of all constituencies, compared with under one-fifth in England (Hutchison, *Scotland*, p. 314).

74. Searle, G. R., *Country Before Party: Coalition and the idea of 'National Government' in Modern Britain, 1885–1987* (Harlow, 1995), Ch. 6.

75. Perhaps the best brief account of the 'fusion' episode is provided by Morgan, *Consensus and Disunity*, pp. 180–90. See also Wrigley, *Lloyd George and the Challenge of Labour*, pp. 201–2, 242–4.

10 Conclusion

1. Cited in J. A. Thompson, 'Historians and the Decline of the Liberal Party', *Albion*, 22 (1990), 82. When Tanner claims to be demonstrating the 'viability' of the Edwardian Liberal Party in the face of Labour's 'challenge', he is sometimes doing nothing more than explaining why the Labour Party was never to be as electorally effective (Tanner, D., *Political Change and the Labour Party 1900–1918* [Cambridge, 1990]).
2. Cited in Glaser, J. F., 'English Nonconformity and the Decline of Liberalism', *American Historical Review*, 63 (1957–8), 361.
3. Mackail, J. W. and Wyndham, G., *Life and Letters of George Wyndham, Vol. II* (London, n.d.), p. 539.
4. Cowling, M., *The Impact of Labour 1920–1924* (Cambridge, 1971), Chs. 18–20.
5. Cited in Cook, C., *The Age of Alignment: Electoral Politics in Britain, 1922–1929* (London, 1975), p. 183.
6. Samuel Storey, *Newcastle Daily Chronicle*, 12 Jan. 1906, cited in Purdue, A. W., 'The Liberal and Labour Parties in North-East Politics, 1900–14: The Struggle for Supremacy', *International Review of Social History*, 26 (1981), 12–13.
7. Matthew, H. C. G., *The Liberal Imperialists: the ideas and politics of a post-Gladstonian élite* (Oxford, 1973), p. 128.
8. A highly sympathetic article by Carolyn W. White describes the author and the circumstances in which the book was written, showing how indebted it is to to Strachey and also to Jung ('The Strange Death of Liberal England in Its Time', *Albion*, 17 [1985]), 425–47).
9. Bentley, M., 'The Liberal Response to Socialism, 1918–29', in Brown, K. D. (ed.), *Essays in Anti-Labour History* (London, 1974), p. 72.
10. Spender, S., *Forward From Liberalism* (London, 1937), esp. Chs. 2–3 and p. 89.
11. Clarke, P., 'Liberals and Social Democrats in Historical Perspective', in Bogdanor, V. (ed.), *Liberal Party Politics* (Oxford, 1983), pp. 39–42. Clarke's thesis in 1983 was that, with the Labour Party apparently disintegrating, its 'social democratic' wing would finally abandon it and, within the ambit of the 'Alliance', reunite with the more ideologically compatible Liberals.
12. Balfour, M., *Britain and Joseph Chamberlain* (London, 1985), pp. 149–50.
13. Clarke, P. F., *Lancashire and the New Liberalism* (Cambridge, 1971), p. 394.
14. Hutchison, I. G. C., *A Political History of Scotland 1832–1924* (Edinburgh, 1986), p. 312.
15. On this subject, see Hannah, L., *The Rise of the Corporate Economy: The British Experience* (London, 1976).
16. James, R. R. (ed.), *Memoirs of a Conservative: J. C. C. Davidson's Memoirs and Papers 1910–37* (London, 1969), pp. 289–90. Pinto-Duschinsky, M., *British Political Finance 1830–1980* (Washington, DC, 1981), pp. 111–13.
17. *National Liberal Federation Report*, 1921.
18. Savage, M., *The Dynamics of Working-Class Politics: the Labour Movement in Preston, 1880–1940* (Cambridge, 1987), p. 144.
19. See for example, MacDonald's remarks at Southampton in 1894, on accepting the invitation to contest the borough as an independent Labour

representative: 'Our movement is neither a party nor a class movement, but a national one', in Marquand, D., *Ramsay MacDonald* (London, 1977), p. 37; this was a claim which he also liked to make in his later 'theoretical' defences of socialism.

20.   McKibbin, R., *The Ideologies of Class* (Oxford, 1990), p. 281.

APPENDIX

A Liberal Party Leaders, 1885–1931

William Ewart Gladstone	to Mar. 1894
Lord Rosebery	Mar. 1894 to Oct. 1896
William Vernon Harcourt	Oct. 1896 to Feb. 1899
Sir Henry Campbell-Bannerman	Feb. 1899 to Apr. 1908
H. H. Asquith (Lord Oxford & Asquith)	Apr. 1908 to Oct. 1926
David Lloyd George	Oct. 1926 to Nov. 1931
Herbert Samuel	from Nov. 1931

B Liberal Cabinets, 1886–1915

Gladstone's Cabinet, Feb. to Aug. 1886

Prime Minister	W. E. Gladstone
Lord Chancellor	Lord Herschell
Foreign Secretary	Lord Rosebery
Home Secretary	H. C. E. Childers
Chancellor of the Exchequer	W. V. Harcourt
Colonial Secretary	Earl Granville
Indian Secretary	Earl of Kimberley
First Lord of Admiralty	Marquess of Ripon
War Secretary	H. Campbell-Bannerman
Sec. of State for Ireland	J. Morley
Scottish Secretary	G. O. Trevelyan (to Apr.)
Pres. of Local Govt Board	J. Chamberlain
	J. Stansfeld (from Apr.)
Pres. of Board of Trade	A. J. Mundella
Lord President of the Council	Earl Spencer

Gladstone's and Rosebery's Cabinets, Aug. 1892 to June 1895

Prime Minister	W. E. Gladstone (to Mar. 1894)
	Earl of Rosebery (from Mar. 1894)
Lord Chancellor	Lord Herschell
Foreign Secretary	Earl of Rosebery (to Mar. 1894)
	Earl of Kimberley (from Mar. 1894)
Home Secretary	H. H. Asquith
Chancellor of the Exchequer	W. V. Harcourt
Colonial Secretary	Marquess of Ripon
Indian Secretary	Earl of Kimberley (to Mar. 1894)
	H. Fowler (from Mar. 1894)
First Lord of Admiralty	Earl Spencer
War Secretary	H. Campbell-Bannerman
Sec. of State for Ireland	J. Morley
Scottish Secretary	G. O. Trevelyan
Pres. of Local Govt Board	H. Fowler (to Mar. 1894)
	G. J. Shaw-Lefevre (from Mar. 1894)
Pres. of Board of Trade	A. J. Mundella (to Mar. 1894)
	J. Bryce (from Mar. 1894)
V-Pres. of Bd of Education	A. H. D. Acland
Lord President of the Council	Earl of Kimberley
Lord Privy Seal	W. E. Gladstone (to Mar. 1894)
	Lord Tweedmouth (from Mar. 1894)
Ch. of Duchy of Lancaster	J. Bryce (to Mar. 1894)
	Lord Tweedmouth (from Mar. 1894)
Postmaster-General	A. Morley
First Commissioner of Works	G. J. Shaw-Lefevre (to Mar. 1894)

Campbell-Bannerman's Cabinet, Dec. 1905 to Apr. 1908

Prime Minister	Sir H. Campbell-Bannerman
Lord Chancellor	Lord Loreburn (Sir R. Reid)
Foreign Secretary	Edward Grey
Home Secretary	H. Gladstone
Chancellor of the Exchequer	H. H. Asquith
Colonial Secretary	Earl of Elgin
Indian Secretary	J. Morley
First Lord of Admiralty	Lord Tweedmouth
War Secretary	R. B. Haldane
Sec. of State for Ireland	J. Bryce (to Jan. 1907)
	A. Birrell (from Jan. 1907)
Scottish Secretary	J. Sinclair
Pres. of Local Govt Board	J. Burns
Pres. of Board of Trade	D. Lloyd George
Pres. of Board of Agriculture	Earl Carrington
Pres. of Board of Education	A. Birrell (to Jan. 1907)

	R. McKenna (from Jan. 1907)
Lord President of the Council	Earl of Crewe
Lord Privy Seal	Marquess of Ripon
Ch. of Duchy of Lancaster	Sir H. Fowler
Postmaster-General	S. Buxton
First Commissioner of Works	L. Harcourt (from Mar. 1907)

Asquith's Cabinet, Apr. 1908 to May 1915

Prime Minister	H. H. Asquith
Lord Chancellor	Lord Loreburn (to June 1912)
	Lord Haldane (from June 1912)
Foreign Secretary	Edward Grey
Home Secretary	H. Gladstone (to Feb. 1910)
	W. Churchill (Feb. 1910 to Oct. 1911)
	R. McKenna (from Oct. 1911)
Chancellor of the Exchequer	D. Lloyd George
Colonial Secretary	Earl of Crewe (to Nov. 1910)
	L. Harcourt (from Nov. 1910)
Indian Secretary	J. Morley (to Nov. 1910)
	Earl of Crewe (Nov. 1910 to Mar. 1911)
	Viscount Morley (Mar. to May 1911)
	Earl of Crewe (from May 1911)
First Lord of Admiralty	R. McKenna (to Oct. 1911)
	W. Churchill (from Oct. 1911)
War Secretary	R. B. Haldane (to June 1912)
	J. Seely (June 1912 to Mar. 1914)
	H. H. Asquith (Mar. to Aug. 1914)
	Lord Kitchener (from Aug. 1914)
Sec. of State for Ireland	A. Birrell
Scottish Secretary	J. Sinclair (Lord Pentland) (to Feb. 1912)
	T. McKinnon Wood (from Feb. 1912)
Pres. of Local Govt Board	J. Burns (to Feb. 1914)
	H. Samuel (from Feb. 1914)
Pres. of Board of Trade	W. Churchill (to Feb. 1910)
	S. Buxton (Feb. 1910 to Feb. 1914)
	J. Burns (Feb. to Aug. 1914)
	W. Runciman (from Aug. 1914)
Pres. of Board of Agriculture	Earl Carrington (to Oct. 1911)
	W. Runciman (Oct. 1911 to Aug. 1914)
	Lord Lucas (from Aug. 1914)
Pres. of Board of Education	W. Runciman (to Oct. 1911)
	J. Pease (from Oct. 1911)
Lord President of the Council	Lord Tweedmouth (Apr. to Oct. 1908)
	Viscount Wolverhampton (Oct. 1908 to June 1910)
	Earl Beauchamp (June to Nov. 1910)

	Viscount Morley (Nov. 1910 to Aug. 1914)
	Earl Beauchamp (from Aug. 1914)
Lord Privy Seal	Marquess of Ripon (to Oct. 1908)
	Earl of Crewe (Oct. 1908 to Oct. 1911)
	Earl Carrington (Oct. 1911 to Feb. 1912)
	Marquess of Crewe (from Feb. 1912)
Ch. of Duchy of Lancaster	H. Fowler (to Apr. 1908)
	Lord Fitzmaurice (Apr. 1908 to June 1909)
	H. Samuel (June 1909 to Feb. 1910)
	J. Pease (Feb. 1910 to Oct. 1911)
	C. Hobhouse (Oct. 1911 to Feb. 1914)
	C. Masterman (Feb. 1914 to Feb. 1915)
	E. Montagu (from Feb. 1915)
Postmaster-General	S. Buxton (to Feb. 1910)
	H. Samuel (Feb. 1910 to Feb. 1914)
	C. Hobhouse (from Feb. 1914)
First Commissioner of Works	L. Harcourt (to Nov. 1910)
	Earl Beauchamp (Nov. 1910 to Aug. 1914)
	Lord Emmott (from Aug. 1914)
Attorney-General	R. Isaacs (June 1912 to Oct. 1913)
	Sir J. Simon (from Oct. 1913)

C   Liberal Cabinet Ministers in Coalition Governments, 1915–22

Asquith's Ministry, May 1915 to Dec. 1916

Lord Buckmaster	Lord Chancellor
W. Churchill	Chancellor of Duchy of Lancaster (to Nov. 1915)
Marquess of Crewe	Lord President of Council
	Pres. of Board of Education (from Aug. 1916)
A. Birrell	Irish Secretary (to July 1916)
E. Grey	Foreign Secretary
L. Harcourt	First Commissioner of Works
D. Lloyd George	Minister of Munitions (to July 1916)
	War Secretary (from July 1916)
R. McKenna	Chancellor of the Exchequer
E. Montagu	Chancellor of Duchy of Lancaster (Jan. to July 1916)
	Minister of Munitions (from July 1916)
W. Runciman	President of Board of Trade
H. Samuel	Chancellor of Duchy of Lancaster (Nov. 1915 to Jan. 1916)
	Home Secretary (from Jan. 1916)
J. Simon	Home Secretary (to Jan. 1916)
H. Tennant	Scottish Secretary (from July 1916)
T. McKinnon Wood	Scottish Secretary (to July 1916)
	Chancellor of Duchy of Lancaster (from July 1916)

Lloyd George's Ministry, Dec. 1916 to Oct. 1922

C. Addison	Minister of Munitions (to July 1917)
	Minister of Reconstruction (July 1917 to Jan. 1919) (not Cabinet post)
	Pres. of Local Govt Bd (Jan. to June 1919)
	Minister of Health (June 1919 to Apr. 1921)
	Minister Without Portfolio (Apr. to July 1921)
Sir F. Cawley	Chancellor of Duchy of Lancaster (to Feb. 1918)
W. Churchill	Minister of Munitions (July 1917 to Jan. 1919)
	War Secretary (Jan. 1919 to Feb. 1921)
	Colonial Secretary (from Feb. 1921)
H. A. L. Fisher	President of Board of Education
Sir H. Greenwood	Irish Secretary (from Apr. 1920)
Sir G. Hewart	Attorney-General (Nov. 1921 to March 1922)
T. Macnamara	Minister of Labour (from Mar. 1920)
I. Macpherson	Irish Secretary (Jan. 1919 to Apr. 1920)
A. Mond	Minister of Health (from Apr. 1921)
E. Montagu	Indian Secretary (July 1917 to Mar. 1922)
R. Munro	Scottish Secretary
Lord Rhondda	Pres. of Local Govt Bd (to June 1917)
E. Shortt	Irish Secretary (May 1918 to Jan. 1919)
A. Stanley	Pres. of Board of Trade (to May 1919)

D General Election Results, 1885–1931

1885	Conservatives 251
	Liberals 333
	Irish Nationalists 86
1886	Conservatives 316
	Liberals 191
	Liberal Unionists 78
	Irish Nationalists 85
1892	Liberals 273
	Conservatives 269
	Irish Nationalists 81
	Liberal Unionists 46
	Independent Labour 1
1895	Conservatives 340
	Liberals 177
	Liberal Unionists 71
	Irish Nationalists 82
1900	Conservative & Liberal Unionists 402
	Liberals 184
	Irish Nationalists 82

Labour 2
1906   Liberals 400
Unionists 157
Irish Nationalists 83
Labour 30
Jan. 1910   Liberals 275
Unionists 273
Irish Nationalists 82
Labour 40
Dec. 1910 Liberals 272
Unionists 272
Irish Nationalists 84
Labour 42
1918   Coalition Conservatives 335
Independent Liberals 28
Coalition Liberals 133
Labour 63
Coalition Labour 10
Sinn Fein 73
Independent Conservatives 23
Irish Nationalists 7
Irish Unionists 25
Others 10
1922   Conservatives 345
Labour 142
National Liberals 62
Liberals 54
Others 12
1923   Labour 191
Conservatives 258
Liberals 159
Others 7
1924   Conservatives 419
Labour 151
Liberals 40
Communist 1
Others 4
1929   Labour 288
Conservatives 260
Liberals 59
Others 8
1931   Conservatives 473
Labour 52
National Labour 13
Independent Labour 4
Liberal Nationals 35
Others 5
Liberals 33

E   Regional Strength of the Liberal Party

General Elections

The percentages refer to the proportion of seats in each region won by the Liberals in general elections during these years. An equals sign (=) indicates that the Liberals achieved identical ratios of success in these regions. For 1886–1910 the regions are those demarcated in Neal Blewett, *The Peers, the Parties and the People: The General Elections of 1910* (London, 1972); and for 1922–9 those demarcated in Tom Stannage, *Baldwin Thwarts the Opposition* (London, 1980).

1886–1910

1.   Forth Valley (87%)
2.   North-East Scotland (86%) = Rural Wales (86%)
3.   Industrial Wales (76.5%)
4.   North-East England (74%)
5.   West Riding, Yorkshire (71%)
6.   Scottish Highlands (67%)
7.   East Midlands (62%)
8.   Clyde Valley (58%)
9.   Southern Scotland (57%) = South-West Peninsula (57%)
10. East Anglia (49.5%)
11. Eastern Lancastria (46%)
12. Lincolnshire (43%)
13. Severn (38%)
14. North and East Ridings (36%) = Cumbria (36%)
15. Inner London (33%)
16. Western Midlands (28.5%)
17. Wessex (19.5%) = Thames Valley (19.5%)
18. Outer London (17%)
19. Western Marches (14%)
20. Western Lancastria (10.5%)
21. South-East England (6.5%)

1922–9

1.   Rural Wales (79%)
2.   Scottish Highlands (75%)
3.   Western Peninsula (46%)
4.   North-East Scotland (36%)
5.   Forth Valley (23%)
6.   East Anglia (22%) = Southern Scotland (22%)
7.   Severn (20%)
8.   Lincolnshire etc (19%) = Eastern Lancastria (19%)
9.   East Midlands (16%)
10. North-East England (15%)
11. Yorkshire, West Riding (13%)

12. South-Central England (12%) = Wessex (12%) = Western Lancastria (12%)
13. Rest of Yorkshire (11.5%)
14. North-West Midlands (11%)
15. Inner London (10%)
16. South-West Midlands (7.5%)
17. Clyde Valley (7%)
18. Salop (5%)
19. Cumbria (3.5%)
20. Outer London (3%) = South-East England (3%) = Industrial Wales (3%)

F   Liberal Women and Parliamentary Elections, 1918–1929 (inc.)

Liberal MPs

Margaret Wintringham (Louth), Sept. 1921, 1922, 1923 (defeated, 1924, 1929)

Lady Terrington (Wycombe), 1923 (defeated, 1922, 1924)

Hilda Runciman (St Ives, Cornwall), Mar. 1928 (defeated, Tavistock, 1929)

Megan Lloyd George (Anglesey), 1929 (later Labour MP for Carmarthenshire, Feb. 1957–May 1966)

(Eleanor Rathbone) (Ind.), Combined English Universities. 1929 (defeated, East Toxteth, 1922)

Though each was a formidable figure in her own right, three of these four MPs were related to male Liberal MPs: Margaret Wintringham being the widow of Tom Wintringham, Hilda Runciman the wife of Walter Runciman, and Megan Lloyd George the daughter of David Lloyd George.

In all, the Liberal Party ran forty-four candidates, involving fifty-six contests. In thirteen of these contests (23.2%), the Liberal lost her deposit.

Thirty-six of the forty-four candidates contested only one election.

Contesting two elections: Helen Fraser, Miss E. B. Mitchell, Hilda Runciman.

Contesting three elections: Lady Terrington, Miss M. P. Grant, Miss A. V. Garland.

Contesting five elections: Mrs Margaret Wintringham, Mrs Margery Corbett-Ashby.

SELECT BIBLIOGRAPHY

Books

Adams, R. J. Q., *Bonar Law* (London, 1999)

Barker, M., *Gladstone and Radicalism: The Reconstruction of Liberal Policy in Britain 1885–94* (Hassocks, 1975)

Bealey, F. and Pelling, H., *Labour and Politics, 1900–1906* (London, 1958)

Bean, J. M. W. (ed.), *The Political Culture of Modern Britain: Studies in Memory of Stephen Koss* (London, 1987)

Bebbington, D. W., *The Nonconformist Conscience: Chapel and Politics 1870–1914* (London, 1982)

Bentley, M., *The Liberal Mind 1914–1929* (Cambridge, 1977)

Bentley, M., *The Climax of Liberal Politics: British Liberalism in Theory and Practice 1868–1918* (London, 1987)

Bernstein, G. L., *Liberalism and Liberal Politics in Edwardian England* (London, 1986)

Biagini, E. F., *Liberty, Retrenchment and Reform: Popular Liberalism in the Age of Gladstone, 1860–1880* (Cambridge), 1992)

Biagini, E. F. (ed.), *Citizenship and community: Liberals, radicals and collective identities in the British Isles 1865–1931* (Cambridge, 1996)

Biagini, E. F., and Reid, A. J. (eds), *Currents of Radicalism: Popular radicalism, organised labour and party politics in Britain 1850–1914* (Cambridge, 1991)

Blaazer, D., *The Popular Front and the Progressive Tradition: Socialists, Liberals, and the Quest for Unity, 1884–1939* (Cambridge, 1992)

Blewett, N., *The Peers, the Parties and the People: The British General Elections of 1910* (London, 1972)

Bogdanor, V. (ed.), *Liberal Party Politics* (Oxford, 1983)

Briggs, A. and Saville, J. (eds), *Essays in Labour History 1886–1923* (London, 1971)

Brown, K. D. (ed.), *Essays in Anti-Labour History* (London, 1974)

Brown, K. D. (ed.), *The First Labour Party 1906–1914* (London, 1985)

Butt, J. and Clarke, I. F. (eds), *The Victorians and Social Protest* (Newton Abbot, 1973)

Campbell, J., *Lloyd George: The Goat in the Wilderness 1922–1931* (London, 1977)

Cassar, G. H., *Asquith As War Leader* (London & Rio Grande, 1994)

Clarke, P., *Liberals and Social Democrats* (Cambridge, 1978)

Clarke, P. F., *Lancashire and the New Liberalism* (Cambridge, 1971)

Clegg, H. A., Fox, A. and Thompson, A. F. (eds.), *A History of British Unions Since 1889, Vol. I* (Oxford, 1964)

Cline, C. A., *Recruits to Labour: The British Labour Party, 1914 to 1931* (Syracuse, New York), 1963)

Coetzee, F., *For Party or Country: Nationalism and the Dilemmas of Popular Conservatism in Edwardian England* (New York, 1990)

Collini, S., *Liberalism and Sociology: L. T. Hobhouse and Political Argument in England, 1880–1914* (Cambridge, 1979)

Cook, C., *The Age of Alignment: Electoral Politics in Britain 1922–1929* (London, 1975)

Cook, C., *A Short History of the Liberal Party, 1900–1976* (London, 1976)

Cowling, M., *The Impact of Labour 1920–1924* (Cambridge, 1971)

Cregier, D. M., *Bounder from Wales: Lloyd George's Career Before the First World War* (Columbia, Miss., 1976)

Cregier, D. M., *Chiefs Without Indians* (Washington, DC, 1982)

Dangerfield, G., *The Strange Death of Liberal England* (London, 1935)

Denley, P. and Hopkin, D. (eds), *History and Computing* (Manchester, 1987)

Douglas, R., *The History of the Liberal Party, 1895–1970* (London, 1971)

Douglas, R., *Land, People and Politics: A History of the Land Question in the United Kingdom, 1878–1952* (London, 1976)

Emy, H. V., *Liberals, Radicals and Social Politics, 1892–1914* (Cambridge, 1973)

Fair, J. D., *British Interparty Conferences* (Oxford, 1980)

Fforde, M., *Conservatism and Collectivism, 1886–1914* (Edinburgh, 1990)

Freeden, M., *The New Liberalism: An Ideology of Social Reform* (Oxford, 1978)

Freeden, M., *Liberalism Divided: A Study in British Political Thought 1914–1939* (Oxford, 1986)

Freeden, M. (ed.), *Minutes of the Rainbow Circle, 1894–1924* (London, 1989)

Fry, M., *Patronage and Principle: A Political History of Modern Scotland* (Aberdeen, 1987)

Gilbert, B. B., *The Evolution of National Insurance in Great Britain* (London, 1966)

Gilbert, B. B., *David Lloyd George: The Architect of Change 1863–1912* (London, 1987)

Gilbert, B. B., *David Lloyd George: The Organizer of Victory 1912–16* (London, 1992)

Gregory, R., *The Miners and British Politics 1906–1914* (Oxford, 1968)

Grigg, J., *Lloyd George: The People's Champion: 1902–1911* (London, 1978)

Grigg, J., *Lloyd George: From Peace to War 1912–1916* (London, 1985)

Hamer, D. A., *Liberal Politics in the Age of Gladstone and Rosebery* (Oxford, 1972)

Harris, J., *Unemployment and Politics: A Study in English Social Policy 1886–1914* (Oxford, 1972)

Harrison, B., *Separate Spheres: The Opposition to Women's Suffrage in Britain* (London, 1978)

Harrison, B., *Prudent Revolutionaries: Portraits of British Feminists between the Wars* (Oxford, 1987)

Hart, J., *Proportional Representation: Critics of the British Electoral System 1820–1945* (Oxford, 1992)

Harvie, C., *The Lights of Liberalism: University Liberals and the Challenge of Democracy 1860–86* (London, 1976)

Hay, J. R., *The Origins of the Liberal Welfare Reforms 1906–1914* (London, 1975)

Hazlehurst, C., *Politicians at War: July 1914 to May 1915* (London, 1971)

Holton, S. S., *Feminism and Democracy: Women's Suffrage and Reform Politics in Britain 1900–1918* (Cambridge, 1986)

Howe, A., *Free Trade and Liberal England 1846–1946* (Oxford, 1997)

Hume, L. P., *The National Union of Women's Suffrage Societies, 1897–1914* (Brighton, 1982)

Hutchison, I. G. C., *A Political History of Scotland 1832–1924* (Edinburgh, 1986)

Jalland, P., *The Liberals and Ireland: The Ulster Question in British Politics to 1914* (Brighton, 1980)

Jay, R., *Joseph Chamberlain: A Political Study* (Oxford, 1981)

Jenkins, R., *Mr Balfour's Poodle* (London, 1954)

Jenkins, R., *Asquith* (London, 1964)

Jenkins, R., *Gladstone* (London & Basingstoke, 1995)

Jenkins, T. A., *Gladstone, Whiggery and the Liberal Party 1874–1886* (Oxford, 1988)

Jenkins, T. A., *The Liberal Ascendancy, 1830–1886* (Basingstoke, 1994)

Jones, G. W., *Borough Politics: Wolverhampton Town Council, 1888–1964* (London, 1969)

Joyce, P., *Visions of The People: Industrial England and the question of class, 1848–1914* (Cambridge, 1991)

Kendle, J., *Ireland and the Federal Solution, 1870–1921* (Kingston, Ont., 1989)

Kendle, J., *Federal Britain: A History* (London, 1997)

Kennedy, P. and Nicholls, A. (eds.), *Nationalist and Racialist Movements in Britain and Germany Before 1914* (London, 1981)

Kinnear, M., *The British Voter: An Atlas and Survey Since 1885* (London, 1968)

Kinnear, M., *The Fall of Lloyd George: The Political Crisis of 1922* (London, 1973)

Koss, S., *Lord Haldane: Scapegoat for Liberalism* (New York, 1969)

Koss, S., *Nonconformity in Modern British Politics* (London, 1975)

Koss, S., *Asquith* (London, 1976)

Koss, S., *The Rise and Fall of the Political Press in Britain, Vol. 2: The Twentieth Century Test* (London, 1984)

Langan, M. and Schwarz, B. (eds.), *Crises in the British State 1880–1930* (London, 1985)

Lawrence, J., *Speaking for the People: Party, Language and Popular Politics in England, 1867–1914* (Cambridge, 1998)

Laybourn, K. and Reynolds, J., *Liberalism and the Rise of Labour 1890–1918* (London, 1984)

Loades, J. (ed.), *The Life and Times of David Lloyd George* (Bangor, 1991)

Loughlin, J., *Gladstone, Home Rule and the Ulster Question 1882–93* (Dublin, 1986)

Lubenow, W. C., *Parliamentary Politics and the Home Rule Crisis: The British House of Commons in 1886* (Oxford, 1988)

Machin, G. I. T., *Politics and the Churches in Great Britain 1869–1921* (Oxford, 1987)

McKibbin, R., *The Evolution of the Labour Party 1910–1924* (Oxford, 1974)

McKibbin, R., *The Ideologies of Class* (Oxford, 1990)

Marquand, D., *Ramsay MacDonald* (London, 1977)

Masterman, L., *C. F. G. Masterman* (London, 1939)

Matthew, H. C. G., *The Liberal Imperialists: The ideas and politics of a Post-Glad-stonian élite* (Oxford, 1973)

Matthew, H. C. G., *Gladstone 1875–1898* (Oxford, 1995)

Maurice, N., *The Maurice Case* (London, 1972)

Morgan, D., *Suffragists and Liberals: The Politics of Woman Suffrage in Britain* (Oxford, 1975)

Morgan, J., *Conflict and Order: The Police and Labour Disputes in England and Wales 1900–1939* (Oxford, 1987)

Morgan, K. O., *Wales in British Politics 1868–1922* (Cardiff, 1970)

Morgan, K. O., *The Age of Lloyd George: The Liberal Party and British Politics, 1890–1929* (London, 1971)

Morgan, K. O., *Consensus and Disunity: The Lloyd George Coalition Government 1918–1922* (Oxford, 1979)

Morgan, K. O. and Morgan, J., *Portrait of a Progressive: The Political Career of Christopher, Viscount Addison* (Oxford, 1980)

Morris, A. J. A., *Radicalism Against War 1906–1914* (London, 1972)

Morris, A. J. A. (ed.), *Edwardian Radicalism 1900–1914* (London, 1974)

Murray, B. K., *The People's Budget 1909–10* (Oxford, 1980)

O'Day, A. (ed.), *The Edwardian Age: Conflict and Stability 1900–1914* (London, 1979)

Offer, A., *Property and Politics, 1870–1914* (Cambridge, 1981)

Parry, J., *The Rise and Fall of Liberal Government in Victorian Britain* (New Haven & London, 1993)

Peele, G. and Cook, C., (eds), *The Politics of Reappraisal 1918–1939* (London, 1975)

Pelling, H., *Social Geography of British Elections 1885–1910* (London, 1967)

Pelling, H., *Popular Politics and Society in Late Victorian Britain* (London, 1968)

Phillips, G. D., *The Diehards: Aristocratic Society and Politics in Edwardian England* (Cambridge, Mass., 1979)

Pinto-Duschinsky, M., *British Political Finance 1830–1980* (Washington, DC, 1981)

Pugh, M., *Electoral Reform in War and Peace 1906–18* (London, 1978)

Pugh, M., *The Making of Modern British Politics, 1867–1939* (Oxford, 1982)

Pugh, M., *Lloyd George* (London, 1988)

Pugh, M., *Women and the Women's Movement in Britain, 1914–1959* (Basingstoke, 1992)

Ramsden, J., *The Age of Balfour and Baldwin 1902–1940* (London, 1978)

Rempel, R. A., *Unionists Divided: Arthur Balfour, Joseph Chamberlain and the Unionist Free Traders* (Newton Abbot, 1972)

Reynolds, J. and Laybourn, K., *Labour Heartland: The History of the Labour Party in West Yorkshire during the Inter-War Years 1918–1939* (Bradford, 1987)

Rosen, A., *Rise Up Women! The Militant Campaign of the Women's Social and Political Union 1903–1914* (London, 1974)

Rover, C., *Women's Suffrage and Party Politics in Britain, 1866–1914* (London & Toronto, 1967)

Rowland, P., *The Last Liberal Governments: The Promised Land, 1905–1910* (London, 1968)

Rowland, P., *The Last Liberal Governments: Unfinished Business, 1911–1914* (London, 1971)

218   Select Bibliography

Russell, A. K., *Liberal Landslide; The General Election of 1906* (Newton Abbot, 1973)
Savage, M., *The Dynamics of Working-Class Politics: The Labour Movement in Preston, 1880–1940* (Cambridge, 1987)
Scally, R. J., *The Origins of the Lloyd George Coalition: The Politics of Social Imperialism, 1900–1918* (Princeton, 1975)
Searle, G. R., *The Quest for National Efficiency, 1899–1914* (Oxford, 1971; new edn, London, 1990)
Searle, G. R., *Corruption in British Politics, 1895–1930* (Oxford, 1987)
Searle, G. R., *Country Before Party: Coalition and the Idea of 'National Government' in Modern Britain 1885–1987* (Harlow, 1995)
Shannon, R., *Gladstone: Heroic Minister 1865–1898* (Harmondsworth, 1999)
Sked, A. and Cook, C. (eds.), *Crisis and Controversy: Essays in honour of A. J. P. Taylor* (London, 1976)
Skidelsky, R., *Politicians and the Slump* (London, 1967)
Stansky, P., *Ambitions and Strategies: The struggle for the leadership of the Liberal Party in the 1890s* (Oxford, 1964)
Swartz, M., *The Union of Democratic Control in British Politics During the First World War* (Oxford, 1971)
Sykes, A., *Tariff Reform in British Politics 1903–1913* (Oxford, 1979)
Sykes, A., *The Rise and Fall of British Liberalism, 1776–1918* (Harlow, 1997)
Tanner, D., *Political Change and the Labour Party 1900–1918* (Cambridge, 1990)
Taylor, A. J. P., *Politics in Wartime* (London, 1964)
Taylor, A. J. P. (ed.), *Lloyd George: Twelve Essays* (London, 1971)
Thompson, F. M. L., *English Landed Society in the Nineteenth Century* (London, 1963)
Thompson, P., *Socialists, Liberals and Labour. The Struggle for London 1885–1914* (London, 1967)
Turner, John, *British Politics and the Great War: Coalition and Conflict 1915–1918* (New Haven & London, 1992)
Waites, B., *A Class Society at War: England 1914–1918* (Leamington Spa, 1987)
Wall, R. and Winter, J. (eds), *The Upheaval of War: Family, Work and Welfare in Europe, 1914–1918* (Cambridge, 1988)
Waller, P. J. (ed.), *Politics and Social Change in Modern Britain* (Brighton, 1987)
Wasserstein, B., *Herbert Samuel: A Political Life* (Oxford, 1992)
Williamson, P., *National Crisis and National Government: British Politics, the Economy and Empire, 1926–1932* (Cambridge, 1992)
Wilson, T., *The Downfall of the Liberal Party, 1914–35* (London, 1966)
Wilson, T. (ed.), *The Political Diaries of C. P. Scott 1911–1928* (London, 1970)
Wilson, T., *The Myriad Faces of War: Britain and the Great War, 1914–1918* (Cambridge, 1988 ed.)
Winter, J. (ed.), *The Working Class in Modern British History* (Cambridge, 1983)
Winter, J. M., *Socialism and the Challenge of War* (London, 1974)
Wrigley, C., *Arthur Henderson* (Cardiff, 1990)
Wrigley, C., *Lloyd George and the Challenge of Labour: The Post War Coalition 1918–1922* (Hemel Hempstead, 1990)
Wrigley, C. J., *David Lloyd George and the British Labour Movement* (Hassocks, 1976)

Articles

Adams, R. J. Q., 'Asquith's Choice: the May Coalition and the Coming of Conscription, 1915–1916', *Journal of British Studies*, 25 (1986), pp. 243–63

Adams, T., 'Labour and the First World War: Economy, Politics and the Erosion of Local Peculiarity?', *Journal of Regional and Local Studies*, 10 (1990), pp. 23–47

Adonis, A., 'Aristocracy, Agriculture and Liberalism: The Politics, Finances and Estates of the Third Lord Carrington', *Historical Journal*, 31 (1988), pp. 871–97

Ball, S. R., 'Asquith's Decline and the General Election of 1918', *Scottish Historical Review*, 61 (1982), pp. 44–61

Bealey, F., 'Negotiations between the Liberal Party and the Labour Representation Committee before the General Election of 1906', *Bulletin of the Institute of Historical Research*, 29 (1956), pp. 261–74

Bebbington, D. W., 'Nonconformity and Electoral Sociology, 1867–1918', *Historical Journal*, 27 (1984), pp. 633–56

Bentley, M., 'Liberal Politics and the Grey Conspiracy of 1921', *Historical Journal*, 20 (1977), pp. 461–78

Bernstein, G. L., 'Liberalism and the Progressive Alliance in the Constituencies 1900–1914', *Historical Journal*, 26 (1983), pp. 617–40

Bernstein, G. L., 'Yorkshire Liberalism during the First World War', *Historical Journal*, 32 (1989), pp. 107–29

Billington, R., 'Women, Politics and Local Liberalism: from Female Suffrage to "Votes for Women"', *Journal of Regional and Local Studies*, 5 (1985), pp. 1–14

Blewett, N., 'The Franchise in the United Kingdom, 1885–1918', *Past and Present*, 32 (1965), pp. 27–56

Blewett, N., 'Free Fooders, Balfourites, Whole Hoggers. Factionalism Within the Unionist Party, 1906–10', *Historical Journal*, 11 (1968), pp. 95–124

Boyle, T., 'The Formation of Campbell-Bannerman's Government in December 1905: A Memorandum by J. A. Spender', *Bulletin of the Institute of Historical Research*, 45 (1972), pp. 283–302

Brooks, D., 'Lloyd George, For and Against', *Historical Journal*, 24 (1981), pp. 74–86

Brown, J., 'Attercliffe, 1894: How One Local Liberal Party Failed to Meet the Challenge of Labour', *Journal of British Studies*, 14 (1975), pp. 48–77

Brown, S. J., '"Echoes of Midlothian": Scottish Liberalism and the South African War, 1899–1902', *Scottish Historical Review*, 71 (1992), pp. 156–83

Chadwick, M. E. J., 'The Role of Redistribution in the Making of the Third Reform Act', *Historical Journal*, 19 (1976), pp. 665–83

Childs, M., 'Labour Grows Up: The Electoral System, Political Generation and British Politics, 1890–1929', *Twentieth-Century British History*, 6 (1995), pp. 123–44

Clarke, P., 'The End of Laissez Faire and the Politics of Cotton', *Historical Journal*, 15 (1972), pp. 493–512

Clarke, P., 'The electoral position of the Liberal and Labour parties, 1910–14', *English Historical Review*, 90 (1975), pp. 828–36

Clarke, P., 'Liberals, Labour and the Franchise', *English Historical Review*, 92 (1977), pp. 582–90

Clarke, P. F, 'The Progressive Movement in England', *Transactions of the Royal Historical Society*, 24 (1974), pp. 159–81

Coetzee, F., 'Pressure Groups, Tory Businessmen, and the Aura of Political Corruption Before the First World War', *Historical Journal*, 29 (1986), pp. 833–52

David, E., 'The Liberal Party Divided, 1916–1918', *Historical Journal*, 13 (1970), pp. 509–32

Dawson, M., 'The Liberal Land Policy, 1924–29: Electoral Strategy and Liberal Division', *Twentieth-Century British History*, 2 (1991), pp. 272–90

Dawson, M., 'Liberalism. Devon and Cornwall, 1910–1931: "the old-time religion"', *Historical Journal*, 38 (1995), pp. 425–37

Douglas, R., 'The background to the "Coupon" election agreements', *English Historical Review*, 86 (1971), pp. 318–36

Dowse, R. E., 'The Entry of the Liberals into the Labour Party, 1910–1920', *Yorkshire Bulletin of Economic and Social Research*, 13 (1961), pp. 77–87

Doyle, B., 'A Conflict of Interest? The Local and National Dimensions of Middle-Class Liberalism, 1900–1939', *Parliamentary History*, 17 (1998), pp. 131–40

Doyle, B. M., 'Urban Liberalism and the "Lost Generation": Politics and Middle Class Culture in Norwich, 1900–1935', *Historical Journal*, 38 (1995), pp. 617–34

Dunne, T., 'La trahison des clercs: British intellectuals and the first home-rule crisis', *Irish Historical Studies*, 23 (1982–3), pp. 134–73

Emy, H. V., 'The Impact of Financial Policy on English Party Politics Before 1914', *English Historical Review*, 15 (1972), pp. 103–31

Fair, J. D., 'The Second Labour Government and the Politics of Electoral Reform 1929–31', *Albion*, 13 (1981), pp. 276–301

Fletcher, I. C., '"Prosecutions . . . Are Always Risky Business": Labor, Liberals, and the 1912 "Don't Shoot" Prosecutions', *Albion*, 28 (1996), pp. 251–78

Fletcher, I. C., '"A Star Chamber of the Twentieth Century": Suffragettes, Liberals, and the 1908 "Rush the Commons" Case', *Journal of British Studies*, 35 (1996), pp. 504–30

Fraser, P., 'The Liberal Unionist Alliance: Chamberlain, Hartington, and the Conservatives 1886–1904', *English Historical Review*, 77 (1962), pp. 53–78

Fraser, P., 'British War Policy and the Crisis of Liberalism in May 1915', *Journal of Modern History*, 54 (1982), pp. 1–26

Fry, M., 'Political Change in Britain, August 1914 to December 1916: Lloyd George Replaces Asquith: The Issues Underlying the Drama', *Historical Journal*, 31 (1988), pp. 609–27

Gilbert, B. B., 'David Lloyd George: The Reform of British Landholding and the Budget of 1914', *Historical Journal*, 21 (1978), pp. 117–41

Gilbert, B. B., 'Lloyd George and the Historians', *Albion*, 2 (1979), pp. 74–86

Gilbert, B. B., 'David Lloyd George and the Great Marconi Scandal', *Historical Research*, 62 (1989), pp. 295–317

Glaser, J. F. 'English Nonconformity and the decline of Liberalism', *American Historical Review*, 63 (1957–8), pp. 352–63

Gooch, J., 'The Maurice Debate 1918', *Journal of Contemporary History*, 3 (1968), pp. 211–28

Goodman, G. L., 'Liberal Unionism: The Revolt of the Whigs', *Victorian Studies*, 3 (1959–60), pp. 173–89

Griffiths, P. C., 'The Caucus and the Liberal Party in 1886', *History*, 61 (1976), pp. 183–97

Gutzke, D. W., 'Rosebery and Ireland, 1898–1903: A Reappraisal', *Bulletin of the Institute of Historical Research*, 53 (1980), pp. 88–98

Hamer, D. A., 'The Irish Question and Liberal Politics, 1886–1894', *Historical Journal*, 12 (1969), pp. 511–32

Hanak, H., 'The Union of Democratic Control During the First World War', *Bulletin of the Institute of Historical Research*, 36 (1963), pp. 168–80

Harrison, B., 'Women's Suffrage at Westminster, 1866–1928', in Bentley, M. and Stevenson, J. (eds), *High and Low Politics in Modern Britain* (Oxford, 1983), pp. 80–122

Harrison, B., 'Women in A Man's House: The Women MPs, 1919–1945', *Historical Journal*, 29 (1986), 623–54

Hart, M., 'The Liberals, the War and the Franchise', *English Historical Review*, 97 (1982), pp. 820–32

Hay, R., 'Employers and social policy in Britain: the evolution of welfare legislation, 1905–14', *Social History*, 2 (1977), pp. 435–55

Hazlehurst, C., 'Asquith as Prime Minister, 1908–16', *English Historical Review*, 85 (1970), pp. 502–31

Hepburn, A. C., 'The Irish Council Bill and the Fall of Sir Antony MacDonnell', *Irish Historical Studies*, 17 (1970–1), pp. 470–98

Heyck, T. W., 'Home Rule, Radicalism and the Liberal Party, 1886–1895', *Journal of British Studies*, 13 (1974), pp. 66–91

Hirschfield, C., 'Fractured Faith: Liberal Party Women and the Suffrage Issue in Britain, 1892–1914', *Gender and History*, 2 (1990), pp. 173–97

Hoskings, G. and King, A., 'Radicals and Whigs in the British Liberal Party 1906–14', in Aydelotte, W., *A History of Parliamentary Behaviour* (Princeton, 1977)

Howarth, J., 'The Liberal Revival in Northamptonshire, 1880–1895: A Case Study in Late Nineteenth Century Elections', *Historical Journal*, 12 (1969), pp. 78–118

Howe, A., 'Towards the "hungry forties": free trade in Britain, *c.*1880–1906', in Biagini, E. F. (ed.), *Citizenship and community: Liberals, radicals and collective identities in the British Isles, 1865–1931* (Cambridge, 1996), pp. 193–218

Howkins, A., 'Edwardian Liberalism and Industrial Unrest: A Class View of the decline of Liberalism', *History Workshop*, 4 (1977), pp. 143–61

Hunter, J., 'The Politics of Highland Land Reform, 1873–1895', *Scottish Historical Review*, 53 (1974), pp. 45–68

Jalland, P., 'A Liberal Chief Secretary and the Irish Question: Augustine Birrell, 1907–1914', *Historical Journal*, 19 (1976), pp. 421–51

Laybourn, K., 'The Rise of Labour and the Decline of Liberalism: the state of the debate', *History*, 80 (1995), pp. 207–26

Little, J. G., 'H. H. Asquith and Britain's Manpower Problem, 1914–1915', *History*, 82 (1997), pp. 397–409

Lloyd, T. O., 'The Whip as paymaster: Herbert Gladstone and party organisation', *English Historical Review*, 89 (1974), pp. 785–813

Lubenow, W. C., 'Irish Home Rule and the Social Basis of the Great Separation in the Liberal Party in 1886', *Historical Journal*, 28 (1985), pp. 125–42

Lubenow, W. C., 'The Liberals and the National Question: Irish Home Rule, Nationalism, and its Relationship to Nineteenth-Century Liberalism', *Parliamentary History*, 13 (1994), pp. 119–42

McEwen, J. M., 'The Coupon Election of 1918 and Unionist Members of Parliament', *Journal of Modern History*, 34 (1962), pp. 294–306

McEwen, J. M., 'The Liberal Party and the Irish Question During the First World War', *Journal of British Studies*, 12 (1972), pp. 109–31

McEwen, J. M., 'The Press and the Fall of Asquith', *Historical Journal*, 21 (1978), pp. 863–83

McEwen, J. M., 'The Struggle for Mastery in Britain: Lloyd George Versus Asquith, December 1916', *Journal of British Studies*, 18 (1978), pp. 131–56

McEwen, J. M., 'Lloyd George's Liberal Supporters in December 1916: A Note', *Bulletin of the Institute of Historical Research*, 53 (1980), pp. 265–72

McGill, B., 'Asquith's Predicament, 1914–1918', *Journal of Modern History*, 39 (1967), pp. 283–303

McGill, B., 'Lloyd George's Timing of the 1918 Election', *Journal of British Studies*, 14 (1974), pp. 109–24

McGill, B., 'Glittering Prizes and Party Funds in Perspective, 1882–1931', *Bulletin of the Institute of Historical Research*, 55 (1982), pp. 88–93

McKibbin, R. I., 'James Ramsay MacDonald and the Problem of the Independence of the Labour Party, 1910–1914', *Journal of Modern History*, 90 (1970), pp. 216–35

Matthew, H. C. G., McKibbin, R. I. and Kay, J. A., 'The Franchise Factor in the Rise of the Labour Party', *English Historical Review*, 91 (1976), pp. 723–52

Morgan, K. O., 'Lloyd George's Premiership: A study in "Prime Ministerial Government"', *Historical Journal*, 13 (1970), pp. 130–57

Murray, B., 'The Politics of the "People's Budget"', *Historical Journal*, 16 (1973), pp. 555–70

Murray, B. K., 'Lloyd George, the Navy Estimates, and the Inclusion of Rating Relief in the 1914 Budget', *Welsh Historical Review*, 15 (1990), pp. 58–78

O'Brien, A. M., 'Churchill and the Tonypandy Riots', *Welsh Historical Review*, 17 (1994), pp. 67–99

Packer, I., 'The Land Issue and the Future of Scottish Liberalism in 1914', *Scottish Historical Review*, 75 (1996), pp. 52–71

Packer, I., 'The Liberal Cave and the 1914 Budget', *English Historical Review*, 111 (1996), pp. 620–34

Petter, M., 'The Progressive Alliance', *History*, 58 (1973), pp. 45–59

Phillips, G. D., 'Lord Willoughby de Broke and the Politics of Radical Toryism, 1909–14', *Journal of British Studies*, 20 (1980), pp. 205–24

Phillips, G. D., 'The Whig Lords and Liberalism, 1886–1893', *Historical Journal*, 24 (1981), pp. 167–73

Powell, D., 'The Liberal Ministries and Labour, 1892–1895', *History*, 68 (1983), pp. 408–26

Powell, D., 'The New Liberalism and the Rise of Labour, 1886–1906', *Historical Journal*, 29 (1986), pp. 369–93

Pugh, M., 'Asquith, Bonar Law and the First Coalition', *Historical Journal*, 17 (1974), pp. 813–36

Pugh, M., 'The limits of liberalism: Liberals and women's suffrage, 1867–1914', in Biagini, E. F. (ed.), *Citizenship and community: Liberals, radicals and collective identities in the British Isles, 1865–1931* (Cambridge, 1996), pp. 45–65

Purdue, A. W., 'Arthur Henderson and Liberal, Liberal-Labour and Labour Politics in North-east England 1892–1903', *Northern History*, 11 (1976), pp. 195–217

Purdue, A. W., 'The Liberal and Labour Parties in North-East Politics, 1900–14: The Struggle for Supremacy', *International Review of Social History*, 26 (1981), pp. 1–24

Richards, N. J., 'The Education Bil of 1906 and the Decline of Political Nonconformity', *Journal of Ecclesiastical History*, 23 (1972), pp. 49–63

Roach, J., 'Liberalism and the Victorian Intelligentsia', *Cambridge Historical Journal*, 13 (1957), pp. 58–81

Robbins, K. G., 'Lord Bryce and the First World War', *Historical Journal*, 10 (1967), pp. 255–77

Roberts, A. W., 'Leeds Liberalism and Late Victorian Politics', *Northern History*, 5 (1970), pp. 131–56

Rubinstein, W. D., 'Wealth, Elites and the Class Structure of Modern Britain', *Past and Present*, 76 (1977), pp. 99–126

Savage, D. C., 'Scottish Politics, 1885–6', *Scottish Historical Review*, 40 (1961), pp. 118–35

Searle, G. R., 'The Edwardian Liberal Party and Business', *English Historical Review*, 98 (1983), pp. 28–60

Sheppard, M. G. and Halstead, J., 'Labour's Municipal Election Performance in Provincial England and Wales, 1901–13', *Bulletin of the Society for the Study of Labour History*, 39 (1979), pp. 39–62

Steele, E. D., 'Gladstone and Ireland', *Irish Historical Studies*, 17 (1970–1), pp. 58–88

Stephens, H. W., 'Party Realignment in Britain, 1900–1925', *Social Science History*, 6 (1982), pp. 35–66

Sykes, A., 'The Radical Right and the Crisis of Conservatism Before the First World War', *Historical Journal*, 26 (1983), pp. 661–76

Tanner, D., 'The Parliamentary Electoral System, the "Fourth" Reform Act and the Rise of Labour in England and Wales', *Bulletin of the Institute of Historical Research*, 56 (1983), pp. 205–19

Thane, P., 'The Working Class and State "Welfare" in Britain, 1880–1914', *Historical Journal*, 27 (1984), pp. 877–900

Thane, P., 'Women, liberalism and citizenship, 1918–1930', in Biagini, E. F. (ed.), *Citizenship and community: Liberals, radicals and collective identities in the British Isles, 1865–1931* (Cambridge, 1996), pp. 66–92

Thompson, J. A., 'The Historians and the Decline of the Liberal Party', *Albion*, 22 (1990), pp. 65–83

Trentmann, F., 'The Strange Death of Free Trade: The Erosion of the "Liberal Consensus" in Britain, c.1903–1932', in Biagini, E. F. (ed.), *Citizenship and community: Liberals, radicals and collective identities in the British Isles 1865–1931* (Cambridge, 1996), pp. 219–50

Wald, K. D., 'Class and the Vote Before the First World War', *British Journal of Political Science*, 8 (1978), pp. 441–57

Walker, L., 'Party Political Women: A Comparative Study of Liberal Women and the Primose League, 1890–1914', in Rendall, J. (ed.), *Equal or Different. Women's Politics 1800–1914* (Oxford, 1987), pp. 165–91

Weiler, P., 'The New Liberalism of L. T. Hobhouse', *Victorian Studies*, 16 (1972–3), pp. 141–61

Weinroth, H. S., 'The British Radicals and the Balance of Power, 1902–1914', *Historical Journal*, 13 (1970), pp. 653–82

Weinroth, H. S., 'Left-Wing Opposition to Naval Armaments in Britain before 1914', *Journal of Contemporary History*, 6 (1971), pp. 93–120

Weston, C. C., 'The Liberal Leadership and the Lords' Veto, 1907–1910', *Historical Journal*, 11 (1968), pp. 508–37

White, C. W., 'The Strange Death of Liberal England in Its Time', *Albion*, 17 (1985), pp. 425–47

Wilson, K. M., 'The Making and Putative Implementation of a British Foreign Policy of Gesture, December 1905 to August 1914: The Anglo-French Entente Revisited', *Canadian Journal of History*, 31 (1996), pp. 227–56

Wilson, T., 'The Coupon and the British General Election of 1918', *Journal of Modern History*, 36 (1964), pp. 28–42

INDEX

Acland, A. H. D., 47
Acland, Eleanor, 116
Addison, Christopher, 130, 131, 145
Agadir Crisis, 81, 82
Agar-Robartes, Thomas, 79
Allan, Maud, 38
'Alliance', 8, 171
Alternative Vote, *see* 'electoral reform'
Amery, L. S., 165
Anti-Corn Law League, 15, 17
Anti-Labour alliances, 96, 152–3
Arch, Joseph, 33
Argyll, Duke of, 20
armed services, 12–13, 80–1, 125
Ashby, Margery Corbett, 121, 122
Asquith, H. H. (Lord Oxford and
    Asquith)
  as Chancellor of the Exchequer, 68
  class, views on, 169–70
  coalition government, head of,
    126–7, 129–30, 134–5
  and Constitutional Crisis, 75, 77
  and 'Coupon' (1918) general
    election, 124, 132
  and electoral reform, 160
  his fall from power, 7–8, 130–1, 136
  his feud with Lloyd George, 2, 132,
    133, 144–8, 158–9, 168
  and foreign policy, 82
  and General Strike, 155, 159
  and the Home Rule crisis, 78–9
  puts Labour in office, 150–1, 154–5,
    158
  as Liberal Leader in the 1920s,
    145, 149
  and women's suffrage, 105, 110,
    111, 112, 113, 117, 119,
    120, 122

  mentioned, 2, 27, 35, 38, 47, 71,
    85, 94, 97
Asquith, Margot, 38

Bagehot, Walter, 3
Baker, Harold, 116
Baldwin, Stanley, 8, 143, 146, 154,
    155, 158, 162
Balfour, A. J., 53, 68, 69, 71, 75, 77,
    97, 113–14, 115, 129, 145
Birkenhead, Lord (F. E. Smith),
    145
Birmingham, 30, 46, 97
Black and Tans, 143, 145
Boer War, 42–3, 64, 68–9, 135
Bonar Law, Andrew, 91, 113–14,
    126, 129, 130, 132, 137, 161
Bradford, 11, 61, 63, 96
Bradlaugh, Charles, 56
Brailsford, H. N., 115
Bright, Jacob, 106, 107
Bright, John, 11, 12, 14, 15, 17, 19,
    23, 24, 28, 57, 74, 106
Bryce, James, 135
budgets
  (1894), 40, 48–9
  (1909, 'People's Budget'), 73, 74,
    77, 86, 94
  (1914), 73, 86
Burns, John, 60, 88, 94, 126
business liberalism, 51–3,
    89–93, 103
by-elections
  Mid-Lanarkshire (1888), 61
  Sheffield, Attercliffe (1894), 61
  Woolwich (1903), 64
  Barkston Ash (1905), 36
  of early 1908, 71

225

Triple Alliance, 98
Tweedmouth, Lord, 33

Ulster, 28, 51, 78–9, 114
Union of Democratic Control
    (UDC), 134–5
Unionist Party, *see* Conservative Party,
    Liberal Unionist Party

Wales, 11, 14, 34, 35, 39, 41, 42, 51,
    52, 71–2, 79, 95, 103, 153, 160;
    see also Welsh Disestablishment
War Emergency Workers' National
    Committee, 140
'war socialism', 140
Webb, Sidney, 47, 49
'Wee Frees', *see* Independent Liberals
welfare capitalism, 169
Welsh Disestablishment, 18, 33, 37,
    75–6, 142–3
Whigs, 16–18, 31–2
White, George, 36
Whittaker, Sir Thomas, 140
Willoughby de Broke, Lord, 82
Wilson, C. H., 51
Wilson, Trevor, 1, 125, 133–4,
    136–8, 150

Wintringham, Margaret, 121
Women's Free Trade Union, 106
Women's Liberal Federation (WLF),
    38, 106, 107–8, 109–10, 115,
    116, 117, 121
Women's National Anti–Suffrage
    League, 118
Women's National Liberal
    Federation (WNLF),
    108, 118, 121–3
Women's Social and Political
    Union (WSPU), 108, 110, 111,
    112, 114
women's suffrage, 9, Ch. 7
working-class stratification,
    138–9
workman's compensation
    legislation, 47, 70
Wyndham, George, 164–5

'Yellow Book', *see* Liberal Industrial
    Inquiry
Yorkshire, West Riding, 46, 51, 52,
    63, 92, 136, 152
Young, Hilton, 155
Young Scots, 95
youth vote, 104, 149